EDITH STEIN AND REGINA JONAS

Religion and Violence
Series Editors: Lisa Isherwood and Rosemary Radford Ruether

This interdisciplinary and multicultural series brings to light the ever-increasing problem of religion and violence. The series highlights how religions have a significant part to play in the creation of cultures that allow – and even encourage – the development of conflict and domestic abuse as well as policies likely to perpetuate violence to citizens.

Edith Stein and Regina Jonas

Religious Visionaries in the Time of the Death Camps

Emily Leah Silverman

ACUMEN

First published in 2013 by Acumen

Acumen Publishing Limited
4 Saddler Street
Durham
DH1 3NP

ISD, 70 Enterprise Drive
Bristol, CT 06010, USA

www.acumenpublishing.com

ISBN: 978-1-84465-718-6   (hardcover)
ISBN: 978-1-84465-719-3   (paperback)

British Library Cataloguing-in-Publication Data
A catalogue record for this book is available from the British Library.

Typeset in Warnock Pro by JS Typesetting Ltd, Porthcawl.
Printed and bound in the UK by 4edge Ltd., Essex.

In memory of my father, Berl "Bernie" Silverman
born 3 May 1920, Zastavna, Bukovina
died 9 September 2006, New York, New York

CONTENTS

ILLUSTRATIONS

FOREWORD

Emily Leah Silverman's book, *Edith Stein and Regina Jonas: Religious Visionaries in the Time of the Death Camps*, is a major contribution to the literature on German Jewish women in the Nazi era. Silverman has written a powerful testimony to the vision of these two women and their ministry in this time of insane violence and attempted extermination of the Jewish people. Silverman writes a profoundly insightful study of these two women and their diverse paths of spiritual leadership.

Edith Stein (1891–1942) grew up in an observant Jewish family in Breslau, Germany, but as a woman received no in-depth knowledge of her faith. She developed a deep desire for knowledge at an early age, receiving a doctorate in philosophy in 1916. She studied under the phenomenologist Edmund Husserl and wrote her dissertation on "The Problem of Empathy." She worked as Husserl's assistant at the University of Freiburg, but was denied a habilitational thesis because she was a woman. In 1932 she became a lecturer at the University of Münster, but was forced to resign in 1933 due to the anti-Semitic legislation of the Nazis that forbade employment of Jews.

Stein was attracted to Roman Catholicism and was baptized into that church in 1922, teaching at a Dominican nun's school from 1923 to 1931. Her loss of her job at Münster opened the way for her entrance into the Discalced Carmelite monastery in Cologne in 1933. To avoid the growing Nazi threat, her order transferred Stein to the Carmelite monastery in Echt in the Netherlands. But when the Dutch bishops had a statement read in all the churches condemning Nazi anti-Semitism, the Nazi leaders there ordered the arrest of Jewish converts to Catholicism. Stein and her sister Rosa, along with many other converts, were rounded up and deported to Auschwitz in August 7, 1942. Stein was gassed soon after arrival on August 9, 1942.

Regina Jonas (1902–1944) grew up in Berlin and studied at the Academy for the Science of Judaism there, developing a vocation to be a rabbi. No woman had been ordained a rabbi before in German Judaism. Jonah wrote an ordination thesis on the topic, "Can a Woman be a Rabbi?," arguing that women were capable of the work of the rabbinate and there was no basis to opposition to it in the tradition. At first her application was refused by the leading rabbis, because she was a woman, but she was eventually accepted and ordained in 1935 Max Dienemann of by the Liberal Rabbis' Association. She worked in several Jewish social institutions as a rabbi, in schools, hospitals and homes for the elderly. She was arrested by the Nazis on November 5, 1942 and deported to Theresienstadt, where she continued her work as a rabbi in the camps, and worked with Viktor Frankl in his crisis intervention service to these people. She worked tirelessly there for two years. She was deported to Auschwitz in October 1944, and was executed two months later.

These two extraordinarily creative women broke at an early age from the standard vocations for women. Both pursued paths of intellectual development and service to others. Both Stein and Jonas were deeply convinced that women were capable of professions beyond the traditional roles of wife and mother. They recognized that this diversity of roles was being pursued in the new generation of women in Weimar Germany. While both Stein and Jonas were clear that women had the capacity for higher knowledge, they also saw women as having particular talents for empathy and care for others. Thus they did not simply see women as the "same" as men, but as combining full human capacities with particular talents for relationships. Both pursued roles – Stein as a philosopher and Jonas as a woman rabbi – for which they had to struggle, and which were not fully received by their teachers, but eventually were accepted. As Jews, both women had to formulate their vocations in the context of Nazi anti-Semitism and ultimately died at the hands of Nazis in the same death camp, Auschwitz.

In the context of their deviant vocations, Stein and Jonas each spent much energy defining who they were as women who "crossed over" and combined identities that were challenging to their societies. Stein sought to combine being a Catholic nun devoted to union with Christ with being a Jew. She sought to understand how her spirituality as a Catholic contemplative did not separate her from, but connected her with, her Jewish community. She came to believe that the suffering she was experiencing because of her public identification as a Jew would itself become a redemptive path. Claiming Jesus as her redeemer who was a Jew, she saw Jewish suffering in the holocaust as linked with Jesus' redemption of all humans on the cross. Through their suffering at the hands of Nazis, Jews would be included in this redemption. Her own suffering would atone for the refusal of Jews to accept Jesus as their Savior, and help include the Jews in redemption, leading to a final transformation of the world. Thus Stein went to her death in Auschwitz with a vision of herself as playing a redemptive role at this fraught time in Jewish and world history.

As Silverman puts it, while Stein saw herself as suffering "for" the Jewish people, Jonas's vision of her work as a rabbi meant that she worked and suffered "with" the Jewish people. Jonas, as well as Stein, had opportunities to escape from Germany to the Americas, but both rejected the possibility of leaving their people. For Jonas, being a rabbi combined teaching and leadership with pastoral care for hurting people. Care for the suffering was itself a key part of what it meant in her Jewish theological vision to bring God's *Shekhinah* (Presence) into society. The cultivation of a relation to God meant not leaving the world, as in Catholic convents, but bringing the sacred into everyday life. Jonas exemplified this ministry in her tireless care and encouragement of others in Berlin, and later in Theresienstadt.

Silverman helps us to see deeply into the spiritual vision and journey of these two very different and yet similar women. We are profoundly moved by experiencing the lives of Edith Stein and Regina Jonas. In the opening chapter to her book, Emily Silverman tells us of her horror and fear as a child in hearing of the Holocaust. She had been told that those who died in the camps, rather than taking the route of armed resistance, were mere "lambs led to the slaughter," victims, who contributed nothing to Jewish survival. Her journey with the two visionaries – Edith Stein, a Catholic Jew, and Regina Jonas, a woman rabbi – opens up an alternative to this judgment. Both died at Auschwitz, but they each did so in a way that humanized and redeemed that path to the death camps. This in itself was a form of resistance to Nazism, and ultimately a theology and practice of liberation in the face of this deathly reality.

Rosemary Radford Ruether

ACKNOWLEDGMENTS

It has taken a village to get this book into the world.

First, I must thank my husband Keith Mostov, who told me in the first ten minutes of our first date that I "have something to say to the world," and he wanted to support me in doing it. He truly has done this in all ways. For the year I was writing this as a dissertation, and now finally a book, he shared the "double burden" of parenting and has taken on most of the childcare of our three kids, schlepping each of them to different schools and to their various appointments and sports each week, all so that I could work. If this weren't enough, he learned citation software and hand-entered over three hundred references for my bibliography.

Rosemary Radford Ruether has been a rock of unwavering support, and I thank her for this. She has believed in this project, encouraged it, and never doubted I would complete it. Even when my life threw me challenges or theological experiences, Rosemary never doubted I would do it. There would not be this thesis and book without Rosemary. I am very grateful for having such a wonderful mentor. I have been truly blessed.

I thank Professor Ibrahim Farajaje for his complete spiritual support, for reminding me not to be afraid to be by myself, when it was hard at times. He has become my older, wiser, spiritual brother, and like Rosemary, a part of my family. We are deeply connected.

Susannah Heschel told me in a car ride: do Edith Stein; you can learn the German. Rabbi Ted Alexander always told me about Regina Jonas and never let her be forgotten. He and Gertrude have always been good friends and family to me. Ruth Callmann z"l (1918–2011) was one of Rabbinerin Regina Jonas's students and I served with her as a synagogue board member of Congregation Bnai Emunah. She shared some great stories about Rabbinerin Jonas with me. Rabbi Elisa Klapheck brought Regina Jonas's ordination thesis out into the world and became a rabbi because of this holy rabbinerin. She has been a spiritual sister and generously sent the Theresienstadt documents. I also have to thank Katharina von Kellenbach for being the first scholar to bring Rabbinerin Jonas to the world.

Susanne and Alfred Batzdorff gave of their time, and Susanne read through the chapter on her Aunt Edith and generously gave me feedback. I am very thankful to my editors – first, Dirk von der Horst, who has been a colleague, a dear friend. We spent many hours sitting in my office, my house and cafés discussing and editing this book. Dirk helped me realize that Jonas offers a critique of Stein, which gave me the ability to turn my dissertation into a book. He has supported me on many levels and is a part of my family.

Roberta Werdinger has been a supportive friend and spiritual colleague in encouraging my work. Polly Pagenhart, who was the major editor on my dissertation, supported me as a friend and shared wonderful insights as a lesbian dad. I want to thank Antonia Barrow, who was very thoughtful and kind in editing the thesis, and also Allan Cummings. I must thank Hanna Bergers for teaching me theological German, and for her support. My dear friend Michele Shields has never wavered in her support of this project and me. I thank all the women and parents who have watched my kids, cleaned my house, or taken over carpool, all so I could finish this project. There have been many people over the years, too numerous to name, but each one indispensable. Dorit Zahavi has been a wonderful *metepelet*; she has become a family member and has been supportive of this thesis. I thank my dear friend Benina Berger Gould for her constant support, as well as Lynn Ponton.

I am grateful to Naomi Seidman for her seminars on queer theory, and on Jews and postmodernism. My dear friend Leslie Choquette has done first edits on part of this thesis, and always supported me towards completing the work, telling me that the thesis broke new ground in many fields, and she always saw it as a book. Jane Redmont edited very early drafts and helped me with understanding aspects of Catholicism. Thank you to Dagmar Theison for translating Jonas's writings and newspaper articles.

I would like to thank Aracely Diaz, Daysi Zepeda, Elizabeth Zepeda for their support and for helping me keep things in order. I thank Tina Krause for her help and support in Berlin. I am so happy to have the support of my friend Eileen David (who got me out to the DC), Monika Sanders and Randy David of the Sword and the Rose, and Dane Morton for urging me to finish. I want to thank the late Tyrrell O'Neil (RIP 1959–2012), who gave me tremendous support to write this book and for a wonderful meaningful friendship of over 30 years.

I want to thank Janet Joyce for giving my first book contract; Janet believed in this book before I completed it as a dissertation. I want to thank Tristan Palmer for his continuing support, and Lisa Isherwood.

I want to thank Chaim Heller, who supported me and my children. Marie Cartier came into my life because of this project and given me great feedback. I want to thank the whole Queer Studies in Religion section at AAR/WR; also Dr Hermann Simon and Barbara Welker of Stiftung Neue Synagoge Berlin--Centrum Judaicum, Martina Siknerova of Patmatnik Terezin (Terezin Memorial), and Dr Sr M Antonia Karmelitinnen-Kloster Maria vom Frieden.

I thank my late father, Bernie Silverman, who is not alive to see me publish this book. To my mother Naomi Gale Silverman, who has been very supportive in helping me focus on finishing, I give thanks. She has been there every step of the way. I thank my brother Daniel Silverman and Rachel Rueben, who has been very supportive of this project. Finally I thank my wonderful children, Ari, Zeke, and Raphie, who have been very patient. They grew up with Edith Stein and Regina Jonas.

I give thanks for all the people who have made this book possible.

Part I

DESIRE

Chapter 1

WHY EDITH STEIN? WHY REGINA JONAS?

To explain the origins of this book, I need to tell a story. It is a story of my growing up, and of my father's family. It is a story of how I came to ask the questions I ask in this book about Edith Stein, about Regina Jonas, and about the intellectual and spiritual traditions that give shape and meaning to their lives and work.

It is the late 1960s, and I am waiting at the New York City harbor. I am a young child. A big cruise ship pulls in, lined with row upon row of decks and windows. It has just come across the Atlantic from Europe, and my relatives, whom I have never met, are on this ship. Three distinguished elderly ladies come down the gangplank. They have a warm, sad feeling to them. We take them home in our Buick station wagon to our suburban house in southern Westchester. They speak a strange language, one that I have not heard before: German interspersed with Yiddish. There is a dark cloud over their heads, but beneath it I can see a golden light that emanates from them. They are my paternal grandmother and *Bubbe* Esther's nieces from Vienna and Geneva.

When they unpack their suitcases in my younger brother's room on the third floor of our 1910 Tudor house, they hand me a German book on the history of ballet. Alma Tannenbaum, the middle niece, has learned in letters from her aunt – my Bubbe – that I am studying ballet. I fall in love with her. My heart goes out to her. I want to know more about her and her sisters. I keep asking my grandmother Granna (my maternal grandmother, who lives with us at our Mount Vernon, New York home), "Why does Paula take pills?" Granna says, "They are survivors of the concentration camps." I ask, "What do you mean, 'concentration camps'? Are they like sleep-away camps where children go in the summer to have fun outdoors, and play games with other children?" "No!" Granna replies, but she does not explain further.

I know something horrible has happened to them there across the ocean, otherwise there would not be a black cloud around them, even though I see through it to their inner light. My five-year-old child-brain cannot grasp the horror that they have been through. It will take another six years until I have any sense of what a concentration camp might be. I feel kindness and love from Alma; I know she has been through something bigger than my mind can grasp.

As I grow older, I begin to make sense of my classmates at the Modern Orthodox Day School. They are children of survivors; concentration camp survivors. The term "survivor" is reserved for those who lived through the camps. People who survived by hiding in the forests, living with righteous gentiles, or passing themselves off as gentiles themselves are not considered survivors among my rabbis and classmates. Such people are something else entirely. And the Jews who escaped to other continents, other parts of the world – China, South America, Africa, Australia, and America – are not considered survivors at all. The survivors and the survivors' children do not have the extended family that others have: no grandparents, aunts, uncles, or cousins, like I do. They were all murdered during the war. Their parents speak with Yiddish and Polish accents. It is not until fifth grade at Westchester Day School that I begin to gain an inkling of what Granna meant when she said, "They are survivors of the concentration camps."

One of my classmates' parents comes to our classroom on Yom Hashoah (Jewish Holocaust Remembrance Day) to talk to us. He is also the school chef. He has the letters KL[1] tattooed on his arm; I have seen them when he walks up and down the lunchroom tables, checking each student and making sure we all get enough to eat. He comes into our classroom, and in a heavy Yiddish Polish accent, begins to tell his story of survival and escape in Poland. Then at the end of his tale, our teacher opens up a book with photos. The pictures of the Shoah are seared into my brain, a tattoo that I never can erase.

The nightmares begin; fear and abject horror creep into my bones, sink into my heart, and wrench my stomach. I realize that fifth-grade day that I am a relic, a walking dinosaur. My family and I should have died out in Europe, but my grandparents and father immigrated long before the war. Without realizing it, I begin to live my life as a concentration camp survivor. Crowded trains turn into cattle cars. Bells ringing are the sounds of roll call; chimney smoke no longer evokes warm fireplaces on a cold winter day, but the burning of the crematoria. When my parents go out at night, I fear that they will not return, because in my child-like imagination I fear the Gestapo will round them up. When I fall asleep, nightmares burn into my dream space. There never is any kind of escape, neither in the days nor in the nights.

The pictures of that afternoon in fifth grade incessantly sizzle in my brain and sear my body. I want to be reassured that it will never happen again, not just to my family, not just to the Jewish people, but to all humanity including myself. (Unfortunately I find it keeps on happening, but in different ways.) I want to fight for peace and justice, and the survival of Israel. I identify with my black brothers and sisters now that I have a better notion of slavery, of the demonization of humans that happened right here in America. I sit in my Granna's lap that fifth-grade Yom Hashoah and I cry for hours. I cry into her marshmallow arms, and she tries to comfort me, rocking me back and forth in her wheelchair. Nothing can comfort me. The connection is made now, back to those dignified women relatives who came off the cruise ship. The nightmares will not cease.

In high school, my classmates and I, along with our refugee teachers from war-torn and Cold War communist countries, start an Amnesty International group. My life will be dedicated to documenting and fighting human rights abuses. Not only will I work for human rights in general, but also, with Survival International, for the human rights of indigenous peoples and tribes being wiped out by industrialization and development. I pursue intensive studies in philosophy, ethics, and the history of science, to try to grasp what happened.

Palpitations and perspiration fill my nights, as does an inability to breathe. I have to sleep with four pillows – almost sitting up – so I will not suffocate. Never can I take a breath without wheezing. "Mommy, I can't breathe!" becomes my most memorable and repeated refrain as a child; memorable, too, are the horrendous migraine headaches that will go undiagnosed until my adulthood. Severe asthma becomes a life-long struggle.

Lying awake in my bed, I read survivor testimonials night after night. I wonder: where could my brothers and I hide in our big house if the Gestapo came for a round-up? Were there places in the woods near our house that we could escape to? Who could we trust? I draw up a packing list: if I had to flee, what would I take with me? What would I leave behind? How would I take care of my younger brothers and make sure they came with me, or had a hiding place to go to? My list includes good-soled hiking shoes, food, water, family photos, jewelry for barter, long underwear, layered clothes, and a strong hiker's backpack with sleeping bag, plus a down jacket and raincoat. I think: maybe I should take a 1970s-style Eskimo parka with the fake fur collar instead of a down jacket and raincoat. This will save me valuable packing space. The items are prioritized over and over again on my nightly packing list. The shoes and family photos are the most important, though: they are at the top of my packing list. Hiking shoes that can be worn all year long in snow and summer heat will ground my feet and take me across America. I can walk to Canada, hide out in the wilderness. I constantly think up new hiding places.

As I become a teenager, I dive into religious texts to find meaning. Freud does not do it for me; I read him for a while when I am in middle school, but don't find answers I'm looking for in his work. He does at least explain to me why humans have created religions: to explain our fear of the unknown. I identify more with the Catholic and Jewish mystics. St Teresa of Avila's *Interior Castle*, St John of the Cross's *Dark Night of the Soul*, and Martin Buber's *I and Thou* especially speak to me. The *Tao Te Ching* teaches me how to be flexible and strong, and to survive as a reed blowing – but not breaking – in the wind, as the wild wind rushes over me. I imagine myself with roots planted, still standing after the storm. Transcendental meditation helps calm me, but the images tattooed into my mind's eye will not leave me. No matter how hard I try to blink them away, they pop right back up. Nothing works: neither the meditations nor the spiritual texts. They soothe my tormented soul, but only temporarily: they are Band-Aids covering the wounds, falling right off as soon as I am done with the reading or practice.

For some reason the Torah does not satisfy me either. Not until divinity school will the prophets Job and Isaiah finally speak to me, as will the Psalms. But for now, in high school, I want to know more about Jewish mystical tradition, and I read Gershom Scholem's classic text *Major Trends in Jewish Mysticism*,[2] which I dig out of a bargain bin in an academic bookstore on 57th Street in Manhattan. Scholem's book provides a tempting glimpse of the moving esoteric texts. My thirst for kabbalistic literature is not quenched, for I still do not find the answers to my questions. I want to read the actual kabbalistic texts, not just Scholem's explication.

Hannah Arendt's *Eichmann in Jerusalem*[3] wakes me up to how evil can encroach both subtly and massively. I want to make sure that I myself will never become complacent and behave with indifference. I keep asking myself: Am I capable of becoming a Nazi?

Political activism keeps up my hopes. In college I protest US intervention in El Salvador, I petition for the release of Leonard Peltier, and I march to stop the sterilization of Native Americans. Anti-nuclear activism is my biggest concern. I actively work for peace and nuclear disarmament by helping scientists and engineers at MIT search for jobs outside of the industrial Star Wars complex of the Ronald Reagan era. Our anti-nuke peace group "High Technology Professionals for Peace" is made up of Harvard and MIT graduate students as well as working scientist and engineers. We communicate with peace groups in India and Russia during the Cold War, and counsel people working in the nuclear arms field. We want to stop nuclear proliferation and start the economic conversion of the nuclear arms industry in order to prevent World War III.

I want to learn how to think critically. As an undergraduate at Bard College I design an independent major in epistemologies in order to understand the difference between philosophical, religious and scientific knowledge. My advisor and I call it the History and Philosophy of Science. I apply to rabbinical school but turn it down to go to Harvard Divinity School, for many reasons, one of which is that I want to understand what I fear, which is Jesus bleeding on the cross. Emotionally, in my mind, the bleeding Jesus' blood, which is Jewish blood, somehow connects to the Nazis. Why do so many people around the world worship this wounded, bleeding Jewish man? I do not understand, and want to.

This desire traces back to early memories as a child, attending Catholic Latin Mass with my "Aunt Kitty" on Sunday mornings. Aunt Kitty was more than our beloved nanny. She was truly a member of our family, and she, along with my Granna, raised my younger brothers and me. She and my grandmother (who died when I was fourteen) took care of us from birth until adulthood. Aunt Kitty lived with us on the weekends. "In church they eat from the body and drink the blood of Christ," she tells us. I tell Aunt Kitty as a five-year-old that I cannot kneel or eat from the sacraments. "I am a Jew," I say to her. "I do not kneel before anyone." I do not want to taste someone else's flesh and blood. But I am curious: what did the body taste like when she went up and stood in the long line for the sacrament? I thought maybe it was like thin mint wafers, without the chocolate. I watch Aunt Kitty and the other kids and people stand in line under the bleeding Jesus, watch the priest giving them their part of Jesus' body. I tell the priest after services, when we go to shake his hand, that I am Jewish.

At Harvard Divinity School, I write a thesis on "The Multiplicity of Evil in the Final Solution" for my Master's in Divinity. I examine Hannah Arendt's notion of the banality of evil, and Kant's notion of radical evil, and plot how all this played out in the Shoah. I carefully examine the Eichmann testimony, and study what he thinks he was doing. In my conclusion, I argue that evil acts on multiple levels: radical, banal, bystander, and sadistic. In the case of the Final Solution, evil is not banal, as Arendt has argued, but banality can become evil. Radical evil does happen in a conscious way – because people like Hitler and Himmler choose not to listen to their conscience, and choose not to follow the categorical imperative.

I am an unusual divinity school student. Instead of studying for a Master of Theological Studies degree, I change to a Master of Divinity program. Jewish students do not pursue this degree. Only one other Jew at that time – a man who had been openly rejected by Reform rabbinical school for being "out of the closet" as gay – is following the same path. He decides to convert, and wants to become a Unitarian minister, but he feels strongly Jewish. At the time, I think: I might be the first Jewish student to graduate with this degree. To me it is practical; I can become a hospital chaplain, and use my internships to work for peace and in synagogue. I have gone through ministry training, but at the same time, I remain true to being a Jew.

All this time, woven throughout my divinity school studies, I wonder about the women who survived. I read survival accounts by men and look carefully at Claude Lanzmann's documentary on the Shoah.[4] And I wonder: Why are there no women in his documentary? What about the spirituality and faith of the people who went through it? I turn to thinking: What about my own women relatives? All four of my paternal grandmother's sisters managed to survive, and I wonder how.

The only book on spirituality and the Holocaust that I find inspirational at the time is Yaffa Eliach's *Hasidic Tales of the Holocaust*,[5] miraculous tales of Rabbi Israel Spira and his community surviving under incredible odds. But again, I wonder: Where are the women? Where are their stories? What is their spirituality? Is there any attempt to discuss a post-Holocaust theology? There is nothing; I find scarcely any articles or books during my early investigations except for those of Emil Fackenheim, Richard Rubenstein, and Arthur Cohen's *The Tremendum*. Not one woman has written a theological response to the Shoah by the 1980s. The literature of Elie Wiesel is the only possible theology I find – if I can even call his work a theology.

When I was young, I could challenge the rabbis in school about Jewish *Halakha* and Torah, but none of us was ever allowed to ask: Where was God during the Shoah? Our Talmud teacher, Rabbi Bermann, would put his finger to his mouth: "Shah, shah. Never ask this question, Emanuella," he would say, calling me by my Hebrew name. And so the largest of all the questions remains unanswered; the intense insomnia follows me into divinity school, never giving me a moment's rest or any space to breathe. I want to be exorcized of these nightmares of the Shoah. But writing my divinity school thesis does not solve the problem. It just enables me to grasp intellectually how it could be that the Reich trains always managed to run on time, how a majority of people were not motivated to intervene and stop them from running on time, to their final destination in the east.

From my relatives, those who lived through the Shoah, I look for more answers. During my last year in high school, I take all my life savings – from babysitting and my part-time earnings as a retail clerk – and buy an airline ticket to fulfill my dream to go the Holy Land. Once there, I go to Jerusalem and visit Hulda, the fourth niece of my paternal grandmother, Bubbe – the only one who had not come from Europe to visit when I was a child.

My Great Uncle Moses Tannenbaum – my Bubbe Esther's older brother – was a well-off man. He sat on the board of the *kehilla* – the Jewish community – in his hometown in Kotzman, Bukovina, and gave each of his four daughters – Gisele, born in 1900, Hulda in 1902, Alma in 1904, and Paula in 1908 – a university education. When I arrive at Hulda's home in Jerusalem in the spring of my high school senior year, I speak only English and Hebrew. For her part, Hulda speaks no English and barely any Hebrew; she does, however, speak six or seven other languages fluently. She asks her German-speaking women friends, her peer group, to have tea with me, and to translate our conversation.

The first thing that jumps out at me is her bookcase: full of German chemistry and medical books. Hulda had studied to become a pharmacist/doctor at the University of Prague. Through her friends, Hulda puts me through a mini-oral exam. What are my views on politics? On philosophy? What do I read? What do I think about? What do I study? What profession do I want to pursue? At that time, my answer is the medical profession; I had just completed most of my science courses in high school. Apparently I pass her exam because Bubbe Esther gets a letter in German saying her one and only granddaughter Emily is both smart and beautiful; she does not let the Tannenbaum sisters down, and lives up to these strong, highly educated women's values and expectations. Bubbe is pleased. The one thing I lack, however, is the sisters' fluency in multiple languages.

In the summer of 2001, I travel to Geneva to visit Paula, the last surviving sister of my Great Uncle Tannenbaum. She is lying in pain from heart failure, with big windows overlooking the distant Alps. "Language is golden," she tells me. "It is the key to survival." She knows eight of them. "The more languages one learns," she tells me, "the more cultures you understand, and the better able you are to exist in this world." Paula goes on to explain how she taught herself Hebrew and went to Palestine after the war and became Chaim Weizmann's personal nurse for the last four months of his life. The imperative to learn languages: this is the wisdom she wants to convey to me. We converse fluently in Hebrew, interspersed with a little English and a little German, which I have studied in the time since my youthful visit to Hulda. Still, Paula's English is much better than my broken German.

The pieces of her sisters' stories start to come together. Strand by strand, they untangle, and weave into a visible pattern. These women inspire me in a way very different from my American relatives on my mother's side. They are fluent in many languages. They have received professional educations, and have gone through something that is not completely comprehensible. But I also want to learn their personal stories, how they managed to survive and continue on with their lives, while not all the men in my family did. Why did they choose to stay in Vienna and Geneva? Why did only Hulda make *aliyah* (literally, to " go up" to the Holy Land) to Israel after the war?

I learn from Paula that Hulda gave birth to a baby boy in Nice, in June 1943. She was 41, and it was one year after the Jewish children of Paris were being rounded up for deportation to the east. They named him Marius, a French name, probably starting with "M" to honor the memory of her father, Moses Tannenbaum. They chose not to circumcise him, so no one would know he was a Jewish baby. They decided to pass him off as a French Catholic.

Choosing to have a child in the midst of the Shoah was a major act of heroism. Indeed, many Jewish women had abortions when it was feasible, so as to increase their chances of survival. Marius later explains to me the irony that it was only because of the Nazis that he was born. His parents attempted to escape to Switzerland but were turned away at the border and told that if they wanted entrance Hulda would have to be pregnant. They went back to Southern France and had Marius. Marius survived; he had himself circumcised at the age of his Bar Mitzvah and made aliyah to Israel after his university studies in Paris in 1968. Hulda eventually followed Marius to Israel, to live near her only child.

Marius's young cousin, however, Paula's son Manfred, did not survive. Neither my father nor I knew his name until I visited Paula in Geneva that summer. Paula's Egyptian Jewish husband Nino, eighteen years her junior, warns me not to ask Paula anything about what happened during the war. "It is forbidden ground," he says. Even Nino, married to her for fifty years, does not know the whole story.

So I do not ask any questions about the war. I ask only about Paula's life before and after the war. I have brought photos with me from her older sister Alma; I had made copies of them when I visited her a decade earlier in Vienna. I show them to Paula, and ask her to identify the relatives and people in the photos. She thumbs through them and then she sees him. He is about six or seven years old in the photo, her beloved young son. She starts crying out, "Freddie! Freddie! Freddie!" Freddie is short for Fredel (Manfred, or "man of peace," in German). I learn after Nino's passing that he had been the same age as Manfred and born on the same day and year. It appears that Paula had married a man who was the same exact age her son would have been if he had survived.

The conversation with Paula suddenly comes to a halt. It is over! We can no longer converse; Paula is shut down, and I feel horrible for causing her so much pain. But from this terrible state of inexpressible agony for her, I learn new information about our family that nobody, outside of her sisters, nieces, and maybe Nino, knows: that her only child, the one who did not survive the Shoah, was named Manfred. I can honor Manfred; his name is no longer lost and will be taken to the grave along with his aunts.

I visit Marius and his first cousin in Israel years later, and they tell me that Fredel died in the Czernowitz ghetto from typhus. He was fifteen years old, and had written a note that a close friend had buried in a bottle during the war. His friend survived, retrieved the note after the war, and gave it to the family. The note stated that he did not know what was going to happen in the future; nevertheless he urged others to have hope and stay left (meaning politically left). Manfred's grandmother, Bertha Gottleib Tannenbaum, followed him in death soon thereafter. She was 66. Bertha was so hurt, so broken that her only grandson had died, that she lay down in the snow determined to die. Her daughter Alma convinced her to stay alive for another six months. She did, and then died two days before Fredel's cousin Marius was born in the south of France.

In June 1943, Paula, along with her sister Alma, survived the Romanian labor and concentration camps in Transnistra. Their sister Gisele and her two children also survived. Gisele had placed her two daughters, then 9 and 11, into the Catholic Monastery of the Holy Mother in Czernowitz. The nuns kept the Nazis away by telling them that their mother had died and that their father was an SS solider. The girls stayed there from 1939 until 1942, until it was too dangerous for the nuns to hide Jewish children. Then they were forced to live in the ghetto in Czernowitz before being deported to Transnistra.

Alma was a medical doctor who had graduated from the University of Vienna in 1929. Viktor Frankel, a year behind Alma, was a colleague. After her medical studies, Alma had returned to Czernovitz, Bukovina, to work as a specialist in infectious diseases. Then she was sent to Transnistra. She survived and was liberated by "Uncle Joe" Stalin, thereafter joining his army and joining the invasion of Poland. There she became captain of general field surgery. She set up her surgeon's operating room in the orphanage of Janusz Korczak, the radical Polish Jewish pediatrician who chose to remain with his orphans and walk with them to their death in the gas chambers. Alma survived the war, and was honored by the Red army in the Russian Red zone of Vienna. She was given a beautiful apartment in the fifth district to live in, and she resumed her medical practice, treating ex-Nazis as well as Jews.

My young husband and I visit her in early 1990, a few months after the Berlin wall falls. She is still a hardcore communist. She hates Gorbachev and fears the re-unification of Germany. In her apartment there is a black-and-white picture of her Aunt Esther's granddaughter hanging on the wall; the girl is in a ballet outfit. I am stunned to see the picture of myself. She has not seen me in over twenty years. I speak neither German nor Yiddish; she does not speak English. We sit with a German–English dictionary between us and communicate. I tell her how much I loved her from the moment I met her in New York some twenty years before. She explains that she had felt the same warm feeling toward me. I attempt to gather her story. She gives me pieces of her writing about the Shoah, published in German journals. I take photographs of her photographs: her Red Army pictures, her pictures before the war, her pictures after the war, a photograph of her nephew Manfred when he was a boy of six or seven.

Before we leave, she presses a pendant into my hand. It is a silver fertility goddess given to her by Paula, which she got when she worked in Africa, setting up nursing schools on behalf of the State of Israel. This African fertility piece is Alma's legacy – and Paula's – now passed down to me. In that moment, I feel I have been accepted as one of the Tannenbaum women.

The women. I want to study more about the nature of evil from a feminist perspective. After beginning Harvard Divinity School as a "blind thinker" in the Arendtian sense, with no concept that gender could affect ideas, I become awakened to feminist readings of gender. Previously, ideas had been genderless to me, even if they had a life of their own. But Harvard Divinity School broadens my perspective, and my Christian feminist sisters teach me that I live in a body, with a gender. They help show me the oppression of women in all the major world religions, especially Christianity and Judaism. I had always fought for the rights of women, but until my encounters with feminist thought in divinity school, I had not coupled my anti-oppression work with my life-long religious study. At Harvard, I work with others to found Jewish-Christian feminist dialogue groups, and I start a Jewish feminist group called Kol Ishah – Voice of Woman. A whole new world opens up, familiar and new at the same time.

At the Graduate Theological Union in Berkeley, I pursue that world. I work on Edith Stein, a Jew who did not find spirituality in Judaism but instead in the contemplative tradition of the Carmelites, while still identifying as a Jew. And then, half-way through my doctoral studies, I join a small conservative synagogue in San Francisco, Congregation B'nai Emunah, led by Rabbi Ted Alexander. Rabbi Ted, as we call him, had survived in Shanghai and immigrated to San Francisco after the war. Through Rabbi Ted and the older congregants from Germany I learn about Rabbiner Regina Jonas, a woman whom Rabbi Ted's father had helped ordain more than sixty years before. Some of the congregants had been Jonas's students. Rabbi Ted had also known Edith Stein's niece. Piece by piece, stories about Jonas and Stein come together to form a portrait.

Ruthie Callmann z"l,[6] a long-standing board member of the synagogue, tells me that Regina Jonas would have been proud of me, a terrible student but the first female board member in our synagogue. When I learn of her, I wonder: Why had I never heard anything about Regina Jonas when I was growing up, and thought that the first woman rabbi was Sally Presind, ordained in 1972? Why was Jonas never mentioned in all the Holocaust literature I had read?

I turn my questions toward my work on this book. Of Stein, I want to know: Why had she left the Jewish tradition? Or had she? And now, of Jonas, I want to know: Why had the Jewish tradition I had known left her out? Both these women were trying to spiritually serve the Jewish community, a quest I shared. Studying them and giving voice to them could bring me back to the four amazing sister–survivors on my father's side of the family; on their behalf, I could bring insights about that generation's story to a broader community. Even though Gisela, Alma, and Paula had gone back to live the rest of their lives in Europe, in a way the Atlantic boat that brought them to New York for that mid-1960s visit had come back around to stay with me here in this small San Francisco congregation.

What I learn from these older German Jews is that we must always have joy in every moment, no matter how tough life becomes. I take this as a precious gift, and know that both Regina Jonas and Edith Stein were trying actively to give it as well, to do something to help their people spiritually during one of the most horrific periods in Jewish history. They did not survive the Shoah, but they left behind their voices in their documents. In this work, I recover and engage their voices, for them, who did not survive, and for my relatives, who did.

My quest to discover whether meaning is possible, whether there is any form of redemption, whether there is any place we can find God, leads to my engagement with Edith Stein and Regina Jonas. I have been on a quest to find meaning in something that seems so incomprehensible and meaningless. To me the Holocaust was about the production of death and I wonder if something good could be found in what appears to be incomprehensible absurdity. As my teenage daughter said to me after she overheard me discussing this book with one of my daughter's friends, "Now I understand, Mom, why you do what you do – it is because you are trying to find the good." In Edith Stein, a Jewish nun, and Regina Jonas, a woman rabbi, I found some good and this is the essence of the meaning of their lives.

When I encounter Edith Stein and Regina Jonas, two German Jewish women born a decade apart from each other but both on a mission to envision something greater than what their circumstances had dictated, I feel I am in the presence of two beings who can teach us the nature of good and give new meaning to the meaningless. Edith Stein was born October 12, 1891 in Breslau, Germany, and Regina Jonas was born August 3, 1902 in Berlin, Germany, both to liberal German Jewish families. They did not know each other during their lifetimes, but both died in Auschwitz two years apart. Stein was taken from Echt Carmel on the eve of Jonas's 40th birthday, August 2, 1942, and Jonas was deported two years later from Theresienstadt to Auschwitz on October 12, 1944 (Stein's 53rd birthday). I find this to be uncanny, even though their paths never crossed in their historical lives.

These two German Jewish women share some commonalities with my relatives the Tannenbaum sisters, who were born in the same decade as Regina Jonas. They all were highly educated women who pursued their passions. The difference between them and my relatives is that Stein and Jonas were religious visionaries. This book will trace how their deviant desires unfolded into religious visions that brought God into the world, from the Catholic and Jewish traditions respectively. Stein teaches us that suffering on the cross brings redemption and Jonas teaches us that *mitzvoth*, acts of compassion, bring the face of God into the world even in Theresienstadt.

Stein's and Jonas's deviant religious desires to be true to themselves as a Jewish Carmelite nun and a woman rabbi enabled them to bring God into the world when the Nazi regime shut down their physical spaces, which forced their desires to grow ever stronger. Stein always quested after the Truth with a capital "T." Jonas envisioned that women could be rabbis. Both Stein's and Jonas's vision quests were groundbreaking on many levels until they both met their fates in Auschwitz, two years apart from each other. They were atypical for their time and place but their truths and lives brought God into the world.

Their stories raise many important issues and questions about religious identity and what it meant to be a Jewish woman in Nazi Germany. Why did one become a Carmelite nun and the other a rabbi? What did Judaism have to offer Regina Jonas that it did not offer Edith Stein? Why did Edith Stein and Regina Jonas choose their particular spiritual paths at this time in Jewish history? Who supported Regina Jonas's ordination in 1935 – and who did not? What were Stein's and Jonas's philosophies of women and how did their philosophies influence their choices? How did these women take on their roles as nun and rabbi as the situation grew worse for the Jewish community in Europe? Were these strategies for dealing with the horrors of the Nazi period? How did Edith Stein handle her transport to Westerbork? How did Regina Jonas handle her transport to Theresienstadt as a woman and as a rabbi?

I will compare and contrast Stein's and Jonas's deviant desires, religious visions, and means of manifesting God in their own lives and the lives of their community. In order to draw my analysis I have had to work with an uneven amount of surviving documents. Stein loved to write and produced many philosophical and theological manuscripts, which the Carmelites have scrupulously preserved. Jonas was literally almost written out of history. She was not naturally a writer like Stein, but an orator who loved to teach and preach. What we have are her rabbinical ordination thesis, lecture and preaching notes, newsletter and newspaper interviews along with correspondence, which she had left in the Jewish Community Archive before her deportation to Theresienstadt. The archive was not fully opened up until the Berlin Wall fell in 1989. Kathrina von Kellenbach, a German-American Christian feminist theologian, was one of the first scholars to go into the Regina Jonas archives and publish articles. Rabbi Elisa Klapheck published the only biography of Jonas, with an annotated ordination thesis. Both of these scholars rescued Rabbinerin Jonas from being written out of history. I am concentrating on the historical theologies Stein and Jonas produced that came out of their experiences of the Nazi period.

BRINGING GOD INTO THE WORLD

The greatest question I had for my Yeshiva rabbis was how could they believe in God after the Holocaust. Is not the Holocaust direct proof there is absolutely no such thing as God? If God existed the Jewish people (or for that manner any people) would have been spared its horrors. A loving God would never have let the Holocaust happen. If a God did indeed exist it was very hard to imagine. I was upset, angry and thought anyone who believed in a God after the Holocaust had to be deluded, but I wanted to find out what had happened to God. I wanted to scream into the universe, "Where is God?"

When I discovered Edith Stein and Regina Jonas I found some theological meaning. These women showed me that God does exist. They were able to maintain their religious practice and their faith and relationship to God in precisely the situation that made me question God's existence.

Stein's faith was in a male, embodied, personal God, Jesus Christ, to whom I cannot relate. I can relate to Jonas's disembodied, impersonal, compassionate God, which is brought into the world by *tikkun olam* ("to repair the world"). I do have a bias towards Jonas because she shows us that we humans have a stake in bringing God into the world through our actions. It is not just a matter of pure faith, but that acts of compassion help us to see the face of the other and thus the power of the divine in the face of the other.

Stein felt that her family's Jewish tradition lacked a spiritual connection; she was alienated from Jewish practice and faith because it did not have connection to a personal, embodied God. She did see the practice of being a contemplative as a way to bring God into the world. She wrote in a letter to a Catholic sister:

> But gradually I realized that something else is asked of us in this world and that, even in the contemplative life, one may not sever the connection with the world. I even believe that the deeper one is drawn into God, the more one must "go out of oneself," that is, one must go to the world in order to carry the divine life into it.[7]

The more she withdrew from the world, the more she was able to go out and bring God into the exterior world.

For Jonas, the secularization of German Jews kept them from recognizing God's presence in their lives and in the world. For Stein, Judaism did not give any sense of spiritual fulfillment. Judaism did not dwell on an afterlife nor did it give her any space to be a contemplative. She found that she had to seek outside of the religions to which she was born and it was in Christianity, and Catholicism in particular, that she found meaning and a practice that satisfied her yearning for a spiritual life. She needed to convert to find God. As a Catholic mystic she was seeking to bring God into her interior world.

Stein brought God into the world through her pursuit of truth. Jonas brought God into the world through *mitzvoth*. Both were enabled by deviant desires. Both brought God into the world in the worst of circumstances. As the Nazis shrank Jewish space, Stein's and Jonas's deviant desires to be a Catholic contemplative and a woman rabbi grew stronger and stronger. Jonas's responsibilities as a woman rabbi expanded. Jonas brought her rabbinate to every space she was in, from working as slave laborer to being an inmate in a concentration camp. Stein's interior life blossomed inside the convent. Stein, in her mystical visions within the Carmel monastery, brought her people back to their redeemer in order to save them.

I treat Jonas as a critique of Stein because Stein turned away from Judaism in the way that Jonas feared Jews would – out of ignorance of their own tradition.[8] The fact that Stein and Jonas were contemporaries proves that Stein had the opportunity to learn about her own heritage. Instead, she rejected it without knowing it.

Many questions surface in the process of examining Stein's and Jonas's lives. What if Stein had met a woman rabbi like Jonas? What if Jonas could encourage Stein to study some Jewish texts with her? Stein's mother Auguste Stein was unsuccessful in getting her daughter to take any interest in Judaism. She would take her to lectures at the Breslau Rabbinical Seminary to listen to learned rabbis. What if Jonas could have understood Stein's struggles? Stein's truth is alien and horrifying to me, as a Jew who has a great love for my own tradition. Stein does teach us how suffering brings redemption on the cross, which speaks to many people. Stein's truth was that she was suffering on the cross for the sins of her people – the Jewish people – who did not accept one of their own as their Savior. This was the Catholic theology of her time and this was Stein's deepest faith. Stein's niece Susanne Batzdorff points out that Stein died because the Nazis saw her as a Jew and her death is no more sacred then any of the other six million Jewish deaths. Stein's life does not need to be elevated above those of her fellow Jews, for each life is just as holy as all the others.

I have experienced a sense of hubris when delving into Stein's thoughts and apparitions about Catholicism, particularly close to the time of her deportation. For a Catholic it may not seem like hubris, for this is the work of a Catholic monastic. My Jewish voice does not fully grasp Catholicism. I feel that Stein was betraying her people by offering herself as a sacrifice for their sins for something that was not part of their religion, although in her *Weltanschauung* she was saving them. Stein found a new path. It lacked an understanding of her family's religion, but in order for her to accept her new religion she had to embrace their anti-Jewish theology. The way she bridged her Jewishness was in her realization that she and Christ had the same Jewish blood. She saw herself as a Catholic Jew. So it is with a sense of disappointment that I use the word hubris to describe her actions at the end of her life, for the young philosopher Stein might have been more open.

Using Jonas as a point of critique allows me to question both Catholic and Jewish readings of Stein. For example, when I began to work on Edith Stein I came across a German illustrated children's book that was published just before Stein's canonization.[9] At the end of this book was a picture of Jewish children and Stein waiting in line at Auschwitz while over the building (presumably a gas chamber) was a cloud in which Jesus was welcoming Stein with all the little children.

When I saw this picture I was shocked and thought it was wrong. I had not yet read all of Stein and wanted to prove that the Carmelite nun who wrote this book was wrong about Stein's theology in this illustration. I talked to my dissertation advisor Rosemary Radford Ruether, a leading scholar on Christian anti-Semitism, and she agreed that it was anti-Jewish theology because the illustrator was trying to show that the Jewish children had converted. I then interviewed Stein's niece, Susanne Batzdorff, who told me that she talked to the Viennese nun who wrote the book. The nun explained to her that the little children were not Jewish. Batzdorff responded that of course the little children were Jewish.

I sadly learned that the nun was correct: this was Stein's contemplative thought, as we will see as I unpack her theology in this book. Stein had prayed for the Jews to accept one of their own as their Savior just as she did with her conversion to Catholicism. A couple of prominent Jewish scholars who have studied Stein cannot wrap their minds around this theological truth about her. Joyce Avrech Berkman explains away Stein's last will and testament, which calls for her death to be received for the sins of Jewish unbelief in God. Berkman argues that Stein believed her sacrifice was not for their sins of not accepting Christ as their Savior and God, but instead "meaning their unbelief in their Talmudic God, not their failing to be Christians."[10]

Rachel Brenner, who believes this story is hagiographical, writes that "it is possible to conjecture, as some of the Carmelite biographers do, that Stein intended to sacrifice herself for her people in order to bring forth the conversion of the Jews."[11] Brenner attempted to explain away Stein sacrificing herself for the sin of the Jews not accepting Christ as their redeemer, by arguing that Stein never reneged on her Jewish identity, her Jewish roots and her Jewish family, but held both religions as a hybrid identity or as a convergence of Jewish and Christian identity.

I agree that Stein did have a hybrid identity because of her identity with Jesus as a Jew, but this does not erase or lighten the fact that Stein in her interior life was praying and sacrificing herself on the cross for all Jews to convert and accept Christ as their own. Stein's unique view was that she recognized the historical Jewish Jesus long before the Catholic Church, but it did not change Stein's implicit anti-Jewish theology.

It is too hard for Berkman and Brenner to accept that one of their own people who was a brilliant philosopher would go to this point. I will show why it was important for Sister Teresa Benedicta of the Cross (aka Edith Stein) to pray for the sins of the Jews not accepting the Jewish man Christ as the Savior; but I think I can still learn about the meaning of redemptive suffering on the cross. Stein's convictions will not speak to the Jews who read this book, for it is part of a long history of Christians forcing Jews to convert. It is shocking that one of their own who converted would do what the enemy wanted to do. If the Jews had accepted the Savior then they would not have been sent to the gas chamber. Christians have to understand that Stein's hope for Jewish conversion is unacceptable to Jews and that it feels like blaming the victim for the horrors of the Holocaust. If only those stubborn Jews had accepted the Savior, then all this horror would stop; this was Stein's prayer. But Stein's message of suffering on the cross will resonate with Catholics and others, conveying the greater meaning that suffering can bring redemption. There is meaning to suffering.

I take full responsibility for what might be my lack of understanding of Catholicism, but it is hard to have engaged all these years with Stein and not have strong feelings about her. As someone who is not a practicing Catholic I cannot experience the practice the way I do Judaism. There is a level of knowledge and insight when one practices religious ritual and tradition, or grows up within one faith community, that cannot be grasped by someone writing outside of it. As Stein has shown in her dissertation, we can never know someone's primordial experience but only have a secondary or a non-primordial experience.

I will never fully grasp Stein's conversion epiphany or her faith, but I can investigate it from a scholar's perspective. For Catholics there may not be a problem that Stein was a Catholic Jew, but it is a serious problem for Jews because it conjures a sense of betrayal. One of many insights I have learned on my journey with Stein is that Catholicism is a religious tradition of faith in which one can be an Italian Catholic, French Catholic, African Catholic, and so on. From a Catholic perspective there might not be a difference to contemplate a Jewish Catholic. "Jewish" is viewed in this case as a nationality or ethnicity.[12] As a Jew this insight about faith was not obvious to me. My scholarly side respects Stein's truth, but the Jew in me has found myself at great tension with her. Many times I have found myself angry at her for not choosing her path from a place of knowledge, for (from my perspective) she made her decision to convert from a chosen ignorance. There are many things that did not satisfy Stein about Judaism. Jews do not dwell on the afterlife; Jews do not have contemplative orders for women; Jews do not have churches that one can go into and pray quietly in without interruption. There have been times in the middle of this project that I have thrown my books across my office, arguing with her. I see her brilliance and wonder what would have happened if she was allowed to submit a habilitation and been accepted as a philosopher.

In all fairness, I need to say that I would like to have engaged with Stein the philosopher and have been a member of her philosophical kindergarten at Göttingen. It would have been interesting to have had a theological discussion with Stein the contemplative nun.

Likewise, I wish I had been able to meet Regina Jonas. She seems to have had a sense of joy that she wanted to convey about the practice of Judaism. She wanted the youth not to stray; one of the many important roles of a woman rabbi would have been her ability to talk to young people who were losing faith in their traditions. Jonas felt a woman's heart was naturally more open to pastoral counseling and to reaching out to teach and comfort people.

DEVIANT DESIRES: THE DOUBLE-TAKE

How strange it must have been for people to see Edith Stein as Sister Teresa Benedicta of the Cross, dressed in the religious garments of a Carmelite nun with a yellow Jewish star sewn on to her brown scapular and black nun's habit. Rabbinerin Regina Jonas dressed in the long robes of a male rabbi. There was a sense of disbelief, of "how can this be?" P. O. Kempen and Pierre Cuypers reported that when they told the guards at Westerbork (a Nazi holding camp where Edith and Rosa Stein were being detained before their deportation eastwards) that they had come to visit a nun, the guards "were amazed ... 'Surely there are no nuns in the camp,' they said. Only after they had inquired that it was true did they believe us."[13]

The reaction of the Nazi guards was one of amazement. The idea that there would be Jewish nuns in a Nazi camp was indeed strange or queer. The guards' first reaction speaks to this strangeness. In the same light Herta S., who was a student of Jonas's, wrote in a letter to Katharina von Kellenbach, "Who had ever heard of a female rabbi? We challenged her accordingly."[14] Herta S.'s reaction is similar to that of the Nazi guards at Westerbork: it was a strange notion to consider that a woman would be a rabbi. It had never happened before.

These testimonies display the strangeness, the double-take, of how out of place a Jewish nun and a woman rabbi must have been. According to queer theorist Sara Ahmed:

> I have used "queer" as a way of describing what is "oblique" or "off line." [And] I also describe the presence of bodies of color in white spaces as disorienting: the proximity of such bodies out of place can work to make things seem "out of line," and can hence even work to "queer" space; people "blink" and do "double turns" when they encounter such bodies.[15]

People's disbelief that Stein was a Jewish nun and Jonas was a rabbi goes "off line," out of place. Queer theory is also a way of talking about deviant religious desire and fluid religious identities. Stein's and Jonas's religious desires led them to dress, act, and perform in the world in a way that was "disorienting" to others. How do we begin to grasp the multi-hybridization of these disorienting identities? Stein considered herself to be a German, Catholic-Jewish nun, and Jonas was a rabbinerin, *Fraulein Rabbiner*, a woman rabbi.

I argue that we can derive, in the cases of these two women, an ethics of multiple and mixed identities. How do we choose the communities that we identify with? And when do we choose our loyalties to them? As I investigate these questions, I develop a philosophy of identity and ethics. Even though these two women cross over to a new world, they still have part of themselves in the world that they have left behind. For example, Edith Stein converted to Catholicism, but she did not feel that she had abandoned the Jewish community. While she was in the convent, she wrote a book about what it meant to grow up Jewish. She referred to herself as Queen Esther. She did not do so because she was a Catholic, but because she was a Jew. The Queen Esther motif in queer theory refers to the motif of hiding and revealing. The King did not know Queen Esther was Jewish; she passed as a Persian but when the Jewish community was in trouble, she revealed her true identity as a Jew. Edith Stein saw herself as doing the same thing centuries later. Edith Stein staked her claim of her Jewishness when she was cloistered in a convent as a contemplative nun.

In a parallel but also contradictory move, Jonas staked her claim as a woman in the Jewish and rabbinical community. Like Stein, Jonas was crossing over, not in the sense of converting, but in terms of gender. Jonas crossed over from the Jewish women's community into the male world of the rabbinate. She challenged the system by posing the question "Can Women Be Rabbis?"

in her rabbinical thesis of the same title. Jonas's rabbinical thesis demonstrates that there is no reason why women cannot be rabbis from the perspective of Talmudic and *Halakhic* authority. Jonas achieved this crossing by maintaining her connectedness to the world of Jewish women and not hiding her intentions. Like Stein, Jonas was making a claim of being in both worlds.

Stein's and Jonas's dramatic and highly personal moves occurred at a critical historical moment in Jewish history. Stein claimed her Catholic spirituality as a Jew and her Jewishness as a Catholic contemplative, while Jonas sought a rabbinical ordination as a woman. Both women made this claim under Nazi rule. Stein began writing *Life in a Jewish Family* in 1933 in the convent at Cologne and stopped writing it in 1939 in the convent at Echt in Holland. Jonas first wrote her ordination thesis in 1930 in Berlin under the Weimar Republic. She was at first rejected for ordination but ultimately received her ordination in 1935 after the Nazis came to power. Jonas went on to give sermons and lectures as a woman rabbi to her people in the late 1930s in Berlin, and then later in Theresienstadt against the wishes of the Chief Rabbi.

These women's spiritual pursuits led them to cross over from one world into another world, but they refused to make the rupture complete – a move that disrupted the normative cultural boundaries. In this way they created a new form of mixed identities and revealed a multiplicity of communities of belonging. I use the word "queering" as a verb meaning "crossing", and to demonstrate that crossing is a form of deviant desire. I borrow the concept of crossing from queer theorists Elspeth Probyn and Eve Kosofsky Sedgwick.

This crossing over is a deviant desire in that I understand Stein and Jonas as crossing over a space of culturally constructed boundaries of religion and gender into another space, creating a new way of being in the world. They ruptured the boundaries of a singular identity by demanding to be in both spaces simultaneously. Hence I define queering as "crossing over" because one is moving across boundaries in space. The outcome of Stein's and Jonas's queering is hybridization: a whole new form of presenting oneself in the world that demonstrates one's allegiance to multiple communities simultaneously and enables them to bring God into the world in very confined, devastating spaces. Their deviant religious desires are journeys, which are a disruption and jarring of the traditionally established boundaries, opening up a new space and creating a new way of performing and being in the world.

Stein and Jonas were breaking out of and liberating themselves from the dominant cultural paradigms and discourses on religion and gender by turning these paradigms upside down, which is a form of self-liberation and an ethical stance. Both perceived themselves in the role of spiritual service to the Jewish people in opposite ways: one seeming to leave the world of Judaism as a contemplative Catholic nun and the other going deeper into the tradition as a woman rabbi. Both these women sought their deepest spiritual truths at one of the most difficult moments in Jewish history and made their truth claims in a significant Jewish historical moment, Nazi Germany, which raised the stakes of their choices.

I argue that the role of queer identity is a form of resistance to dominant cultural identities. When one acts queer, as Jonas and Stein did, one rejects the normative cultural boundaries and liberates one's sense of self, which is an ethical act. Stein was not passing as a Catholic to survive in the dominant culture, she was queering her identity by asserting her sense of spiritual self. When Jonas gave sermons as a woman rabbi in Berlin and Theresienstadt, her queering not only liberated herself but also inspired other Jewish women to resist Nazi oppression.

In the case studies of Edith Stein, a Jewish nun, and Regina Jonas, a woman rabbi, their religious desires and practices, dress and performance, social orientations as Jew and woman, and the spaces they performed in and inhabited because of their religious claims are all queer. Stein and Jonas are considered strange in many ways due to the sense of how they perform their "out-of-line" religious desires in the world. They have crossed over two forbidden boundaries for their historical time and place. Modern identity is characterized by an emphasis on an inner voice and capacity for *authenticity*, that is, the ability to find a way of being that is somehow true to oneself. [16] Although the outside world might have perceived Stein and Jonas to be queer for their time, both of them claimed that they were being true to themselves. Jonas wrote on the back of her ordination photo from Exodus, "I will be what I will be"; Stein claimed she found the big Truth that she was looking for when she read St Teresa of Avila's autobiography.

What is religious desire? What is queer desire? How can religious desires be deviant? How do dress and performance signify these desires, which in a binary culture could be noted as strange? Do dress and performance instill a sense of identity that matches with desire? What if someone's religious desire does not fit into acceptable religious categories? In Stein's and Jonas's time women did not become rabbis and Jews did not become Catholics who claim to be both Catholic and Jewish at the same time. I make the case that their religious desires were deviant in the same way that queer sexual desires are viewed as deviant in a heterosexual paradigm. In order to grasp why these religious identity claims would seem strange, I need to find a method that would address the hybridities of their claims: Stein's claim as a German Catholic Jewish woman nun, and Jonas's as a woman rabbi who states that a whole new way of addressing her is required. Stein and Jonas demonstrate what Hannah Arendt points out about the uniqueness of human beings:

> The fact that man is capable of action means that the unexpected can be expected from him, that he is able to perform what is infinitely improbable and this again is possible only because each man is unique, so that with each birth something uniquely new comes into the world.[17]

Queer theory gives us a language and a way of talking about a Jewish nun's and woman rabbi's out-of-placeness; it argues for the infinitely possible ways of acting and being in the world through performance. How they perform, dress, speak, and desire reveals who they are and not what they are. Queer theory shows us how uniqueness is possible by arguing for the social construction of fluid identities.

Ultimately, what I feel queer theory is showing us is how it is possible to see through to the uniqueness of human beings. Hannah Arendt was the first to recognize this. I contend that she has paved the way because she understood, like the postcolonial theorist Frantz Fanon, that we are oppressed when our biological characteristics are reified. This applies to Jews because they were essentialized by the Nazis in order to oppress them, as modern anti-Semites have also done. We know who someone is through their actions, which means speech and performance in the world. Human identity is not to be confused with the physical attributes that we are born with. Fanon demonstrates that oppression operates through constructing ontological identities based on physical attributes such as skin color, and that the Nazis tried to prove that the Jews were physically inferior by inventing physical attributes that demonized them, such as calling them vermin.

Before there was something called identity politics and something known as queer theory, two thinkers framed the debate of how we identify ourselves, not by asking the question "What are we?" but instead asking, "Who are we?" Both thinkers were writing from their own experience of oppression, of being a subjugated and oppressed minority in an anti-Semitic and racist world. The first thinker, Hannah Arendt, a German Jew who escaped the Nazi persecution to America in 1941, has not usually been viewed as being part of the discourse of identity politics. The second, Franz Fanon, a black man from French-colonized Martinique, is considered to be the father of the theory of identity politics in colonization. Both Arendt and Fanon were responding to having had to deal with anti-Semitism and racism. Hannah Arendt is one of the first philosophers to have recognized that identity is not about "what" we are but about "who" we are. Arendt writes in her 1958 book *The Human Condition*:

> In acting and speaking, men show *who they are*, reveal actively their unique personal identities and thus make their appearance in the human world, while their physical identities appear without any activity of their own in the unique shape of the body and sound of the voice. *This disclosure of "who" in contradistinction to "what" somebody is* – his qualities, gifts, talents, and shortcomings, which he may display or hide – is implicit in everything somebody says and does.[18]

Arendt points out, as queer theorists such as Judith Butler, David Halperin, Susan Phelan, Eve Sedgwick, and others will forty years later, that physical attributes such as one's gender does not tell us anything about "who" someone is and that it is a mistake to attribute a personal identity to physical attributes and qualities. Identity is not about "what" somebody is. "What" is a question about essence that can be associated with physical qualities. Arendt is asserting that when an individual speaks and acts in the world they are informing us, the audience, "who" they are. Franz Fanon, in his revolutionary 1952 book *Black Skin White Masks*, makes the ground-breaking statement: "black is not the man."[19] In other words my skin color does not tell someone who I am. My skin color is just a physical attribute, as Arendt has stated.

Unfortunately, in a racist world black skin signifies – as Fanon goes on to argue – a negative biological quality, which is demonized and has to be subjugated and enslaved by the white oppressor. Black is viewed as a biological essence and the unique person cannot be seen – only skin color and the evil it implies. The unique human being is erased or obliterated by the objectification of the physical qualities. Just as Fanon has argued that oppressors reify biological categories in order to oppress, the Nazis went to extremes to reify nonexistent biological attributes of Jews, which is why they had to resort to the Yellow Star. Stein and Jonas exemplify a form of liberating themselves from these Nazi categories, exemplified in their religious identity and dress. So, a nun with a Jewish star sewn onto her habit totally subverts the Nazi system.

Arendt's response to the Holocaust was to state that we cannot reduce people to all or nothing categories, such as the nation state. She told Gerschom Scholem in a famous exchange of letters in response to Scholem's outrage over her book *Eichmann in Jerusalem* that she never had a love for her people – the Jewish people or nation – but she loves her individual friends; what matters is the particular, the individual:

> I have never in my life "loved" any people or collective – neither the German people, nor the French, nor the American, nor the working class or anything of that sort, I indeed love "only" my friends and the only kind of love I know of and believe in is the love of persons.[20]

Arendt had a love of the unique individual, which is what queer theorists are arguing: that there is no thing, no substance, no general essence. She did not love a nation, a collective or a political movement such as the women's movement. Arendt refused to subsume who she was. If we take as an understanding that our identities are not tied to our physical attributes, what is left is the performance in the world which expresses uniqueness. Also, a failure to recognize uniqueness leads to making people superfluous, which was the core dynamic of the Holocaust. Stein and Jonas both exemplified the uniqueness that resisted the way the Nazis tried to make populations superfluous.

Queer identity is defined through its opposition to the normative, but also through its claims to achieve the so-called "norm." The idea of "no thing" in particular implies that there is no essence. This is why I choose to use queer theory in my investigation into Stein and Jonas's religious identities. They are queer because they do not fit into any previous set categories. No one had conceived of a woman rabbi and no one had conceived of a Catholic Jew. Stein's use of Jewishness was different. It would not be recognized by any normative Jew in her day or ours. I investigate the crossing of Stein and Jonas through a non-essentialist socially constructed lens but Stein and Jonas believe in a foundation of essence. In terms of the category of woman, Jonas's crossing of becoming a woman rabbi is oppositional to the notion of rabbi, which had always been male. The boundary she was breaking was the concept that all rabbis are male. The opposition that Stein was defined by was Catholic Jew, especially when most Jews converted to Catholicism to escape the Nazis. It threatened one's life to say that one was still a Jew in Nazi Germany. Queer theory asks *how* Stein and Jonas identify themselves and *where* Stein and Jonas identify themselves, not *as what* they identify themselves.

OVERVIEW

This first part of the book will examine Stein's and Jonas's deviant desires. Their desires culminate with Stein becoming a Jewish Carmelite nun and Jonas a rabbinerin. I will demonstrate that the foundations for their inner yearnings and deviant desires were laid down by their essentialist worldviews on women. This is not the essentialism we think of today, in which the biology of the body dictates destiny, but an essentialism that viewed women as having a propensity towards certain innate qualities, such as nurturing and caring, which Stein locates on a spectrum. There is an implicit but not explicit feminism in the essentialist arguments of both Stein and Jonas.

Part II will describe how they handled their religious visions. What is religious vision? In the case of Stein and Jonas it meant two different things. For Stein, it was apparitions of a mystical vision of the future, a mystical vision of the present and a mystical vision of the soul's reunion with its beloved. For Jonas, it was instead a vision of the possibilities of a new type of rabbinate, a new type of rabbi, a woman rabbi. It was also a vision of bringing secular German Jews back to their Jewish roots. For Stein vision meant that her mysticism led her to become a contemplative, whereas for Jonas vision meant that she practiced as a woman rabbi. Religious vision is different than mystical vision because it envisions the role that one's religion can play in one's life and historical circumstances.

Part III demonstrates how the two women manifested their vision of community and God: for Stein, through interior life via her writing in the Carmel monastery, and for Jonas, through teaching as a woman rabbi in Berlin and then in Theresienstadt.

I am not a historian. This work is a historical theology that demonstrates how two out-of-place women – a Jewish nun and a woman rabbi – brought God into the world.

Chapter 2

STEIN'S AND JONAS'S VIEWS OF WOMEN: THE PHILOSOPHY STUDENT AND THE RABBINICAL STUDENT

What drove Stein and Jonas to pursue their paths toward bringing God into the world as a Jewish Carmelite contemplative and a woman rabbi? What underpinned their desires were their views and conceptions of women as being naturally empathetic, whole, and nurturing, which they then brought to professions outside of the private domain, to which women had been conventionally relegated. They needed to bring what they saw as their innate natural feminine qualities to what had originally been male professions. This chapter addresses the fundamental questions asked and answered by Stein and Jonas: What is woman? What are the innate qualities that each associated with being female? How did their perception of woman affect their religious calling and practice? Whom do Stein and Jonas perceive to be the "new women" of Weimar? How did they respond to these women in their writing and lectures? Finally, how did they perceive themselves in light of their concepts of woman?

Both women wrote major academic works at the beginning of their careers. In 1916, Stein completed her dissertation on empathy, which she wrote under the supervision of the phenomenologist Edmund Husserl. In 1930, Jonas completed her ordination thesis, titled "Can Women Serve as Rabbis?," which she wrote under the supervision of Rabbi Dr Eduard Baneth. In this chapter I will unpack Stein's doctoral dissertation on empathy and her writings on women, as well as Jonas's ordination thesis, which set up the trajectories of both of their life's work.

Neither Stein nor Jonas had role models to mentor them as they were pursuing their goals of being a woman philosopher and a woman rabbi.[1] Unlike in England and America, where women had been pursuing higher education since at least the 1860s, in central Europe women were not admitted to universities until 1908.[2] Just eight short years later, Stein became the one of the first women in central European history to receive her doctorate in philosophy (as noted below, Grete Henschel was the first), and the first to receive it from Husserl. No European woman that we know of had formally trained for the rabbinate. Jonas achieved her goal in 1935. It is possible that

27

Jonas would have known of women aspiring to the rabbinate in America –
the question of women becoming Rabbis was discussed in *Jüdischer Frauenbund* circles – but Jonas would not have been able to turn to American
women for support and advice, in any case.[3] Not having role models meant
that Stein and Jonas had to blaze their own paths in their own way; there
were no other women from whom they could seek counsel. In Stein's case,
a number of her women friends were also studying for PhDs in philosophy
and mathematics, including her sister-in-law Nellie Courant *née* Neumann,[4]
but all of them were forging a new path together. Not having a role model
meant that Stein and Jonas both followed their inner compass. They had
something in sight, but they didn't know what it looked like or how to con-
figure it. They had to figure it out along the way. Stein felt called to seek
the truth; Jonas felt called to serve her people as a spiritual leader. Stein's
quest for truth was a moving target, whereas Jonas always had a clear idea
that she wanted to be a woman rabbi. Their inner visions would guide them
along their lives' journeys to pursue their personal truths. Stein's journey
went from being a phenomenological philosopher to being a Carmelite contemplative. Jonas went from being a Hebrew school teacher to being a fully
ordained woman rabbi.

Both Stein and Jonas shared the liberal or bourgeois feminist view of
women associated with the women's organizations *Bund Deutscher Frauenv-
ereine* and the *Jüdischer Frauenbund*: they believed that there was a "unique"
difference between men and women.[5] A woman's uniqueness did not, however, limit her talents, nor did it restrict the professions she might choose
to enter. Each gender brought a particular set of qualities that complement
the other, they believed. These notions were aligned with the German and
German Jewish traditions of feminism in which they found themselves, which
"was also built upon the assumption of certain natural differences between
the sexes. It conceived of 'equality' not in formal or inalienable terms, but
rather in terms of equal possibilities for the fulfillment of the unique potential
of each sex."[6] A woman's unique potential was that that she "naturally seeks
to embrace that which is *living, personal* and *whole*."[7] Stein and Jonas both
saw a moral dilemma to the sexually active, daring "new woman". While they
embraced the celebration of women's multiple talents and gifts, they both
found a moral decay in some of the behavior. Historians Renate Bridenthal,
Atina Grossman, and Marion Kaplan point out that:

> While the "new woman" did not signal female emancipation or the
> collapse of the patriarchy, she did represent – to some – a moral
> crisis. This definition of the female in Weimar period included
> images of women, as victim, threat, and salvation. Thus the "new
> woman" captured the imagination of progressives who celebrated
> her, even as they sought to discipline and regulate her, and of con-
> servatives, who blamed her for everything from the decline of the

birth rate and the laxity of morals to the unemployment of male workers.[8]

Both Stein and Jonas lamented in their discussions of women that there was a moral crisis over the young woman, and especially their new-found sexual practices. The type of women that Stein and Jonas were attacking were women who are known as flappers: they dressed in a very masculine style, with bobbed hair, straight dresses, or pants. Their dress accentuated no curves; they chewed gum, smoked cigarettes, and were not afraid of the power of freely expressing their sexuality. They were self-supporting and did not necessarily believe in legal marriage. In contrast, both Stein and Jonas felt that a certain amount of modesty and piety should be brought to the male professions, which they were attempting to enter, and they considered themselves role models in this respect.

Despite their similarities with regard to their understanding of the role of women, their paths would diverge on religious grounds. There is an indirect personal connection between Edith Stein and Regina Jonas, which perfectly illustrates the divergent theological routes of the two women: Dr Rabbi Julius Guttmann. One of Stein's Jewish friends from her philosophical circle, Dr Grete Henschel, who was the first woman in central Europe to receive a doctorate in philosophy, studied and wrote a thesis under Eugen Kuhnemann, who was a Kantian. Henschel married Guttmann, who was also a Kantian and opposed on principle to phenomenology. Stein only met Guttmann once at a friend's house where they had a philosophical discussion. Stein wrote of Guttmann, "In every way he was as totally the opposite of Grete Henschel as I was. Short, unprepossessing in appearance, and modest in bearing, he was a fine but reticent scholar and thoroughly kind person."[9] Guttmann, in turn, went on to become a full professor at the Hochschule fur die Wissenschaft des Judentums, or the Liberal Rabbinical Seminary in Berlin, when Regina Jonas was a Rabbinical student. On March 4, 1931, he signed, along with other faculty members, a get-well card to Jonas.[10] He was her examiner for religious philosophy and signed her diploma on December 12, 1930 "Academic Teacher of Religion" at the Hochschule.[11]

It is probable that Guttmann had been influenced by Hermann Cohen, the neo-Kantian at Marburg and then a professor at the Rabbinical Seminary in Berlin from 1912 to 1918. Guttmann later replaced Cohen as the Professor of Jewish Philosophy at the Rabbinical Seminary in Berlin when Cohen passed away in 1919:

> Cohen defined God as the conjunction of two ideas: the concept of ideal ethical laws unifying all humanity into a harmonious realm of ends, and the faith that, at the end of history, this ideal would be realized. Thus Cohen's ethics seem to offer complete, systematic accounts of both of religion's central concepts.[12]

Cohen's Kantian concept of God partially reflected Jewish practice's emphasis on ethics. Judaism is predominantly about the practice of Jewish law and ethical practice of good deeds known as *mitzvoth*. It teaches a faith in a non-personal God that is greater than one can imagine and is all-knowing, but also is not possible to know personally. Jonas accepted this understanding of God. Stein did not.

EDITH STEIN

Edith Stein was born in Breslau on October 12, 1891. Starting from a very young age, Stein was looking for the ultimate meaning of life, which led her on her journey to find the truth. Around the time they entered university, Stein and her sister Erna visited their uncle in Lublinitz, where he counseled them on their education. Stein had desired to get a PhD in philosophy and psychology, and her sister had desired to obtain a PhD in literature. Their uncle told them that it would be much better if they went to medical school instead, because then they would be able to have a practice and support themselves. Stein's sister followed their uncle's advice of abandoning her dream of pursuing literature and trained to become a gynecologist and obstetrician. Stein ignored the advice and went on to pursue a PhD in philosophy. She was adamant that she was going to pursue philosophy, for Stein's desire was always to discover the truth. This incident with her uncle shows from the beginning that nothing could sway Stein from her desire to pursue the truth. Stein became the first woman to receive her doctorate in philosophy from the most eminent philosopher of her day, Edmund Husserl.

Stein went to study psychology in Breslau, but it did not have the deep answers she was looking for in her pursuit of psychology and philosophy. Stein had been part of a group that was studying with the psychologist William Stern, who was then more interested in methods for studying the psychology of early childhood and children's speech and pedagogy than in the deep philosophical questions that interested Stein. What truly inspired her to study with Husserl was a photo in a journal of a talented female philosophy student, Hedwig Martius. Stein writes, "One day, an illustrated journal carried a picture of a woman student from Göttingen who had won a prize for a philosophical thesis. She was Husserl's highly talented student."[13] Her friend Dr Moskewicz (a medical doctor and doctoral candidate in philosophy), who had studied with Husserl, told her that students spent every moment philosophizing about phenomena, which was a dream for Stein. When Stein approached Stern for a dissertation topic, he gave her a rigid one, which was to stick to his ideas on the thought process of children. He did not let her choose her own topic, and was adamant that she accept his thesis and not challenge it. Stern's approach to psychology was an experimental one, and this restriction did not please her. For all these reasons she went off to become a phenomenologist with Husserl and his circle.

Figure 1 Edith Stein as a student in 1913 (© Edith Stein Archiv, Karmel Maria vom Frieden).

She went to Göttingen to study under Husserl, the father of the philosophy of phenomenology. In contrast to the standard procedure of a *Doktorvater* assigning a dissertation topic, Stein and Husserl discussed the matter and decided she would write on empathy. Stein had been fascinated by the philosopher Max Scheler (one of the only people she described as a genius) and his book, *The Nature of Sympathy*.[14] Stein felt that Scheler's book was especially significant because she had just begun thinking about the problem of "empathy."

During World War I, in the middle of her studies, she decided that she *must* serve her country. As a German patriot, she enrolled in the Red Cross and trained to be a nurse. She served the wounded and learned first-hand the meaning of war and suffering by serving in the *Lazeretto*, an infectious disease unit, at Mahrisch-Weiskirchen. Her experiences on the front serving wounded, traumatized soldiers had a deep impact on her.

Nursing was an act of direct empathy on the front. Stein practiced the art of caring and had to learn how to navigate different classes of soldiers with typhoid, and how to confront illness, trauma, and dying. When Stein served in the *Lazaretto* there were wounded and diseased soldiers from many different nations under the rubric of the Austro-Hungarian Empire. These included Germans, Czechs, Slovaks, Slovenes, Poles, Ruthenians, Hungarians, Romanians, and Italians. The German nurses had to learn how to communicate with them when they did not know one of the nine different languages, so they signed to the wounded soldiers when they did not have a language in common. What Stein experienced in the ward could have impacted her dissertation on empathy. We do not have any letters or texts from Stein about trying to communicate with sick soldiers and how this impacted her dissertation topic on empathy, but we can surmise that it enriched her dissertation question on how we understand or empathize with another person, especially when language barriers are present.

When she finally returned from serving on the front, she completed her dissertation. During the summer of 1916 she was at her mother's house, bedridden from exhaustion. After she returned home and completed her state examinations for her dissertation she was asked to teach at her old gymnasium in Breslau since all the teachers had been called to serve in the War. This left little time for her to finish writing her dissertation, so she had to dictate it to her two cousins. When she tried to work on her dissertation while she was a nurse in Weisskirchen she would get anxious as she examined the literature, but now back at home she was able to put her anxieties aside and begin anew:

> [T]hat dreadful winter of 1913–14 was not yet forgotten. Now I
> resolutely put aside everything derived from other sources and
> began, entirely at rock bottom to make an objective examination
> of the problem of empathy according to phenomenological methods. Oh what a difference compared to my former efforts![15]

Her dissertation was in the field of philosophical phenomenology. Her thesis "On the Problem of Empathy" attempted to explicate the essence of inter-subjectivity between human beings, who exist in the form of living human bodies in a spatial world. Stein asks: How are we "to consider the phenomenon of givenness in and of itself and to investigate its essence?"[16] How is it that we experience someone else's experience of emotion, feelings, desire? How do we acquire knowledge and communicate with another human? What is the essence of this type of inter-subjectivity between human beings? How is something given to us and how do we experience another's experience? Stein states:

The individual is not given as physical body, but as a sensitive, living body belonging to an "I" – an "I" that senses, thinks, feels and wills. The living body of this "I" not only fits into my phenomenal world, but is itself the center of orientation of such a phenomenal world. It faces this world and communicates with me.[17]

In this initial statement, the "I" whose acts of empathetic awareness provide the subject matter for her investigation is characterized both as subject and as object and indeed as "a subject who is aware of herself as an object of awareness of other subjects."[18] The "I" becomes aware that it is both a subject and object simultaneously. The "I" is the object to the other as the object is an other to her, which the "I" investigates from the subjective perspective of the object being presented to her. The "I" holds two perspectives at the same time that it is both subject and object. Empathy is "what is given." It is a mental act that we perform from the knowledge of what is given from the other living body.

Stein's dissertation was groundbreaking in that it was the first fully fledged, in-depth attempt to describe a phenomenological approach to empathy.[19] She proposes that our investigation of phenomena begins from the zero point orientation, which is the "I" in our own selves. Stein goes on to argue that empathy becomes the bridge to the inter-subjective experience between myself and the outer world, which creates "the condition of the possible knowledge of the existing outer world."[20] The approach of phenomenology was an epistemological rejection of Kant's argument that we can never know things in themselves; we can only know their appearances. Unlike Kant, we are not imposing static categories from our mind on our sensory impressions of objects, which then come together from our sense impression to form a representation of the thing in itself that does not exist outside of experience.[21] For Husserl, things in themselves do exist outside of our experience – it is our mental acts that present us with these objects, such as judging, thinking, hearing, seeing. Stein wanted to understand how we experience what is given to us through communication with others who share living bodies outside of our own lives in a spatial world. The other has a living body just as much as I who is being given the communication. Perhaps her experience as a nurse made her wonder how we can understand what is given to us in a communication even if it is not in language we comprehend.

For example, when we as a subject have the experience of encountering another person as a living body who is feeling the emotion "joy," we immediately become an object to them as another living body who also has feelings. In the experience of empathy, we are being given the emotion of joy as our object, a non-primordial experience of the other's joy. We cannot have a direct experience of another's particular joy; we can only have an experience of the act of memory that triggers our memories of joy, which we are projecting on to it. Our projection tells us something about ourselves, and our experience of the other is always informing us about knowledge of ourselves as both subject and object:

> Knowledge reaches its object but does not "have" it. It stands before its object but does not see it. Knowledge is blind, empty and restless, always pointing back to some kind of experienced, seen act. *And the experience back to which knowledge of foreign experience points is called empathy.*[22]

I know of another's grief through a communication with them. This can be communicated by gestures from our bodies, language etc., but is always a physical body. Stein explains that my experience of the other's grief which is given in this communication is experienced non-primordially through a trigger in myself of a reflection of the memories and feeling I have about grief. "Should this be the griever himself, it is primordially given to him in reflection. Should it be the third person he comprehends it non-primordially in empathy."[23]

Empathy is an act of cognition that happens when there is a communication between two living beings that gives the subject non-primordial experience of the emotion of the object, which then triggers memories of the feeling that was given to them in the communication with the other. Is it possible then to experience empathy with a spirit who is not a living body and can a being who is not in a living body have communication with someone who is in a living body? She reasons that we can know the spiritual life of others through their corporeal work such as their writings or any other form, which is connected to a physical body:

> But does not live communion unite me with contemporary spirits and tradition unite me immediately with spirits of the past without bodily mediation? Certainly I feel myself to be one with others and allow their emotions to become motives for my willing. However this does not give me the others, but already presupposes their givenness. (And I consider as my own that which penetrates into me from others, living or dead, without knowing it. This establishes no exchange of spirits.)[24]

She goes on to wonder how we can have empathy for spiritual people's experience of God's grace or those who feel they have been guided by protective spirits. She concludes that she cannot really answer these questions, which are for the study of religious consciousness. Her last words of the dissertation are, "It is not clear."[25]

The irony is that in the dissertation she says that it is not clear if knowledge exchange in the form of empathy can take place between a disembodied being and a being who is in the body. As a Catholic mystic and contemplative she will experience direct exchange of being. The questions that she posed as a 25-year-old philosopher and Jewish woman did not become clear to her until she converted to Catholicism, and especially when she entered the Carmelite as contemplative nun. As a bride of God she was literally married to disembodied being and she had a mystical experience of this union.

One area that Stein later developed is that of the nature of the human person. This comes out in her lectures on her views and concepts of women:

> I had examined the act of "empathy" as a particular act of cognition. After that, however, I went on to something which was personally close to my heart and which continually occupied me anew in all later works; the constitution of the human person. In connection with my original work, research along this line was necessary to show how the comprehension of mental associations differs from the simple perception of psychic conditions.[26]

Stein's thesis demonstrates that empathy is one of the keys with which we unlock the essence or gain knowledge not only of other people's experiences but of being itself. Stein carries this philosophical approach into her investigation of the nature of women and eventually into a mystical relationship with the divine, which is the ultimate experience of being. Both her reflections on woman and her relation to the divine would be guided by her conversion to Catholicism – she was baptized on January 1, 1922. I will discuss her conversion in detail in Chapter 3.

STEIN'S CONCEPT OF WOMAN

We can glean the answers to the question "What is the nature of woman?" from Stein's academic lectures, delivered on a lecture tour and in radio addresses in Germany, Switzerland, and Austria. A tour for her was organized by Stein's friend Fr Erich Przywara, who between 1928 and 1932 was involved with the Catholic Women Movement. Her main exploration was of the question, "Is there a feminine nature, and if so how should we educate human beings who possess this nature?" She answers that young women should be prepared for a professional life, married life, or a consecrated life to Christ as a nun. During the time of Stein's speaking tour, she was a teacher at St Magdalena's secondary school and training institute, instructing young women to be future Catholic school teachers in Spreyer, Germany. She was a practicing Catholic living with the Dominican sisters of St Magdalena. Her academic career had fallen flat; no university would accept her habilitation, simply because she was a woman. Husserl had not really supported her application to Göttingen. He wrote a disappointing recommendation, basically refusing to battle or break down the gender barriers in academia and support her, his talented female student. Husserl stated, "If the career of university teaching was open to ladies, then I would be the very first to be able to recommend her enthusiastically for admission to habilitation."[27] Stein wrote a letter of protest to the Prussian Ministry for Science, Art and Education for discrimination against her as a woman. Stein wrote to her philosophical friend Fritz Kaufman after her rejection and protest in 1920:

> I am not thinking of trying again for habilitation. That circular to the universities regarding the habilitation of women was due to my request, certainly, but I promise myself very little by ways of results. It was only a rap on the knuckles for the gentlemen in Göttingen.[28]

The Prussian ministry issued a statement in 1921 that a person's gender should not be a barrier for habilitation. But change would come very slowly: the first woman was not hired until thirty years later. In the interim, Stein had converted and became a devout Catholic.

Stein experienced first-hand the limits of women's emancipation. She was not welcomed inside the walls of the academy, and had to fall back on the more traditional career path of a school teacher. Ironically, the most important male mentor in Stein's philosophical career, Edmund Husserl, did not take on her battle for acceptance into the world of academia. He simply wanted to keep her as his glorified assistant until she married. It is possible that Husserl, being a converted Lutheran Jew, was hesitant to take on the struggle to admit a woman to the university when so few Jewish *men* had been hired as professors at German universities because of anti-Semitic discrimination. In this way, Stein had the double burden of being not only a woman but also a Jew at the time of her habilitation, which was a major handicap in Imperial Germany.

Stein addressed her view of the moral laxity of Weimar women when she described the drop in marriage and the high divorce rate; she tried to explain why women were led astray. In 1932, she wrote a reflective paper, "Problems of Women's Education," for the Catholic German Institute of Scientific Pedagogy. She served there as an Instructor for one year, before her dismissal with the rise of the Nazis in 1933, and was well aware of the sexual revolution that was taking place in Weimar. She cautioned that "we must admit that the situation of woman differs according to generation, status and *Weltanschauung* [worldview]; and these differences must not be overlooked."[29] She recognized that married people between the ages of 20 and 30 were having more childless marriages, more divorces, and more unmarried unions. Also she noted an increased significance attributed to eroticism and sexuality in scholarly writing as well as in *belles lettres*, in public discussion, and in daily life, such that even children are confronted with them at every turn:

Modern Youth has proclaimed their sexual rights. ... If these ideals [sacred marriage] are abandoned, it results in the practice of free unions or absolute promiscuous intercourse. The latter has increased in frightening proportion in all circles from year to year. This is partly a manifestation of the universally growing uninhibited drives: partly, it is an exact consequence of the negative theories aired in public discussion on marriage, which a more traditional morality cannot withstand.[30]

Stein felt that the new attitude towards sexual freedom was pervasive in every sphere, even the scholarly. Pioneers such as Magnus Hirschfield had set up the Institute for the Scientific Study of Sex to investigate sexual choices and practices such as lesbianism or homosexuality. Different sexual practices were freely expressed outside of the domain of marriage. The new generation was seeking companion marriages, getting married, but using birth control during the first years of marriage in order to decide whether they were compatible before launching a family. If not, they reasoned, they could easily get divorced. Or the couple would live together as comrades in the communist or socialist sense: as equals, with no difference between them. Stein argued that the remedy for the moral decay, the destruction of the sacred institution of marriage, and the sexual promiscuity was to understand women's unique, innate nature. Based on this understanding, one could then design an education system that addressed the needs of women. After all, education had been designed for men as the normative model student, without any thought of young women.

As with her reticence to affirm sexual innovations, Stein's political stance shied away from radicalism. She was a suffragist, but not a socialist. She joined the Prussian Society for Women Right's to Vote, which was made up of mostly socialists. She was a member of the women's student union at the University of Breslau, which was more of a social group. In contrast to her friends, she was a supporter of the Prussian state because it had educated her and given her access "to the wisdom of mankind,"[31] for which she felt deep gratitude, which was part of her inspiration to make a professional contribution. She felt a deep sense of social responsibility to give back to the people and the state for all that it had done for her.

In order to comprehend women's nature, Stein begins with the question: What is gender? Is gender a type, a species, or a form? And was there such a thing as a species of woman? She notes that "By species we understand a permanent category which does not change."[32] She goes on to explain that the term "form" refers to an "inner form which determines structure,"[33] the term used by Thomistic philosophy. The concept here is of type as a subcategory of species that is mutable and can change. Species is immutable and unchanging. Stein states that if gender were not *species* but only a *type*, then gendered man or woman could transform from one type to another. Her statements on this in 1932 anticipate queer and gender theorists of the late twentieth and early twenty-first century:

> It is quite clear that species is the core of all questions concerning woman. If such a species exists then it cannot be modified by environmental, economic, cultural or professional factors. If we question the concept of species, if man and woman are to be considered as types as we have defined them, then *the transformation of one type to another is possible under certain conditions.*[34]

She goes on to say, "this is not *as* absurd as may appear at first glance." Stein is arguing that if woman is not a *species*, meaning a structure and form that is immutable and not affected by external environment, then woman could be a *type*, something which changes and can transform. This opens up the possibility that there could be many positons betwixt and between any single concept that we would have of women. Stein continues:

> At one time this view was considered valid on the basis that, although physical differences were unchanging, the psychological differences were considered of infinite variation. But certain facts such as the existence of hybrid and transitory forms can be quoted to dispute immutability of physical difference.[35]

Stein is stating that our concept of female and male is not limited to a binary category by the genitals of our physical bodies. Gender is not limited to our physical differences. Gender is made up by our psyche, and it could express a contrast with what would be expected based on the physical body. This hybridity appears in what, in queer language, is known today as a butch lesbian, or a transman. These individuals, common to queer culture today, are those whom Stein is describing as a hybrid. A butch lesbian feels what some would view as more masculine: she lives in a body with female genitals but does not feel that she wants to have sexual reassignment surgery. Others are born with a female body but know that they are men and want a gender reassignment, and as such, are "transmen." Both are people who, in Stein's language, would be examples of a hybrid.

At the time Stein was lecturing, a whole discourse was going on about the nature of sex and gender. German sexologist Magnus Hirschfeld, one of the leaders of the discourse, argued in 1900 that there was an intermediate or third sex. Havelock Ellis, in England, was also part of this discourse. Stein was philosophically proving their arguments possible. Stein was writing as a Catholic feminist; she did not mention the discourse directly with this statement. Her critique of Weimar sexuality distances her construction of gender from Hirschfeld's and Ellis's, but still, in her argument she is proposing that flexibility is possible. She argues that we need a theological and philosophical anthropology to further the investigation into the nature of woman. We ultimately need to understand the connection between gender, species, type, and individual. It seems as if Stein's flexibility in her understanding of gender comes from phenomenology, as opposed to her Catholic theology.

WHAT IS A HUMAN BEING?

The root of Stein's definition and exploration of woman lies in her exploration of what it means to be a human being; in other words, an understanding of the nature of woman is located within the philosophical discipline of ontology. Ontology asks the question, what is being? What is essence? It is the study of being or beingness. Stein states, "I regard ontology, i.e. a science of the basic forms of Being (Sein) and beings (Seienden), as the fundamental discipline."[36] She argues that one needs to view the question "what is a human being?" in terms of what the *nature* of being is. This approach is meant to help us differentiate the division between beings. The highest form of being is pure Being with a capital "B." This is the equivalent to God, which is formless; "It holds nothing of non-being in itself, has neither beginning nor end and holds in itself all which it can be."[37] Finite being with a lower case "b" has a beginning and an end. All living organisms are some gradation or another of being. Human beings, for Stein, are organisms that are form, directed from within by a potential that is like a seed or a kernel that unfolds and develops. Human beings are composed from material bodies that have a soul, and they are ultimately spiritual beings. Human beings have the ability to act and reflect on their own initiative. As Stein explains:

> [A human being is] an *organism, which* is formed and activated from within ... an *organism* with a *soul* who in the sensitive manner peculiar to him is open to himself and his environment. ... He is a *spiritual being* who is consciously cognizant of himself and others and can act freely to develop himself and others.[38]

Stein makes the case that:

> anthropology clarifies the meaning of sexual differences and proves the substance of the species: moreover it is proper ... to prove the place of the species in the structure of the human being, the relationship of the types to the species and to the individual and the relationship of the types to conditions in which they develop.[39]

WHAT IS WOMAN?

Stein's answer to the question "what is a woman?" is complex. First and foremost, women and men are human beings. We need to figure out the relationship or connection of woman and man to the structure of the human being. Once we establish and grasp the relationship of woman and man to the structure of the human being first, then we can figure what the *type* of man or the *type* of woman might be within that structure. The environment in which they develop will affect the type of woman or the type of man a human being becomes. So what are these types and qualities of woman and types and qualities of man that develop as human being? Stein gives us a working definition of human being that is informed by her theological understanding of the verse in Genesis: "God created man according to His Image. He created them as man and woman. Here we find the fact of oneness and differentiation."[40] In other words, human beings are the reflection of the image of God and in this reflection there exists a dual nature within the core of human beings. This duality and differentiation is embraced in oneness, which is the expression of our image of God within human beings: "I am convinced then that the species humanity embraces the double species man and woman; the essence of the complete human being is characterized by this duality; and that the entire structure of essence demonstrates the specific character."[41] Two immutable structures are present within the structure of the human beings themselves, says Stein. Human beings are not just *species man* but both the species of man and the species of woman.

At first appearance it seems as if Stein is arguing for an innate and essentialist understanding of man and woman, but she believes that the species of woman and the species of man do determine a different relationship between body and soul. The species of woman has different qualities than the species of man. It would appear that Stein is saying that there is a core, black-and-white duality between the two, but she argues differently. Within the species of woman there are different types ranging from the more masculine to the more feminine. It is a spectrum for Stein. For her there is core form, deriving from a Thomistic perspective, that develops within a human being. This core form will dictate the primary difference, but within that difference there are multiple variations.

Although Stein considered the possibility, philosophically, that woman and man are types and not species, she ultimately ruled this notion out. She decided, based on her theological anthropology, that they each are indeed a discrete species; they possess natures that are immutable within the structure of the human being. She went on to argue that many variations of the species *woman* exist within the species *humanity*, and that they can belong to more of one type that leans towards the qualities of the other species:

There is a difference not only in body structure and in particular physiological functions but also in corporeal life. The relationship of soul to body is different in man and woman; the relationship of soul to body differs in their psychic life as well as that of the spiritual faculties to each other.[42]

So the innate form or species or structure drives the type, but within each type there is multiple variation.

WHAT ARE THE QUALITIES OF THE FEMININE SPECIES?

Stein explains then that the feminine species has some major qualities, which are different than the male species. "The feminine species expresses a unity and wholeness of the total psychosomatic personality and a harmonious development of faculties,"[43] says Stein, whereas the male species "strive to enhance individual abilities in order that they may attain their highest achievements."[44] Females, in other words, are whole, and can approach the world from a holistic perspective, whereas males are singularly driven in purpose, not necessarily seeing the whole. Furthermore Stein states that "To reveal God's Image in themselves is the mission assigned to man and woman; it belongs to the criteria of finite being imparted to them that they also must do this in specific ways."[45] Human beings are the reflection of God, and the female and male reflect different attributes of the image of God. The teleology of human beings is to reflect God's image by ruling over the earth, which means, according to Stein, knowing, delighting, and creating things in the world. But Stein acknowledges that we each reflect the image of God in our own unique way:

> The species humanity as well as the species femininity is revealed differently in different individuals. Man and woman have the same basic traits although this or that trait predominates not only in the sexes but also in respective individuals. Therefore women may closely approximate the masculine type and conversely.[46]

Women are a female species who, according to talent and vocation, can exhibit different types of qualities, some more male or more female. A woman can bring the qualities of the species of femininity to traditional female vocations, such as marriage and motherhood, or to the more masculine type of vocations, such as law, academics, and engineering. However it is directed, the human impulse is to express a creative force in a multiplicity of vocations, which does not limit women to one type.

Stein draws on a contemporary Weimar psychologist, Else Corner, to identify five different feminine types that she has encountered in her teaching experience:

the *maternal* type's outlook regarding children emerges distinctly
in play, favorite pastimes, and desires; the *erotic* type shows a
predominantly male directed mentality and recognizable marks
of high sexuality; the *romantic* type longs for experiences and is
impelled to surrender unconditionally to a leader, this possibly
without any sexual impact; the *level-headed* type emerges in life's
practical duties and adapts easily to surrounding circumstances;
lastly, the *intellectual type* is predominantly involved with objec-
tive interests and perhaps capable of creative achievements. Those
of us teaching girls will surely recall students representing one
and another of these types as well as those of mixed types, and
still others belonging to types we have not mentioned.[47]

Just as Stein identifies the maternal, romantic, level-headed, and intellectual
types of expressions of the species woman, she also recognizes that within
these types there are some who are mixed and others that we have not even
considered. Stein grasps the uniqueness within the innate structure of the
species woman. Given this, how does Stein view types in light of the imperative to emulate the Holy Mother or Mary?

STEIN, MARIOLOGY, AND THE SPECIES WOMAN

Stein recognizes that the "new woman" of Weimar could not square with the
image of Mary. Most women could not live the life of one called to a religious
vocation, becoming the spouse of Christ, as did nuns of the different Catholic
orders such as the Dominicans, the Franciscans, or the Carmelites.

Stein views Mary as stepping outside of her time and its cultural demands
that women be companion to man as a mother and wife. God created Eve as
a companion to Adam. This was the prototype of the old model of woman
before Mary, and before Jesus came into the world.

Mary stands at the crucial point of human history and especially
at the crucial point of the history of woman; in her, motherhood
was transfigured and physical maternity surmounted. ... The most
significant evidence of the eternal meaning and value to be found
in sexual differentiation lies in the fact that the new Eve stands
beside the new Adam on the threshold between the Old and the
New Covenants. God chose as the instrument for His Incarnation
a human mother and in her He presented the perfect image of a
mother, at the service of this mission.[48]

The new Eve is Mary, who is no longer married to an earthly man but to the
new Adam – God – who then inseminated her with His son. Her maternity

brought out and represents a perfect example of total surrender and service – not to a human man, but to God. The son of God is "given to her by God and in fidelity to God she must look after Him."[49] What distinguishes Mary from the old covenant and from her Jewish people was that she wanted to be free of marital obligations. She was not married to Joseph. Jesus' earthly father was a guardian for the Son of God, not a husband to earthly woman. She did not have relations as a normal wife would with her husband, within the practice of the Jewish people. She remained a virgin. "She did not become *one flesh* with him; this marriage was not to propagate his heirs to carry on the human race."[50] Mary had completely surrendered her divine love and divine service to God, which then serves all humanity: "this woman called to the most exalted maternity had not wanted marriage and motherhood for herself; and this was against every tradition of her people."[51] Mary becomes a co-redeemer, a being who sits by His side as support for the Redeemer Christ:

> Both mother and Son spring from the human race, and both embody human nature; yet, both are free from that relationship which makes possible the fulfillment of life's meaning only in union with and through another person. *Union with God replaces the relationship in both.*"[52]

So Mary is in constant union with God. But can everyday woman imitate this?

Stein has taken the pulse of ordinary women around her, and realizes that they cannot live in constant union with God. Stein sees the stress of the "new woman" of Weimar. She recognizes that more and more women are working outside of the home, and have to handle the stress of taking care of their husbands and children and home on top of tending to their jobs: "Many of the best women are overwhelmed by the double burden of family duties and professional life – or often simply of only gainful employment. Always on the go, they are harassed, nervous and irritable."[53]

Stein asks, "where are they [women] to get the needed inner peace and cheerfulness in order to offer stability, support and guidance to others?"[54] Even with women who are home full-time, or who have a spouse who respects women's work inside and outside the home, Stein notes the stress. "Even when there is mutual love and recognition of achievements there are small daily frictions between a woman and her husband and children: this results in uneasiness throughout the entire household and a slackening of relationships in the home."[55]

Stein realized that women cannot be expected, as wives, mothers, and working professionals, to lead lives in flawless emulation of the image of the Divine Mother Mary. It is only the nun, the virgin who consecrates herself to Christ in one of the Catholic religious orders, who can hope to achieve

Mary-like attributes. The life of the nun gives women the opportunity to achieve inner peace, and the stability to provide support and guidance to others. It is difficult for regular women to achieve this, which Stein recognizes. But Stein points out that even if women are overburdened as mothers, wives, and professionals, they do have the opportunity to bring the innate qualities of feminine virtue to the male species and the rest of humanity, and that this is a benefit to whatever profession they might choose: "the participation of women in the most diverse professional disciplines could be a blessing for the entire society, private or public, precisely if the specifically feminine ethos would be preserved."[56]

Of their choice of profession, Stein notes that women are capable of anything. Stein asks, "Are there feminine vocations other than the *natural* one?"[57] And then she answers her own question: "Only subjective delusion could deny that women are capable of practicing vocations other than that of spouse and mother ... And there is no profession which cannot be practiced by a woman."[58]

Stein's language is emphatic. She uses the term "subjective delusion" to describe the condition of one who failed to realize that women were capable of any type of profession. You would have to be blind, Stein says, not to see that the "experience of the last decades, and for that matter, the experience of all times, demonstrated this."[59] Throughout human history women have always accomplished much more than the roles of wife and mother. Stein's feminist beliefs are shining through in her word choice and her argument about the nature of woman. "A self-sacrificing woman can accomplish astounding achievements when it is a question of replacing the breadwinner of fatherless children, of supporting abandoned children or aged parents," she writes.[60] It is hard not to think of Augustus Stein, her mother, as the example that Edith Stein might have had in mind. Augustus Stein lost her husband at a young age and then became very successful, taking over her husband's lumber business, even taking care of other families' children.

Women are not only capable of any professional career; in addition, if they find themselves drawn to professions that are not in the domain of conventional feminine virtues, she can bring her innate qualities to the profession, seeking the concrete within the abstract, the whole in the part:

> Everything abstract is ultimately part of the concrete. Everything inanimate finally serves the living. That is why activity dealing in abstraction stands in ultimate service to the living whole. Whoever can take hold of this view of the whole and make it active will feel himself bound to it.[61]

Stein demonstrates that women's unique feminine qualities can be of service in any profession she chooses, even the most abstract profession like philosophy. A woman in a profession such as philosophy – Stein's original one

– used it to serve the living whole. As a philosopher, Stein wrote about the phenomenological foundation of empathy. Empathy in and of itself is a form of compassion and caring, something that Stein argued women bring to their professions in service of the whole. Stein shows in her dissertation that without empathy, without intersubjectivity, we would not have the condition that enables our knowledge of the outer world and of others, which Stein considered to be part of the living whole.

JONAS'S CONCEPT OF WOMAN

Jonas, in contrast to Stein, was not a philosopher. She was a woman who was passionate about Judaism and about becoming a woman rabbi. Jonas's mastery was of Jewish holy texts, legal reasoning, and historical understandings of the perception of women within Jewish tradition. She did share with Stein a deep interest in empathy and caring, not in the philosophical sense, but in a practical one: to her mind, modern rabbis needed to have more nurturing and empathic qualities, for their roles had fundamentally changed.

Regina Jonas was born in Berlin on August 2, 1902. She was a little girl when the war broke out. She shares with Stein the tragedy that both of them lost their fathers young. She actually lost her father, not to the war, but to illness when she was eleven years old. Stein's father died of heat stroke when she was barely two and Jonas's father died in 1913. Jonas had had at least a chance to develop a relationship with her father, which Stein was unable to do. One can surmise there was a warmth of Judaism that Jonas's father imparted to her; he used to take her to the old Orthodox *shuls* (synagogues) in the poor neighborhood that they lived in.

During this same period – 1924 to 1935 – Jonas was, like Stein, teaching young Jewish girls and boys. Jonas had finished her rabbinical studies, but did not receive her ordination in Liberal Judaism because the Talmud professor who was to give her her oral exam unexpectedly died. Jonas worked as a religious school teacher at Annenstrasse Synagogue and taught religious studies classes to the Jewish students in public schools, which were, at that time, an official part of the German public school system. While Stein was seeking a position as the first woman philosophy professor in a university, Jonas was figuring out how to become the first ordained woman rabbi – not an eternal rabbinical candidate.

Jonas received her ordination after the Nuremberg Laws went into effect. In a newspaper interview by Mala Laaser of *Frauenblatt C. V. Zeitung* following her ordination, her sincere theological view that, first and foremost, we are human beings who have a God-given duty to fulfill our unique talents: "Everyone has the duty, regardless if they are a man or woman, to use the gifts given by God to work and to create ... one would accept woman and man as they are, namely human beings."[62] Jonas argued that the custom of modesty, which would traditionally prevent a woman from being seen upon the pulpit, before man, should not get in the way of her expression of these God-given talents. Jonas emphasized that a woman rabbi's dress should be modest:

> That something such as *tzniut* should prevent her from preach-
> ing is also not acceptable, for her rabbinical dress should not be
> taken for "fashionable frivolity," something to which unfortunately
> the world of our women have surrendered, as she must wear the
> clothing befitting to her job.[63]

What does Jonas mean by fashionable frivolity? Here Jonas might have been responding to the vogueish flappers that were all the rage in mid-1920s Berlin. Theirs was known as a "masculine" type of dressing. Women cut their hair short into a bob. They wore short dresses that exposed their knees. They even chewed gum: a new Wrigley's chewing gum factory had opened in Frankfurt in 1925.

In *The Berliner Illustrate Zeitung*, one of the most widely-read maga-zines in 1925, an article denounces this type of dressing. "Enough is Enough! Against the Masculinization of Women" paints the following grim picture:

> At first it was like a charming novelty: that gentle, delicate women
> cut their long tresses and bobbed their hair; that the dresses they
> wore hung down in almost perfectly straight line, denying the
> contours of the female body, the curve of the hips; that they short-
> ened their skirts, exposing their slender legs up to calf level.[64]

A woman rabbi, by contrast, would wear robes that rabbis traditionally did: garb certainly in harmony with what Jonas believed was modest. Her hair would be covered with the cap that the rabbis wore during services, probably the very one that Jonas is pictured with in the photograph that accompanies her ordination thesis. Jonas describes how it would be that a woman rabbi's dress could conform to *Halakhic* dictates:

> Her hair likewise is covered and the appearance of the woman to
> man during the sermon need not give rise to any Halakhic objec-
> tions as it can only be a fleeting glimpse, and it is to be expected
> that a serious man pays attention in strictly *religious* mood during
> services.[65]

In the same newspaper article, the author laments what women were doing with their hair: "And we observe ... that the bobbed haircut with its curls is disappearing, to be replaced by the modern masculine hairstyle: sleek and brushed straight back."[66] Women were becoming men, much to the chagrin of bourgeois women. This transformation was an expression of the newly emancipated woman. "The new fashion in women's coats is also decidedly masculine: it would scarcely be noticed this spring if a woman absentmindedly put on her husband's coat."[67] As Jonas had stated, a woman rabbi should not be subjected to fashion frivolity. The article echoed her sentiment: "Fashion is like a pendulum swinging back and forth."[68]

Jonas says, "How beneficial it could be to have a woman in the rabbinic role to reclaim the lost meaning of *tzniut* by example and teaching."[69] She rebuts the Talmud and rabbinic sages, such as Rambam, who make negative statements about women's poor intellect, "light-heartedness," and concern with things of menial importance. This is due not to their innate nature, argues Jonas, but their lack of education:

> There is just *one* single *remedy* for all these deficits that 'cling' to the woman, and that is *intellectual education*: because the powers available to humans will atrophy if not used! To give a contemporary example today it is obvious from women's intellectual pursuits and other work that they are more than *capable of concentration and possess the intellectual capacity* necessary for scientific work.[70]

Jonas is making the point that for over two thousand years, women were not taught the holy texts of the Talmud, and were denied training in the logical reasoning that this study entails. Not teaching woman how to read texts and think atrophied their minds.

Jonas comments on contemporary youth and argues why it is even more important that mothers know something of Jewish texts and Jewish understanding.

TZNIUT AND THE "NEW WOMAN"

Jonas had probably been a member of the *Jüdischer Frauenbund* (the JFB), which advocated that "women analyze the Bible and Talmud from a woman's perspective in order to combat male interpretations."[71] Jonas lectured on women in the Bible and the Talmud from before her ordination up until her time as a rabbi in Theresienstadt concentration camp. After she became a rabbi in 1935 she gave newspaper interviews about her thoughts on the woman question for a woman rabbi. She had the same view as Stein: we are human beings before we are a gender, either male or female. "Thus each of us has the duty, whether man or woman, to realize those gifts God has given," said Jonas. "If you look at things this way, one takes woman and man for what they are: human beings."[72] Not only are women human beings who must use their talents just like men, but "God created the world with *two sexes,* and the world cannot be supported by only *one sex.* In her private circle the woman was always a servant of G–d but today times demand that she serve *in public life*."[73] In private circles, the Jewish woman took care of the children and husband. A woman was traditionally of service to her family and community as a wife and mother.

Jonas, like Stein, saw a moral looseness with current Jewish women that could be remedied by reclaiming the Jewish value of modesty known as *tzniut* in a positive way. Traditional Jewish women practiced *tzniut* which traditional Orthodox and Hasidic women still practice. Klapheck explains "A key term repeated in her [Jonas'] work was Tzniut – the Jewish ideal of humility, modesty, also chaste behavior."[74] *Tzniut* was a virtue that German Jewish middle class bourgeois women cherished. It represented the opposite of the wild "new woman", whom Stein had lamented. But while the dicates of *tzniut* were held up as a primary justification for barring women from becoming rabbis, Jonas turns it around and shows how a woman rabbi could *demonstrate tzniut*. She felt that it would be wonderful if they could wear modest fashion and not reveal their body parts, citing Moses Maimonides's *Mishneh: Torah Laws of Woman*.[75] Maimonides states that *tzniut* demands a woman's hair be fully covered and she be completely dressed so that not even her forearm is exposed. Ironically, Stein, who as a Carmelite nun wore "a white coif black veil which hangs over a brown tunic and scapular," provided an excellent example of *tzniut*.[76] Maimonides and ultra-Orthodox women would have understood Stein's modest dress.[77]

Jonas's dress was similarly modest: she was known to wear purple robes when she worked at a Jewish hospital, and in her ordination photo Jonas wore her hair tucked under a rabbi's cap. A woman rabbi would not be subjected to fashion whims like a pendulum swinging back and forth. Jonas demonstrated in this way how a woman rabbi could indeed reclaim the lost meaning of tzniut. Hers was a brilliant approach, addressing the tension in the culture over modern women's immodesty by becoming a role model of feminine qualities in a male profession.

JEWISH WOMAN AND *HALAKHA*

Jonas's views on women and *Halakha* were nuanced, and reflected her views and critiques of modern woman, Weimar culture, and her intense attempt to take on two thousand years of misogynistic, prejudicial views of women.[78] Her ordination thesis was a very bold attempt to bring a woman's voice to male legal interpretation. According to traditional Judaism, 613 laws were given to the Israelites on Mount Sinai. The Torah was not only given to man but, according to Jonas, to woman as well. "Both men and women had gathered to receive the Torah at the fundamental event of our Jewish people, the *Mantan Torah* [giving of the Torah] on Mt Sinai."[79] These laws were then explicated by the rabbis in the Talmud (Mishneh and Gemerah), then commented upon by the later rabbis in the holy texts to which Jonas refers in her *Halakhic* thesis.[80] Jonas herself had an Orthodox perspective: she believed the laws that were revealed to Moses were eternal, outside of the realm of time. She saw herself as an Orthodox Jew, even though she was seeking ordination in the Liberal tradition, one that did not believe the *Halakha* was revealed.[81]

The 613 laws are divided into positive and negative time-bound laws and non-time-bound laws.[82] The rabbis of the Talmud ruled that women were not obligated to observe time-bound positive laws, such as praying three times a day. Women's lives were ruled by the domestic sphere, taking care of their husbands, mothering full-time, and running a household. So the rabbis' ruling showed some wisdom. Indeed, any parent who has stayed home taking care of children knows that parenting is a very demanding job. Time-bound *mitzvoth* would be impossible to practice, and this in turn would interfere with one's ability to fulfill the *Halakhic* obligation. For instance, one could not pull a baby off a breast or away from a bottle or leave a small or sick child unattended to fulfill all the time-bound laws that Judaism requires.[83]

Jewish women were obligated to follow only three time-bound laws out of the 613, and Jonas does mention them.[84] Jonas laments that the meaning and understanding of women's *Halakhic* obligations were being lost. Women's inability to study the Torah and the Talmud contributes to the loss of the deep meaning behind the *Halakha*:

> Today, our Jewish life has become distant from its direct relation to Halakha, due to changed life circumstances. But what affects the woman in particular ... is that she is distant from the thinking of the Talmud, because she was not prepared for such thinking due to constant distancing from learning across the generations. With shocking clarity this holds true for the *modern* woman because modern times and the *notions* of *man* as of *woman* are turned toward completely different pages of life. ... If Jewish woman with such "preparation" were encouraged to fulfill our holy obligation [the *mitzvoth*], she would likely ask why, with amazement: I was not raised with these things![85]

Furthermore, not only were women distanced from the *Halakha* but times had changed; both modern man and woman had other distractions to pull them away from Jewish practice. Could Jonas possibly be referring to such cultural and political distractions as communism and socialism, and the contemporary imperative to be patriotic Germans, more than observant Jews? American and English women had attempted to become rabbis before Jonas, but did not succeed, for good reason.[86] Jewish feminists now, as then, have asked Jonas's question exactly the same: Why was I not raised with these things?[87]

WOMEN IN THE BIBLE

A woman rabbi would exemplify the feminine qualities of compassion, caring, psychological understanding of human nature, and keen intellect, all of which were demonstrated by women in the Torah and Talmud. Jonas points out that there are both positive and negative statements in the Talmud about women, and attempts to dispel the myths about women's negative qualities. Biblical women leaders and prophets include Sarah, Miriam, Deborah, Hannah, Abigail, Hulda, and Esther, who "were graced with salvation, bravery, kindness and gentleness."[88] Jonas explains that the Talmud "attributes to women an understanding of human nature, which is an essential ability for the profession under discussion [rabbinate] almost as important as keen intellect and kind-heartedness."[89]

The Solomonic proverb "Woman of Valor" describes a woman of self-sacrificing kind-heartedness, who also has a wise and sharp business intellect.[90] This proverb was sung every week by the husband to his wife, as the Friday night Shabbat evening meal describes woman's service to God through her care of her family. This wonder woman not only took care of children and husband, but also planted and grew food, spun linen, sewed clothes, sold them, clothed her whole family, cared for the poor, worked into the wee hours of the night, and was up before dawn. She accomplished all these tasks with kindness and spoke words of wisdom. Jonas observes that these same attributes, previously limited to women's roles in the private sphere, were now being brought to bear in the public sphere:

> Those were the activities seen by the Talmud as ideal for the married woman, because it was easy for them to marry and fulfill their beautiful profession of being housewives. However today many women are denied this role, because in some countries there are not enough men available: aside from that woman today is not simply married off, but rather approves of the match or chooses her husband herself. In addition, the modern, unmarried woman has a considerable number of opportunities within the sphere of public professions.[91]

Jonas's comments reflect the cultural context of inter-war Germany. There was a shortage of men in Germany; more women than men had been born in Imperial Germany and during the Republic. Second, many men were lost to World War I. Jonas implies that many women did want to get married but could not because of the shortage of potential partners. But was Jonas implying that if women could get married they would? Was she voicing the Jewish tradition of the importance and value of marriage? It was not legally incumbent upon the woman, but it was upon the man. Jonas points out that modern woman was the "new woman" who had choices: she could choose whom to marry and pursue a professional life. For her part, Jonas was choosing a professional life and yet not getting married.

WOMEN IN THE TALMUD AND MEDIEVAL TEXTS

Jonas cites several interesting passages from the Talmud that point out women's understanding and compassionate nature. BT *Niddah* 45b says, "and the Eternal built the rib; this teaches that the Holy one, blessed be He, gave woman more understanding than the man."[92] The point that woman was created out of Adam's rib denotes a woman's understanding and compassion, but also shows that a woman was a companion and complemented a man as a fellow human being. A man was not whole unless he had a wife. Jonas cites Genesis 27:1 and the comment in BT *Yevamont* 63a: "Any man who does not have a wife is not a complete human being [*continued*: as it says: He created male and female ... and he called their name Adam (human being)]."[93]

Women had already demonstrated their intellectual brilliance in the case of Talmudic female sage Beruria. She lived in the first half of the second century, in Tiberias. She was the wife of Rabbi Meir and the daughter of the martyred Palestinian rabbi Hananiah ben Teradion. She was known to have studied three hundred Talmudic subjects daily. Rabbi Judah was said to have endorsed a ruling of hers on the questions of purity and impurity. She was known for dialoguing with her rabbinical contemporaries. In one of her notes at the end of "Can Women Serve as Rabbis?," Jonas describes Beruria's lasting influence: "She also explained verses of the Bible, closing with the words 'Look at the end of the verse'; this expression would become the norm among later Talmud scholars during discussions."[94]

Many stories attest to Beruria's vast Talmudic knowledge and tenderness, yet the tragedy of Beruria was that she was made into an example of women's light-headedness in Rashi's comments. Beruria's death is connected to a legend mentioned by Rashi ('Ab. Zarah 18b). To explain Rabbi Meier's flight to Babylonia, the commentator relates the following:

> Once Beruria scoffed at the rabbinical saying, "Women are light-minded" (Kid. 80b), and her husband warned her that her own end might yet testify to the truth of the words. To put her virtue to the test, he charged one of his disciples to endeavor to seduce her. After repeated efforts she yielded, and then shame drove her to commit suicide. R. Meier, tortured by remorse, fled from his home.[95]

This rightfully upset Jonas, as it would any woman. Jonas responds, "Poor Beruria, who after a long moral conflict untimely fell victim to trickery! No one today would abuse this highly esteemed personality of a woman."[96]

Although the Bible and Talmud illustrate positive qualities of feminine nature, some of the rabbis espoused awful views. The Talmud complains of women's over-talkativeness and shallowness, which Jonas cites: "In BT *Kiddushin* 49b, it is referred to as 'Ten Kab [a measure] of talkativeness came down into the world and women received nine of them."[97] Jonas, however, turned this criticism into an attribute: "so can speech be either talkativeness or eloquence capable of moving the heart; the latter is an attribute not to be underestimated in the professional work of the female rabbi."[98] Other negative comments include accusations of women's shallowness. A major complaint of the Talmud of later sages, such as Maimonides, was that women had limited intellect. He stated, *"lefi aniut da'atan"* [because of their poor intellect]."[99] Women were also accused of being only interested in matters of beauty. Jonas notes that "the words *nashim da'atan kalah aleyhen* [women are light-headed] are used as a weapon against women's ways."[100]

Jonas strongly rebuts the sages' hostile comments, explaining that women did not have the opportunity to study the Torah and develop their intellects like men. Women's ostensibly "poor intellect," "light-headedness," and propensity to speak "of things of menial importance" was due not to their innate nature, but to their lack of education. Jonas strongly contends that for over two thousand years, women were not taught the Torah in the same ways as boys. Jewish boys learned in Hebrew and Aramaic, studying the Bible, the Talmud, and the method of logical legal reasoning. This had a devastating impact not just on Jewish women's intellect, but on the future Jewish children who were tempted by outside culture.

Jonas clearly demonstrates that children have left Judaism precisely because of a mother's lack of Jewish education, her lack of knowledge of Jewish texts and Hebrew language. Nothing was (and is) more tragic to Jews than to lose a child to conversion. These comments of Jonas's astutely apply to the case of Edith Stein:

> One must remember that today the critical voices of children penetrate their mother's ears: skeptical expressions through which the environment external to Jewish life and cultural activity apply the tone of doubt and criticism to our sacred values. The mother can arm her child with the knowledge and Jewish self-confidence, due to the wisdom and gentleness that the Talmud attributes to her, particularly those mothers who learned much about Judaism in their own childhood, and are, like the son and the father, steeped in the Jewish Spirit. But if the mother stands ignorant before these questions and before her unsteady child, then her son or daughter will turn from her. One must be honest and admit that one factor that creates a gap between parents and children and destroys the beautiful family life is the inability of parents to understand the doubts of youth. But a mother who herself has studied also

has had her time of doubting and so can recognize that which her own child must go through as a reliving of her own past. She will therefore hold fast to the child by sharing her own tribulations and showing how she herself found the way from darkness to light. No matter that the child goes it own way – that must be the case; but understanding and love, harmony, and thankfulness unite young and old.[101]

Jonas tellingly observes that the child will turn from the mother, and this was exactly what Edith Stein did when she converted to Catholicism.

STEIN AS AN EXAMPLE OF IGNORANCE OF JEWISH TRADITION

I constantly wonder if Stein would have had a different view of Judaism if she had met and studied with Jonas. Jonas was not a philosopher, like Stein. I wonder if Stein would have dismissed Jonas or respected her for becoming the first woman rabbi. Jonas loved people, as testified by the survivors who remembered her and her views of the rabbinate. Although Stein had many friends and many people wanted her counsel, she does not share openness to people and acceptance of their natures in the same way as Jonas. Stein's autobiography *Life in a Jewish Family* clearly reflects her critical view of family and friends. I found that Stein's character never fully let go of such critical judging of human beings. I think it made it possible for her to truly soak in her later anti-Jewish Catholic Carmelite theology of praying for the sins of her people to accept Christ, the Jewish Jesus, as their Savior. Stein wrote her autobiography as a Catholic; she started it as she was about to become a postulant in the Cologne Carmel and continued it in the convent. Her reflections on her early life are colored by Catholic lenses.

In her autobiography *Life in a Jewish Family*, Stein criticized various aspects of the Jewish tradition. Yet Stein's own family and some scholars wonder whether, if she had known more about Jewish practice and studied Jewish texts the way she studied philosophy, she might not have converted. Edith Stein's niece, Susanne Batzdorff, echoes Jonas's sentiment in her biography *Aunt Edith: The Jewish Heritage of a Catholic Saint*:

Edith Stein had little real knowledge of Judaism, and despite her bent for scholarship and research she had never seemed to have shown for making up for this *lack* of knowledge. In Judaism in those days girls were never given more than a superficial Jewish education. My mother never learned Hebrew or Jewish history and liturgy. As a youngster Edith witnessed in her family an attenuated Judaism.[102]

Stein never had a father who would impart a love of the Jewish tradition. She looked to her older brothers, but in Stein's judging, critical way, she found their practice of Judaism unsatisfactory, even though their mother was very devout and had a pious practice of Judaism. Stein admits that she was very critical of others and had thought of herself as perfect since she was admired and adored for her brilliant mind. This was a part of her nature. When one of her student friends, Hugo Harmsen, bid her farewell at Göttingen, he told her that she had become far too critical. This shocked her because he was the first person to reflect back to her judging hubris. She felt that her Catholicism had tempered her and made her realize that she was not a perfect human: "So I had been living in the naïve conviction that I was perfect. This is frequently the case with persons without any faith who live an exalted ethical idealism."[103] In an indirect way Stein's comment reflects that she did not experience her family's Jewish practice as having a strong faith in a redeeming God.

Stein's mother, Auguste Stein, had been educated in the traditional ways for a Jewish woman of her time: she had learned how to keep a kosher home, to bake challah, to light the Sabbath candles. She used a woman's book of Jewish prayers in German, known as *The Book of Hannah*.[104] Still, she had no knowledge of Hebrew, nor could she read the Torah, despite the fact that she was a pious woman, an exemplar of both the "woman of valor" and the "new woman." The widowed Auguste Stein could not pass on the same knowledge that her husband would have been able to pass on to his sons. Auguste Stein was not ignorant, but she did not have an education equal to a Jewish male. She could not answer all of young Edith's questions, even if Edith were to have brought them to her.

Stein's attenuated knowledge indeed attenuated her Judaism, no doubt contributing to the very consequence that Jonas feared most, when Jewish women do not receive the same education as Jewish men. Stein had rejected her own tradition. Jonas pleads, of the uneducated Jewish woman, that we must "guard against the danger of her rejecting it [*Halakha*] all out of accidental ignorance, because one cannot treasure what one does not know, it becomes an *urgent necessity* to make the incomprehensible comprehensible."[105]

Stein's niece Susanne Batzdorff explains that her parents Hans and Erna Biberstein, *née* Stein (Edith's closest sister), wanted to make sure that she and her brother Ernst recieved a solid Jewish education. They sent them, beginning in 1928, to an after-school Liberal Jewish religious school in Breslau, similar to ones that Jonas had taught at in Berlin. Batzdorff was taught "beginner's Hebrew, some biblical history, Jewish customs and holiday observances," essentially the entire curriculum that Jonas strongly argues Jewish girls needed to learn in her time.[106] The Bibersteins sent their children consciously to religious school because of what happened to Aunt Edith. The Bibersteins felt directly that Aunt Edith strayed from Judaism and converted to Catholicism because of her lack of knowledge and understanding. They reasoned that Aunt Edith "might have followed a different path, had she been given a thorough grounding in her Jewish heritage."[107]

This grounding in Judaism was not as readily accessible to Edith and her sister Erna during the 1890s and early 1900s. It was only during Jonas's time that religious school became accessible to young Jewish girls in the same way that it had always been for Jewish boys. Traditionally, interested girls would have learned about Jewish law and practice from their fathers and brothers. They would have asked their husbands or fathers to clarify a legal point. "If women earlier did not understand something [related to *Halakha*], it was easy enough for them to ask their well-informed husbands or, if they were not married, their father or other relatives," says Jonas.[108] But Stein's father had passed away before she was two, and her much older brothers did not take Jewish practice seriously.

Jonas clearly explicates the problems that Edith and her sister Erma encountered growing up in a fatherless household, with a mother who was herself minimally knowledgeable about Judaism. Ideally, for Jonas,

> The mother can arm her child with the knowledge and Jewish self-confidence, due to the wisdom and gentleness that the Talmud attributes to her, particularly those mothers who learned much about Judaism in their own childhood and are, like the son and the father, steeped in the Jewish spirit.[109]

And, in turn, Stein demonstrates Jonas's major point: woman can turn away from Jewish practice if they do not know enough, if their intellects and spirit are not engaged in the tradition. The only way future Jewish women can be enthusiastic about Jewish practice and spirit is if they themselves are respected and taught the same subjects, alongside the Jewish boys. Educated Jewish mothers would then be able to pass on to their daughters what Jewish men have always passed on to their sons: the wisdom and spirit of Judaism. Women in Jonas's day were highly educated. There was no reason why they could not be just as learned in Jewish tradition. Edith Stein was brilliantly erudite in philosophy, but if she had learned the Talmud and kabbalistic texts, who knows if she would have left her religious tradition? Susanne Batzdorff herself says, "I can testify to the fact that religious affiliation becomes much more meaningful with the opportunity to delve into the deeper layers of Jewish existence and practice."[110]

Despite the handicaps that Jonas diagnosed and Stein experienced, Stein did have many opportunities to learn about her Jewish heritage. Stein had a number of opportunities where she could have found out more about Judaism and figured out a way to access the Jewish study of texts such as the Torah. We know that she was not afraid to pursue knowledge when she wanted it. There were books that had been written about Judaism, and there was the Rabbinical Seminary in Breslau. Some of her missed opportunities were as follows:

First, Stein had a number of friends both male and female during her university days who were practicing Jews. In Breslau she had the chance to speak to Dr Julius Guttmann who was *privatdozent* at the university and was probably studying for his rabbinical ordination at the same time. He was there until 1919 before he moved to Berlin to serve as a professor and rabbi at the *Hochschule*. Stein was very aware that Guttmann's father was the famous Rabbi Jakob Guttmann, who was also well known as a scholar. She had a conversation with Guttmann and could have asked him questions about Judaism, which she chose not to. Julius Guttmann would go on to write an important book, *The Philosophies of Judaism*,[111] but that was after Stein had converted to Catholicism.

Secondly, when Stein did seek out information on Judaism, she was closed to it. Stein had asked her only Orthodox Jewish friend Eduard Metis to explain to her his concept of God. "I asked him once by letter about his idea of God: His reply was succinct: God is spirit: nothing more could be said on the subject. To me, it seemed I had been handed a stone instead of bread."[112] Stein's response that her friend's answer only gave her a stone comes from Stein's Catholic perspective. Stein lacked enough knowledge of Judaism to understand that most Jews do not believe in a personal God and that God is omnipresent – even to have a sense of a personal God would be to limit God. It is true she asked an Orthodox friend about Judaism by the form of a letter. Maybe she thought he would have an answer that would suit her since he had an Orthodox observance of Judaism, but without an understanding of his tradition she would not grasp that Orthodox Jews do not have a theology in any traditional sense. As a Catholic who believed in a personal God, she was disappointed with her friend's answer. For Judaism is about practice of the 613 Jewish laws, ethics, and study of the Torah. Jews have faith that the Torah was revealed to Moses on Mount Sinai. There is faith in a God that is greater than can be imagined, but not faith in a personal God.

Finally, Susanne Batzdorff explains that Auguste Stein asked her daughter to go with her to lectures by prominent Rabbis and scholars at the Rabbinical Seminary in Breslau. This had no influence on Stein. We will never know whether, if Stein was able to study Torah and engage her independent mind with Talmudic and kabbalistic texts, she would have stayed a Jew. She made her decision to convert on a religious experience and from an ignorance of the tradition that she had been born and raised in. While from a Jewish perspective, her decision to convert placed her outside of Jewry, we will see that her self-understanding was one of a Catholic Jew who refused the normative boundary between Jew and gentile.[113]

CONCLUSION

For their many differences, both Stein and Jonas would agree on three major points. First, before we are man or woman, we are human beings. Woman does have unique feminine qualities. Stein identifies these qualities as living, personal, and whole. Jonas identifies these qualities as a unique understanding of human nature, kindness, and compassion. Women's feminine nature ought not to limit them to the private sphere any longer, and both agree that women are just as smart and as gifted as men, and that in fact women are more whole. They argue that women are innately whole and caring (Stein), nurturing (Jonas), and it is time for women to bring these qualities into professions that men normally hold. Everything is possible for women.

For her part, Stein argues that woman is a species, an immutable structure within a human being. Stein contends that women must bring their feminine qualities into their profession, just as Stein did as a philosopher in her dissertation on empathy. She even notes that if a woman does not bring her feminine nature into her chosen profession, she will be unfulfilled: "this is due to their having taken pains to fill their post, just like a man."[114] Ultimately, Stein believes that women should not pretend to be men.

Jonas, for her part, does not argue that the feminine qualities are necessarily innate. The Torah and history of Jewish women's deeds do demonstrate women's unique qualities, however. Jonas shows that keeping women away from studying the Torah and Talmud has atrophied their minds, and it is now an urgent necessity that young women be given the same education as young men. In her work, Jonas takes on two thousand years of misogyny, during which Jewish women have been kept from the Torah because of some rabbis' negative views of women.

Stein and Jonas differ in their views of women's education, reflecting the differences inherent in a Catholic and Jewish perspective. Stein argues that because woman is innately different from man, she needs a curriculum that is woman-centered and reflecting of the virtue of Mary. Jonas, on the other hand, argues that women must learn the exact same texts and liturgy, in Hebrew and Aramaic, as do Jewish men. Jonas wants Jewish girls to have access to what they have been denied, because this denial has potentially caused great damage. Both Stein's and Jonas's texts on women's nature reflect the tension each felt between chaste womanhood and the wild "new woman" of modern Weimar culture. But Jonas thought that education and the role model of a woman rabbi could remedy the problem; Stein thought a gynocentric education was the answer.

Writing these specific arguments about philosophy, *Halakha*, and women were milestones in Stein's and Jonas's journeys toward bringing God into the world because they showed how women can serve God not only as mothers and wives, but in the public sphere as a philosopher, rabbi, or contemplative and in diverse professions of the day, such as doctor, teacher, social worker, or lawyer. Their arguments provide the foundation of their desires, illustrating what is possible for women outside the private sphere. Like men, women have multiple talents, which need to be brought into the public sphere. It was in these new public roles that Stein and Jonas would act in redemptive ways.

Part II

VISION

Chapter 3

ST TERESA BENEDICTA OF THE CROSS REVEALS
THE WHOLE MEGILLAH AS EDITH STEIN

Edith Stein died in Auschwitz in 1942. Her niece Waltraut Stein explains in the translator's note to Stein's spiritual texts that she was both "hidden in a convent and hidden in God during a time when the world around her was caught up in the conflagration ignited by Adolph Hitler."[1] This statement is only partially true. For while Stein spent the last decade of her life cloistered, to her mind she was responding to the "conflagration" in the most direct way she knew how: she came out of "hiding" by way of the words she wrote from the convent, and she paid for this revelation with her life.

In this chapter I intend to draw aside her nun's veil to show how Stein located and expressed her Jewish identity while she practiced as a Carmelite nun. Through close examination of her autobiography *Life in a Jewish Family*, I will show Stein's sense of her Jewish voice. Further, I want to demonstrate, by looking at Stein from a postmodern perspective, that her sense of identity is queer – not in a gendered or a sexual sense, but in a religious and social sense. To look at her from this angle deepens our understanding of Stein as a multifaceted person who was loyal to her Jewish origins, and it helps shed light on the complex nature of religious identity. Ultimately, my study of Stein offers a response to this larger question: how can one simultaneously portray oneself to the world as both self and other? In my answer to this question, I propose a new metaphor we might consider as a means to represent the paradoxical "truths" about identity that Stein's life forces us to acknowledge.

Because Stein compared herself to the biblical Queen Esther, I will structure this chapter predominantly around this narrative motif. First, I explore what identities Stein was hiding. I follow that with a look at how Stein paints an ambiguous picture of her Jewish identity. I next show how – and why – Stein proclaims her Jewishness. To explore this matter further, I turn to gender and queer theory. I attempt to resolve the problem of Stein's simultaneous embrace of her Jewishness and Catholicity by applying Judith Butler's and Elspeth Probyn's formulations to the problem of identity politics that her life raises. Finally, I suggest a metaphor which might help disentangle the theoretical contradictions seemingly inherent in identity – a metaphor which shows how identity is "written" and "read" in many ways at numerous times, thus adding a needed depth to our notion of the nature and formation of identity, not just in Stein, but in general. To this end, an exploration of the illustrative potential of the megillah closes the chapter.

EDITH STEIN AS QUEEN ESTHER

On October 31, 1938, Stein – now Sister Teresa Benedicta of the Cross – wrote a letter from the convent of Carmel in Cologne to Mother Petra Bruning of Dorsten expressing how she viewed herself during these ominous years. In it, she compares herself to Queen Esther and to a Christian:

> I keep having to think of Queen Esther who was taken from among her people precisely that she might represent them before the king. I am a very poor and powerless little Esther, but the King who chose me is infinitely great and merciful. That is such a great comfort.[2]

Sister Teresa Benedicta had more in common with Queen Esther than she might have realized. Comparisons between their life narratives demonstrate myriad similarities: "marriage" changed each of their names, since beforehand Sister Teresa Benedicta was known as Edith Stein, and Queen Esther was known as Haddasah and as Esther.[3] They both dressed in new attire for the roles they assumed as Queen and nun. Once "married," each lived in closed quarters, hidden away from the Jewish people: Queen Esther lived cloistered in the palace of the Persian King, while Sister Teresa served her king in the convent in Cologne and Echt. Both lived, to use Hannah Arendt's term, during "dark times," attempting to save their people, the Jews, by revealing themselves to be Jews.[4] We know that Stein was encouraged by a priest friend to reveal herself by writing about her experiences as a Jew. Similarly, Esther was urged to reveal herself to the Persian King by her Uncle Mordecai. He sent news, through messengers, about the injustices happening to her people outside, and Esther first reacted with ambivalence. We see in Stein's introduction to her book that she, too, was ambivalent as she began the process of writing. We can see a final parallel in a moral interpretation of the Esther story. It was Esther's destiny to be picked by King Ahasuerus as the new Queen of the Persian Empire so that she could eventually save the Jews; likewise Stein came to consider herself guided by God to become a contemplative nun so that she could save her people. Their narratives conclude quite differently, however. Queen Esther succeeded in saving her people and became a hero, whereas Sister Teresa Benedicta did not succeed in doing so, and became instead a Christian martyr.

THE CIRCUMSTANCES OF HIDING

> And Haman said unto king Ahasuerus: There is a certain people scattered abroad and dispersed among the peoples in all the provinces of thy kingdom; and their laws are diverse from those of every people; neither keep they the king's laws: therefore it profiteth not the king to suffer them. If it please the king, let it be written that they may be destroyed.   (Esther 3:8-9)[5]

To appreciate the emotional stakes of Stein's revelation of her identity, we need to consider the historical context and personal circumstances under which she wrote the (auto)biography in which this revelation takes place.[6] Like Haman two thousand years before him, Hitler wanted to destroy all the Jews. The Nazis viewed the Jews just as Haman did: they were a dispersed and hidden threat, and needed to be eliminated. Haman asked the King of Persia to destroy Jews throughout the Kingdom; a declaration was written and sent out to all the Persian provinces to annihilate them. The Nuremberg Laws began this same process in Germany in early 1933.

However, unlike Esther, who was hiding only her Jewish identity, Stein was simultaneously hiding two identities. To her friends, family, and mother she needed to "come out of the closet" as a practicing Catholic who would soon become a cloistered nun.[7] To herself and the non-Jewish community she needed to reveal herself as a Jew. Yet, it is crucial to our understanding of her that we see Stein as neither a Jew nor a Catholic, for she saw herself as both Jew and Catholic.

It was under these tense circumstances that Stein began writing the foreword to *Life in a Jewish Family* in her home town of Breslau, in the autumn of the year the Nuremberg laws went into effect. She went on to write the first three chapters over the next two years, cloistered in the Carmelite convent in Cologne, and stopped working on it while in the convent at Echt in 1939. Her narrative ends in 1916, at the point that Stein, then still a young woman, had just completed her PhD. Her autobiography remained unfinished, and what we have of it was published posthumously: she was taken from her convent, transported to Auschwitz, and gassed there virtually as soon as she arrived, August 9, 1942.[8]

The settings in which Stein wrote are vital to both the nature of her reflections and to the transition she makes from the biographical format to the autobiographical. Her geographic and temporal locales helped create for her an eddy of sorts, in which her attempts to navigate her multiple identities as a Jewish–Catholic–woman philosopher in a modern era bore fruit in her recognition of a multifaceted identity. This realization was exceptional, since universal meta-narratives about identity still constituted the dominant paradigm.[9] One could be either a Jew or a Catholic, but not both. And a Jew, in this horrific time, could never be anything but a Jew; indeed, conversions of any sort were never recognized by the Nazis.

At the time Stein began to write, she had just lost her job as lecturer at the German Institute for Educational Studies at the University of Münster. She lost it because she was of Jewish descent, despite the fact that she was a full practicing Catholic, and had been baptized over ten years earlier. Yet rather than see it as a disaster, Stein read the loss of her job as a sign of divine providence. It signified to her that it was time she entered the convent and lead a contemplative life as a Sister. In a letter to her friend Hedwig Conrad-Martius, she writes: "I do not regret that I no longer give lectures. I believe that a great and merciful Providence is behind all of it."[10]

Stein had wanted to enter the Carmelite order earlier but was denied permission by her mentor, Abbot Walzer. She wrote: "Even before beginning my work in Münster, I had pleaded for permission to enter the convent, which he had refused on the grounds of my mother's reaction and my own contribution to Catholic life."[11] Recognizing the change in her circumstances – essentially, the loss of her voice as a teacher – the Abbot finally conceded, and granted her permission to serve God in this way.

Stein was her mother's favorite and the youngest of seven children. She had decided to return to Breslau and spend a month with her family to say goodbye and to prepare her mother – an observant, pious Jewess to whom she was extremely close – for her coming entry into the convent. Stein expressed to a friend the worries she felt about confronting her mother and family with her Catholicism:

> [My mother] particularly rejects conversions. Everyone ought to live and die in the faith in which they were born. She imagines atrocious things about Catholicism and life in a convent. At the moment it is difficult to know what is causing her more pain: whether it is the separation from her youngest child to whom she has ever been attached with a particular love, or her horror of the completely foreign and inaccessible world into which that child is disappearing, or the qualms of conscience that she herself is at fault because she was not strict enough in raising me as a Jew.[12]

This, then, is the burden under which Stein wrote the foreword of her (auto) biography: the severe anxiety about informing her family of her controversial decision to enter the convent. The news resulted in shock and grief for both mother and family.

Stein's "otherness" was pervasive: she was writing, in many ways, under the pressure of being "other" as a Catholic to her mother and family, and "other" as a woman philosopher and Jew to her male academic colleagues, to the Nazis, and to her fellow Catholics. But to her family she was even more than "other." Her family viewed her decision to join the convent as an abandonment of the family, and worse, a betrayal of her people in a menacing time; recall that the Nuremberg Laws had gone into effect just that same year. Her sister Erna Biberstein, the second youngest, writes about Stein's last visit home in her contribution to the editor's foreword to *Life in the Jewish Family*: "The weeks that followed [her revelation] were very difficult for us all. My mother was truly in despair, and never got over her grief. For the rest of us too, the farewell this time cut much deeper."[13] Yet, Erna continues, "Edith herself did not want to admit it, and even from the convent continued to take part in everything."[14] Stein worked hard to keep a close connection with her Jewish family and her Jewish roots, in spite of the rift caused by her Catholicism.

Stein regarded her conversion as an act with quite the opposite effect than the one so feared by her family: she believed that in the cloistered community of the convent she could be of greater help to Jews. In her interior and spiritual life – to which she felt called – she saw herself as "carrying the cross" for her people, just as she felt Queen Esther was anointed – indeed, called – to save her people.[15] She describes experiencing this epiphany in the midst of her decision to enter the convent: "I spoke with the Savior to tell him that I realized it was his Cross that was now being laid upon the Jewish people, that the few who understood this had the responsibility of carrying it in the name of all, and [asked, was] I myself willing to do this?"[16]

In response to the Nazi persecution of her as a Jew, Stein dove deeper into her spiritual identity as a Catholic – not to escape, but in order to work for the salvation of her people.

For Stein, the consequences of her conversion to Catholicism were painful. But the pain, interestingly, led a part of her back to her Jewish identity. Once home with her mother and family in Breslau, Stein writes of her confrontation with her mother: "It was a step that had to be taken in the absolute darkness of faith. Time and again, I asked myself during those weeks, "Which of us is going to break first – me or my mother?" But the two of us held out to the very last day."[17]

To her dismay, Stein realized that she was doing more than breaking her mother's heart; for her, the act had broader consequences, since her mother represented to Stein all the positive and pious attributes of the Jewish people. It was under this severe anxiety about her mother (both as an individual and as a metonym for pious Jewry) that Stein began to mull over and write the foreword to *Life in a Jewish Family*. In less than a few months, she would exchange her identity as Dr Edith Stein, Catholic academy professor, for that of Sister Teresa Benedicta of the Cross. But it is also in this moment, the moment she felt she broke her Jewish mother's heart, that she was inspired to educate non-Jews about what it was like to be one. To forge this connection to her mother at this time required of Stein deep self-reflection, as well as great moral fortitude.

WERE THEY HIDING THEIR JEWISH IDENTITIES?

> Esther had not yet made known her kindred or her people, as
> Mordecai had charged her.   (Esther 2:20)

> R. Judah says that although Hadassah was her original name she
> was called Esther "because she hides facts about herself."
>   (Talmud Megillah 13a)

Stein's opening statement in the foreword to her (auto)biography *Life in a Jewish Family* is riddled with ambiguity. "Recent months have catapulted the German Jews out of the peaceful existence they had come to take for granted. They have been forced to reflect upon themselves, upon their being, and upon their destiny."[18] This is an interesting statement given that the reader cannot be sure where Stein is locating either her identity or her voice. Was she speaking as someone who *is* a Jew or someone who once *was* a Jew? Was Stein implying that she is being forced to reflect upon her destiny? Or was it her observation that it was her family and the Jewish community around her – of whom she is no longer a part – who were being forced to reflect upon themselves, their being and their destiny?

The more one examines the statement, the more questions emerge: is it true that the German Jews before that time lived a peaceful existence? Or is this a myth?[19] In the next sentence she points out that not only must Jews respond to "the Jewish question," but non-Jews must do so too: "But today's events have also impelled many others, hitherto non-partisan, to take up the Jewish question. Catholic Youth Groups, for instance, have been dealing with it in all seriousness and with a deep sense of responsibility."[20] Did Stein feel the need to point out that "others" or outsiders to the Jewish community were responding to the Jewish problem, in order to justify her concern, because she considered herself one of them, being no longer a Jew?

From these sentences we cannot accurately determine where she has located her religious identity, for Stein could plausibly be speaking from either of two distinct voices, one Jewish and the other Catholic. One could read her as proclaiming that she is indeed an outsider to non-Jewish life, and that this is the reason she decided to write an autobiography. Reporting on a conversation with the priest friend who urged her to write about growing up in a Jewish family, Stein notes that "In that discussion I was urged to write down what I, child of a Jewish family, had learned about the Jewish people, *since such knowledge is so rarely found in outsiders.*"[21] In other words, her audience (unlike her) was outside the Jewish community and thus needed to be educated.

On the other hand, one could argue that at the time she wrote her memoir, Stein saw herself not as an insider to Jewish life, but, from the perspective of her adoptive Catholic identity, as an outsider to Jewry who had at one time, in her pre-Christian life, been a Jew. Unfortunately, the word "outsider" as she employs it in her remarks above remains ambiguous. Did her friend mean to imply that the "outsider" is outside the Christian community? That is, was Stein herself even at that point an outsider to the Christian community because she never denied her Jewishness? Or was she rather an outsider to the Jewish community? Through *my* Jewish lens, I see the priest referring to a perspective coming from outside the *Jewish* community. But in her writing Stein seems about as easy to contain as a droplet of mercury.

Occasionally, we can find clues outside her own slippery voice. In her essay "Witnessing My Aunt's Beatification," Susanne Batzdorff describes a moment in Breslau when she was twelve – it was 1933 – and she ran into her Tante (Aunt) Edith Stein. Batzdorff summoned the courage to ask her Tante why she had decided to enter the convent. Stein's answer sheds crucial light on her identity as a Jew: "What I am doing does not mean that I want to leave my people and my family," she said. "I will always be close to you, the family and the Jewish people. And don't think what is happening in a convent is going to keep me immune from what is happening in the world."[22]

Interestingly, Stein's autobiography – which she considered, on an individual scale, to be a record of the Jewish people – eerily anticipates the events to come. It is as if she sensed that her people were on the brink of extinction, and, acting as something between an anthropologist and a paleontologist, took it as her responsibility to fix an accurate picture of the Jews into public memory for the sake of posterity, if not for their salvation.[23] She saw her story not only as an instance of the life of a Jewish family, but also as an apologia of sorts, a treatise demonstrating that Jews were humans, not monsters.

Even in this work, her ambivalence is apparent. When she describes the atrocities that are happening to the Jewish people, and wonders aloud why they were taking place, she is trying to come to terms with the horrific caricatures of the Jews prevalent at the time – yet she does not fully refute them. Instead, she suggests that they might indeed be modeled on actual characteristics: "Possibly, the specific traits may have been copied from living models."[24] Did she believe there might be an element of truth to Nazi propaganda against the Jews? If this is the case, it is difficult to imagine her making such statements while thinking of herself as a fully fledged member of the Jewish community. In the next sentence, however, she turns around and raises what we now would regard as a postmodern question. She asks, "But does having 'Jewish Blood' cause an inevitable consequence in the Jewish people?"[25] That she placed quotation marks around "Jewish Blood" shows she is consciously challenging the old meta-narrative regarding Jewish identity – the one that says you are born a Jew, and you will always be a Jew, no matter what your religious beliefs are. Even in the Nazi imagination, Jewishness is not a *constructed* ethnic and religious identity – a notion Stein's statement seems to lay the groundwork for – but a biologically, racially determined one.

Her voice in the foreword, previously so noncommittal on the matter of her own identification, begins to become clearer, however. Stein next explains why she is motivated to write this memoir at this historical moment. She worries that the attacks against the Jews do not portray the truth about the nature of the Jewish people and the Jewish community. She fears for the youth and the people who had not associated with or had any personal relationship with the Jews – they were likely to believe the propaganda they were force-fed. She wants her audience to be able to empathize with the "other":

> But many others lack this kind of experience. The opportunity to attain it has been denied primarily to the young who, these days, are being reared in racial hatred from earliest childhood. To all those who have been deprived, *we who grew up in Judaism have an obligation to give our testimony.*[26]

She reasons that if she were to write a memoir describing the everyday life of a Jewish family, readers would see that the people in this family – and by extension the Jewish people – were no different than anyone else. But she emphasizes that she does not want to write a definitive tract on Judaism: "To develop 'the idea' of Judaism and to defend it against false interpretation, to present the content of the Jewish religion, to write the history of the Jewish people – for all this, experts are at hand."[27] Stein clarifies her intentions: she is no authority on the philosophical, historical, and spiritual aspects of Judaism; she does not identify herself as a scholar of Judaism or as a rabbi; instead she locates her Jewish voice in a very specific genre which is outside these domains.[28] She locates her authority in her own life, and, significantly, aligns her narrative with a specific genre:

> I would like to give simply a straightforward account of *my own experience of Jewish testimony, to be placed alongside others* already available in print or soon to be published. It is intended as information for anyone wishing to pursue an unprejudiced study from original sources.[29]

So Stein retrieved her Jewish identity by "testifying" to her experience growing up as a Jewish woman. As we see in the next section, she compared her writing to other "testimonies": specifically, the autobiographies and ethical wills of other Jewish women. Her use of the word "testimony" to describe her narrative was cunning: in the Christian Bible the four gospels give "testimony" to their experience of Jesus. Might Stein be employing this term in a deliberately Christian sense, implying that not only did she *experience* Judaism, but she also *bore witness to* Judaism, in the way the four disciples were witness to the life of Jesus? Perhaps she was well aware that her use of the word "testimony" would help her Catholic and non-Jewish audience empathize with her story of a Jewish woman.

SECLUSION IN MARRIAGE: KING AHASUERUS
OR THE CATHOLIC CHURCH

Then Mordechai bade them return answer unto Esther: *Think not with thyself that thou shalt escape in the king's house, more than all the Jews.* For if thou all together holdest thy peace at this time, then will relief and deliverance arise to the Jews from another place, but thou and thy father's house will perish; and who knoweth whether thou art not come to the royal estate for such a time as this?   (Esther 4:13-14)[30]

And don't think that my being in a convent is going to keep me immune from what is happening in the world.   (Edith Stein)[31]

Stein mentions in her foreword to *Life in a Jewish Family* that other autobiographies were soon to be published. In a footnote she identifies two: those of Glückel of Hameln and Pauline Wengeroff.[32] Her reference to these two texts written by Jewish women – the first an ethical will[33] and the second an autobiography – reveals how learned her Jewish feminism was. Further, by naming them she indicates her implicit allegiance to a genre of literature written by Jewish women. Glückel's ethical will and Pauline Wengeroff's autobiography offer testimony, like hers, to their experience not just as Jews, but as Jewish *women* during dark times. Glückel was inspired to write on the occasion of the death of her husband; Wengeroff was inspired by the onslaught of the Haskalah, the prevalence of nihilism, and the destruction of tradition. Stein could have referred to other autobiographies by non-Jewish women, but she did not. In a construction offering a mirror opposite of Stein's narrative, both Glückel and Wengeroff were mothers and grandmothers writing to their children. While Glückel wrote in the eighteenth century, and Wengeroff in the nineteenth, both of their life stories bear some strong resemblance to the life of Stein's mother, Frau Auguste Stein. But if Edith Stein was consciously aware of the parallels in these testimonies to figures in her own life, she did not acknowledge this in her own diaries and letters.

Glückel began writing her ethical will when she was forty-four and had just been widowed, left to cope on her own with her twelve children. She took over the family business and married off the children yet unwed. Frau Stein, Edith's mother, was widowed when she was in her forties, when Edith was less than two years old. Like Glückel, Frau Stein was left with children to raise, and took over the family business to survive. The primary difference between them was that Frau Stein did not write her autobiography; instead, the daughter who was closest to her decided she should write her mother's memoirs.

Grief figures strongly in all three women's stories. It is what spurred Glückel to write her memoirs:

> In my great grief and for my heart's ease I begin this book the
> year of creation 5451 [1690–91]. May God soon rejoice us and
> send us His redeemer! ... I began writing it, dear children, upon
> the death of your good father, in the hope of distracting my soul
> from the burdens laid upon it, and the bitter thought we have lost
> our faithful shepherd. In this way I have managed to live through
> many wakeful nights, and springing from my bed shortened the
> sleepless hours.[34]

It was the pain of Edith Stein's mother (ironically caused by Stein herself)
which sparked her daughter to begin her memoirs. The inspiration for both
of these memoirs – Glückel's and Stein's – emerged because the writers were
living in difficult times: for the former, the difficulties were individual; for the
latter, they were global. The parallel between Pauline Wengeroff and Frau
Stein appears in the fact that both mothers suffered the loss of their children
to Christianity, though for different reasons. Over this event, both mothers
suffered despair. Wengeroff writes in her autobiography:

> The baptism of my children was the hardest blow of my life. But
> the loving heart of a mother can bear a great deal. I forgave them;
> the blame was on us parents. My sorrow gradually lost its personal
> meaning, but evermore took on the character of a national mis-
> fortune. I mourn it not only as a mother, but as a Jewess mourning
> the Jewish people that has lost so many of its noble sons.[35]

Wengeroff laments that her son converted in order to be accepted at the university in St. Petersburg. However, his motivation was strictly to gain access
to education and to a career, and had nothing to do with an interior motive;
in contrast, Stein's motivation was spiritual. Significantly, Stein's sister also
converted to Christianity and joined her in the same convent at Echt. But
her conversion was made after their mother's death and so it did not have an
impact on her.[36]

By employing these two Jewish women as her "chosen others" – a term
critic Carolyn Heilbrun uses to describe the relational guideposts so often
found in women's autobiography – we can see evidence of Stein's identification with her mother as a Jewish woman.[37] Furthermore, Stein tells us that
her narrative began as an account of her mother's life:

> Originally I had intended to sketch my mother's memoirs. She
> was always an inexhaustible source of stories. ... To achieve this, I
> have had to ask specific questions, and often it has been impossi-
> ble to ascertain tangible and positive facts. In what follows I shall
> begin with sketches based on these conversations with my mother.
> After that I will present, to the best of my ability, an account of my
> mother's life.[38]

Unfortunately, she never got to that story.

It is certainly intriguing that Stein's testimony to Judaism began as a biography of her mother's life and not of her own. To make sense of this we have to go back to the strain Stein was feeling as she wrote. She felt she was breaking her mother's heart, and decided – not coincidentally, as a salve perhaps to herself, or to her mother – that it was time to reflect on life as a Jew. Thus, using her mother as her precursor and writing in her mother's house, Stein confronted her own strong Jewish identity. It is indeed paradoxical that it was the rupture of her mother's pious Jewish legacy that brought Stein to claim her Jewishness.

In the chapter entitled "My Mother Remembers," Stein describes why she had such a close connection to her mother. She was the youngest and was less than two years old when her father died suddenly on a business trip. Her mother had been holding Stein in her arms when the two saw him off, and it had been Stein herself who was the last one in the family to say good-bye. She writes:

> I have already told how my mother held me in her arms as he bade her farewell when he set out on a journey from which he was not to return alive, and that, when he had already turned to leave, I called him back once more. So, for her [Edith's mother] I was the final legacy from my father. I slept beside her, and when, weary after a day of work, she would return home, her first steps led her to me.[39]

Thus Stein represented to her mother a unique and intense connection to the father, creating a bond with her not shared by any of her other siblings. Stein explains that she was also so close to her mother because she was born on the holiest day of the Jewish year:

> She laid great stress on my being born on the Day of Atonement, and I believed this contributed more than anything else to her youngest being especially dear to her. And since our destinies are intertwined in such a unique way, it is probably appropriate that in this portrait of my mother I say more about my own development than about that of my brothers or sisters.[40]

It is after establishing this strong connection to her mother, deeply inflected with Jewish religious significance, that Stein breaks into her own voice. In the second chapter – "The World as the Two Youngest Knew It" – she breaks into autobiography.[41] So it comes to be that the memoirs Stein hoped to write for her mother become an account of her own development, told through the lens of her relationship to her mother. It is interesting to note that in a way this move represents another form of hiding: she was hiding herself behind her mother, or perhaps even in her mother's story.

Rachel Brenner points out that Stein saw her autobiography as part of her pedagogical Jewish feminism, grounded in both her concept of feminine nature and her concept of empathy:[42] "By referring to their memoirs as precedents that define her own, Stein legitimized her autobiographical effort and affirmed the educational value of Jewish women's self-narratives in teaching the world about Jewish life."[43]

Stein writes, "Women naturally seem to embrace that which is *living, personal, and whole*."[44] She finds these uniquely female qualities exemplary and sees it as her duty also to recommend their merits to men, presumably so that they may emulate them.[45] In her writing Stein never compromises her ethics, which are intertwined with both her notions of pedagogy and her concept of empathy. Stein explores empathy in her doctoral dissertation, seeing it as an encounter with the "other" through time. She divides human experience into primordial and non-primordial, seeing the experience of the moment as primordial, and the experience of remembering as non-primordial. When we encounter the "other" our own experience is primordial, but our experience of the "other" is secondary. Empathy is created when we relate non-primordial experiences to our own. Brenner explains Stein's theory in this way: "The empathic act is thus predicated upon the ability of the individual to perceive himself/herself as a unique and, at the same time, as an integral component of the social network."[46]

Stein's understanding of empathy informed her pedagogical practice. In *Life in a Jewish Family*, these emerge clearly in her meticulous description of how the Jewish holidays were celebrated in her family. Her voice takes on the tone of an educator, enlightening Christians about Judaism, using links between Jewish holidays and the Christian holidays as one of her primary teaching tools:

> Among the most important events of life at home, aside from the family feast, were the major Jewish High Holy Days: particularly Pesach (the Passover holiday) which coincides approximately with Easter; also the holiday of the New Year and the Day of Atonement (in September or October depending on the correspondence of the Jewish to the Gregorian calendar). Most Christians are unaware that the "Feast of Unleavened Bread," in remembrance of the Exodus of the children of Israel from Egypt, continues to be celebrated today in the identical manner in which it was celebrated by our Lord with his disciples when he instituted the Blessed Sacrament and took leave of his followers. Of course, a Passover lamb is no longer slaughtered since the destruction of the Temple in Jerusalem; but the head of the house, reciting the prescribed prayers, still distributes the unleavened bread and the bitter herbs which are a reminder of the suffering connected with the exile. He blesses the wine and reads the account of the deliverance of the

People from Egypt. With the indomitable consistency that marks the Jewish spirit, the observances of the feast are extensive ... (During my childhood, everything was done as prescribed; later, our liberal-minded elder brothers and sisters talked my mother out of some of it.) On the days of preparation, housewives have a great deal of work to get done and are very happy when evening comes and the holiday itself begins (Jewish holidays begin on the eve when the first star appears in the sky).[47]

Stein's description of the holidays is both detailed and didactic. Her voice conveys a conscious awareness of her Christian audience, as she explains what the Jewish terms mean and how the holidays are similar to Christian ones. In all her parenthetical asides Stein attempts to provide for her audience a Christian framework with which to understand the Jewish holy days. We also see that Stein's descriptions emphasize her mother's devotion. When Stein describes the Jewish New Year she again comments on her mother, who "performs the deep devotion, reciting the prescribed prayers."[48]

Stein's knowledge and understanding of the Jewish holidays was considerable. Indeed, she seemed to know more than most non-orthodox American Jews know today. Her favorite Jewish holiday was the Day of Atonement, which resonated with her deep appreciation for the contemplative life. She describes the holiday – her birthday – this way:

The highest of all the Jewish festivals is the Day of Atonement, the day on which the High Priest used to enter the Holy of Holies to offer the sacrifice of atonement for himself and for the people; afterwards the "scapegoat," upon whose head, symbolically, the sins of all the people had been laid, was driven out into the desert. All of this ritual has come to an end. But even at present the day it is observed with prayer and fasting, and whoever preserves but a trace of Judaism goes to the "Temple" on this day. ... I was especially attracted to the ritual of this particular holy day, when one refrained from taking any food or drink for twenty-four hours or more, and I loved it more than any of the others. On the eve, one had to partake of the evening meal while it was still daylight, for the service in the synagogue would begin as soon as the first star appeared in the sky. Not only did my mother attend on this evening but she was accompanied by our elder sisters; even my brothers considered it a duty to be present. The beautiful ancient melodies used on this evening even attract those of other beliefs.[49]

This extensive quote bears close scrutiny, since it so deftly demonstrates Stein's theology. The learnedness is clear, but beyond that, Stein shows a subtle perception – quite ahead of her time–of the fact that one does not need to understand oneself as a practicing Jew to find resonance in these holidays. It would be far later that such a nuanced understanding of secular German Jewry would emerge. Further, her placing "Temple" in quotes makes reference to the ancient Temple of King Solomon. Her love of this holiday – one of fasting and restraint – indicates the asceticism which reappears in her love of the cloistered life. Her intent to connect Judaism to non-Jews reappears in her final statement, in which she gestures to the universal appeal of "the beautiful ancient melodies."

In Stein's description of the Jewish holidays we hear the multiplicity of her voices as teacher, Jew, and Catholic woman. She continually addresses (and embraces) the "other" in her explanations and understandings, whether that "other" is Catholic or Jewish. Even fellow Jews can learn from her descriptions. What emerges in her narrative is her conviction that the mother and other women in the family maintain and preserve the tradition and show pious devotion. She felt that the men in her own family – actually her brothers – dilute the expression of Judaism and the sacredness of Jewish ritual and holidays because of their liberal-mindedness. And yet in spite of her brothers' relative impiety, she portrays her Jewish family as very warm and caring, especially when she describes how they take care of one another during life-cycle events.

One thing which is startling, however, given the historical context, is the passage in which Stein explains how Jews endure hardships. She contemplates why so many Jews were committing suicide during this menacing period of economic hardship and virulent anti-Semitism:[50]

> I believe that the inability to face and to accept the collapse of one's worldly existence with reasonable calm is closely linked to the lack of a prospect of life in eternity. The personal immortality of the soul is not considered an article of faith; all of one's effort is concentrated on what is temporal. Even the piety of the pious is directed toward the sanctification of *this* life. *A Jew is able to endure severe hardship and untiring labor coupled with extreme privations for years on end as long as he sees a goal ahead. ... The true believer of course, is deterred from such a course by his submission to the will of God.*[51]

Stein's explanation that Judaism is a temporal tradition which emphasizes "*this* life" reveals to us one of Catholic spirituality's appeals to her: Judaism cannot offer her a way to understand eternity. She felt that the means to avoid hopelessness and suicide is to submit one's will to God. Although Orthodox Jews certainly believe they are submitting their wills to God by following all the proscribed Jewish laws, Stein did not think this worked, because their piety is directed toward "*this* life." Perhaps Stein believed that the only way to keep oneself together during catastrophic times was to possess Catholic faith.

This, of course, is what worked for her. Yet clearly, while Stein's Catholic faith ran deep, so did her faithfulness to her Jewish identity.

We see then that her autobiography represents not only an ethical act, but an attempt at the educational reform of non-Jews. But it is also, argues Rachel Brenner, a self-investigation:

> The shift of focus from mother to self signifies the seriousness of Stein's self-investigation; it's not merely the desire to placate her mother and make up for the pain she has caused her that prompts Stein to write, but rather the need to both reconstruct and maintain ties with her former, Jewish self at that particular time.[52]

We see how the voice of Stein's Jewish identity was birthed through her mother; it speaks, to her, of a sense of belonging. Through the voice of her mother, as well as those of Glückel and Wengeroff, Stein proclaims her Jewishness, her womanness, and her belonging. In the convergence of time and space, and her anxiety towards her mother, Stein's Jewish identity came to life, and this convergence was made possible only by the catastrophic times in which she and her people lived.

COMING OUT OF HIDING

> The King said, "Whatever thy petition, Queen Esther, it shall be granted thee; and whatever thy request, even to the half of the kingdom, it shall be performed." Then Esther the queen answered and said: "If I have found favor in thy sight, O king, and if it please the king, let my life be given me at my petition, and my people at my request; for we are sold, I and my people, to be destroyed, to be slain, and to perish."   (Esther 7:2-3)

Both Stein and Esther pose some important challenges to current notions about identity politics, by offering up a paradox: each identifies simultaneously as both self and "other." Their narratives of hiding and revelation prompt numerous questions: if we consider facets of identity capable of being "closeted" or concealed, is the process by which they "come out of the closet" as transparent as we might have thought? What if one's fluid sense of identity does not fit into prevailing social paradigms? Is one's identity essentialist or anti-essentialist? Foundational or non-foundational? Do one's appearance and identity have substance behind them, or are we really the masks we wear? Is Jewish identity produced and constructed, or is it an innate quality? Finally, what can we learn about Edith Stein's Jewish identity from the parallel to the Book of Esther in the Hebrew Bible? Let us now return to the discussion of gender and queer theory begun in Chapter 1, which will illuminate some answers to these questions, and give us a sound framework for a new understanding of the layered identity politics of Stein and Esther.

To begin with, gender and queer theorists find essentialism too flawed as a means to make sense of identity. They have found that essentialist discourse on gender and identity politics would not be able to articulate the impossible identity paradox of being "other" and the self, or the same, at once. This discourse limits categories of identity to mutually exclusive, Aristotelian binaries such as male/female, self/other, inside/outside, subject/object. One chief problem with such dualities or binaries is that they can be used to subject and oppress all those who are "other" through hierarchical ordering and a projection on to the "other" of all negative attributes.

Queer theorist Judith Butler demonstrates gender's non-essential performativity.[53] But this paradigm works for the construction of more than just gender. Although they believed in an essential, racialized Jewish identity, the Nazis could not prove someone's Jewishness except in a non-essentialist manner.[54] That is, to prove Jewishness they had to create a marking system by using the "label" of the yellow star, which – to them – signified some sort of racial quality, an innate substance. All people who were identified as Jews by the Nazis were given the name Israel and Sara. Without these devices the Nazis could not distinguish Jewish identity from any other. The yellow star and the naming were markers, signifiers, a type of stylization.

Did this mean that Jewish blood was somehow different from others? Was the blood of Jews a special color? How did one prove one had Jewish blood except through the performative? Recall that Stein posed the question in her foreword: "does having 'Jewish Blood' cause an inevitable consequence in the Jewish people?" However, the only way the Nazis could identify Jews was by resorting to a non-essentialist action and a marking system. Ostensibly the yellow star could be removed at any point and no one would know the wearer had been a Jew unless they claimed to be one. Indeed, the blood of Jews is not a different color, and Jewishness is not an essence located in biology.

The narrative detail on which the Book of Esther turns would seem to reinforce this point, and show the limits of foundational categories of identity. Her desire to survive, coupled with her ability to save the Jewish people, required Esther to double her identity. Yet she simultaneously embraced both identities, and so traditional (foundational) understandings of identity fail to explain her ambivalence. Timothy Beal astutely demonstrates that:

> The Book of Esther ... explores the possibilities of political subversion and transformation produced by the problematic limits and ambivalences of identity – the non-viability of complete integrity. Survival in the Book of Esther relies precisely on the *impossibility* and therefore the *surpassability* of the limits imposed on identity according to the logic of the same.[55]

Beal builds on Butler's reconceptualization of identity in his reading of the Book of Esther, showing how Esther's identity surpasses foundational categories and is constructed as an *effect*, produced and generated by the different possibilities of agency required of her.

But I believe that to begin to make sense of Esther's and Stein's multilayered performance and rhetoric we need to leave both essentialist and anti-essentialist notions of identity behind. Because Esther and Stein acted and dressed as queen and nun, respectively, according to Butler's non-essentialist view of gender identity they cannot *be* anything but what and how they presented themselves in the public spheres. They are the *effect* of their stylized repetition of acting and dressing as a queen and a nun. It would appear, however, that performing and dressing one way in public and then revealing oneself to be something "other" than what one appears would challenge Butler's anti-essentialist identity theory.

So we can't merely understand Esther's and Stein's Jewishness by framing it in the binary debate between an interior and an exterior identity, wherein their identities are labeled as Jew on the interior, and "other" on the exterior. In this approach their acting and dressing as queen and nun would be viewed as a mask for their so-called 'interior' Jewishness, similar in a way to the *conversos*.[56] Acting and dressing then becomes a type of masquerade to cover up their Jewishness. We have seen that this argument does not work for Stein because her interior sense of herself was as a Carmelite Catholic; this was her truth. But she also simultaneously considered herself to be a Jew. Stein's convergence, her being both Jew and Carmelite, does not fit into the binary identity of interior and exterior labeling.

We therefore need to look at them from a different perspective in order to make sense of their identities. Butler's anti-essentialist theory does not illuminate the complex lives of Esther and Stein; indeed, they pose a challenge to her notion of identity as being equivalent to performance and dress. In their respective narratives Esther and Stein rhetorically construct themselves as Jews, while at the same time acting and dressing as non-Jews. They both embody and perform the self and "other" simultaneously. If their Jewishness was a grounded, innate substance then the appearance of being a queen or a nun would be farcical to their 'true' identities, for they would be Jews pretending to be something other. Yet, as we have seen, Stein was not pretending her Catholic faith. Her Jewishness surfaced when it was necessary to take moral action, and at this point, she "came out" with both her identities.

Jewishness, for Stein, is expressed through her sense of longing *to be* or *belonging*. Elspeth Probyn offers this third and final way to view Stein, which I find provides the best way to understand her. Probyn takes Butler's gender definition one step further by examining gender not only in the mode of time but also in the mode of space. Probyn gives us a new language in which to articulate this sense of convergence, this being *both* self and "other." To reveal this dimension of oneself is a form of movement in space. Probyn's insight on gender can thus be applied to Esther's and Stein's identity politics. Their identities were multifaceted; they were "queer" in the literal sense of the word, as defined above. Probyn says, "I want ... to turn queer into a verb (a sense already evident in Butler's proposition that the noun *queer* itself is twisted and queered). As [Eve] Sedgwick notes, 'The word "queer" itself means *across* ...'."[57] Esther's and Stein's senses of self and identity were twisted to adapt to their social settings in time and place. Stein's Jewish friends and family thought her Catholic identity was "queer," and her Jewish identity was "queer" to her Catholic community. To use Probyn's concept of queer as a verb would imply then that one crosses over fixed rules and boundaries to demonstrate identity and communities of belonging.

To this day the Jewish community cannot accept Stein's entwined identity as a Jew and a Christian.[58] She transgressed prescribed boundaries. In the Esther narrative and the case of Stein's life, more light is shed if we think in terms other than mere "identity":

> Here I slide from "identity" to "belonging," in part because I think that the latter term captures more accurately the desire for some sort of attachment, be it to other people, places, or modes of being, and the ways in which individuals and groups are caught within wanting to belong, wanting to become, a process that is fueled by yearning rather than the positing of identity as a stable state.[59]

Thus we should not talk about identities but instead should introduce to the discussion the concept of "belonging," which resolves the problem posed by multifaceted identity. After all, *identity* comes from the Latin root *idem*, which means "the same." This concept of identity is limiting because it is wrapped, as Judith Butler has noted, in the language of approbation:

> Instrumentality and distinction germane to the epistemological mode also belong to a strategy of domination that pits the "I" against an "Other" and, once that separation is effected, creates an artificial set of questions about the known ability and recoverability of that Other.[60]

In other words, when we define our knowledge of ourselves and others through a binary split, hierarchical and static, which pits the self against the "other," we are stuck; the ways we can understand and appreciate a person's multifaceted sense of self are confined to an inadequate, binary system of categories which cannot "cross over." If we think Stein pits her sense of self as a Christian Carmelite *against* her Jewish sense of self, we misunderstand her. Instead, she "be-longs" to the Jewish people just as much she "be-longs" to the Carmelite order. And she performs her "be-longing" to the Jewish people via the courageous act of writing a (Jewish) autobiography in a convent while under the implicit threat of annihilation.

To use Probyn's language, at what point in time did Esther and Stein "come out of the closet" to their non-Jewish communities of belonging about their Jewish selves? And, conversely, when did they come out to their Jewish communities as a Persian Queen and a Carmelite nun? In other words, how did Esther and Stein show their agency? The answer: when the Jewish people's survival was in question. Esther and Stein were what Jean Amery calls "catastrophe Jews," and Brenner shows that Stein defined her Jewishness by these terms. Such Jews, says Brenner, admit that "solidarity in the face of threat is all that links [them] with [their] Jewish contemporaries, the believers as well as the non-believers, the national-minded as well as those ready to assimilate."[61]

Recall that in her foreword to *Life in a Jewish Family*, Stein wrote that "[r]ecent months have catapulted the German Jews out of the peaceful existence they had come to take for granted."[62] In other words, their endangerment catalyzed Stein's narrative, and consequent coming out of the closet – or, more precisely, out of the convent – to declare both her Jewishness and her solidarity with her people. What creates the paradox is that she steadfastly identifies with her Catholic faith as she declares her Jewishness: she insists on her loyalties to both communities of belonging.

I have shown that neither the essentialist construction of identity, nor Butler's anti-essentialist formulation, explain the enigma that Esther's and Stein's identity politics represent. To move us toward some resolution, I propose that the discussion of identity politics be moved out of the essentialist/anti-essentialist debate. I propose that we take the whole conversation in a new direction, one that takes into account Probyn's concept of be-longing. This new direction should also take into account the historical context in which one reveals to oneself and others the various facets of one's multifaceted sense of be-longings. Ultimately, I propose we discard the word "identity," and instead consider only our communities of belonging. What we need now is a means by which to envision the multiplicities of these communities, and the means by which they overlap in our understandings of ourselves.

THE WHOLE MEGILLAH: SOME NOTES TOWARD
A NEW METAPHOR FOR BE-LONGING

I will close by exploring a metaphor which we can use to represent a new means of envisioning be-longing – one that reconciles the paradoxes of Stein's multiple, seemingly mutually exclusive senses of herself as Jew and Catholic. Drawing from Probyn's work, which describes identity's existence in space, and revising Butler's, which describes identity's existence in time, I propose we think of identity as a *megillah*.

The megillah, a holy object to Jewish ritual and community, lends itself well to our study here, since the Book of Esther is known as the Megillah of Esther. Here, I will consider its qualities as an object (skin-like) whose meaning fluctuates depending on its existence in *both* space and time. In Hebrew the word means *scroll*, and refers to the scrolls on which the Torah's five books of Moses are written; most often it is used to refer to the Book of Esther. In its use in Yiddish, and as a Yiddish word borrowed by English, a megillah is a long, involved story or account of an event; as such, it suits our purposes well, since we have seen that accounting for Stein's religious identity is no simple matter. We can look at the word from several different angles to reveal its utility as a metaphor for identity: we can look at its etymology, at the actual process of the megillah's construction, and finally we can examine the means by which the megillah is read.

In Hebrew, the word megillah comes from the root letters gimel, lamed, lamed, which, when used as a verb, means "to roll," and when used as a noun means "wheel." Embedded in the Hebrew word megillah, then, is the notion of some sort of movement. Interestingly, the English translation – scroll – also embraces the word "roll." A scroll then can either be rolled backward or forward to reveal a huge span of parchment; it can be opened just slightly or it can stay in place. When we employ the Yiddish phrase "I will tell you the whole megillah," we mean we will tell the whole story or scroll's worth, not just a portion of it. If we imagine the megillah as a metaphor for our identities, we could choose to unroll and reveal (or "bring out") different sections of ourselves to present to those who would read them. Stein's audience was a predominantly Catholic one, and unaware of her Jewish past; by writing and publishing her (auto)biography she scrolled backwards into earlier portions of her life to reveal her Jewishness. *Life in a Jewish Family* represents the intact, whole "megillah" of Stein's identity/ies, encompassing the past with the present. As she embarked on her new role as Sister Teresa Benedicta of the Cross, as she was on the verge of embracing her new be-longing to the Carmelite order, it was the historical moment – the pending catastrophe – that forced her to scroll backwards to reflect on her sense of Jewish be-longing.

A megillah scroll is constructed out of parchment made from lambskin, which is sewn together and attached at either end to wooden dowels. The fact that the scroll is constructed from skin, and that this skin is then written upon, echoes Probyn's characterization of identity as something which exists at the surfaces of belonging. She argues that rather than talking about identity we should talk about *rendering a surface* or *surfacing*. Further, Probyn suggests we conceptualize surfacing not as an object but as a process. She describes this "sociology of the skin" as "the processes by which things become visible and are produced as the outside."[63] To illustrate Probyn's concept of surfacing, we need only look as far as the Torah service. At the end of the reading known as the Hagbah, the Torah is held up and the parchment of the Torah portion being chanted is shown to the congregation; literally, the opening and display of the Torah scroll is rendering surface. Understanding surfacing and the sociology of the skin forces us, says Probyn, to "constantly place ourselves within the relations of proximity of different forms of belonging. And at the edge of ourselves we mutate; we become other."[64] The metaphor of the megillah gives us an image with which we can animate Probyn's insight: Sister Teresa scrolled backwards to her upbringing as a Jewess so that she could mutate her otherness, her being a Jew, into a new identity, a new surfacing of herself as a Carmelite nun. These are two coexistent forms of belonging written on the same megillah of Edith Stein/Sister Teresa's life.

We can see that this image of the megillah as metaphor for identity implies some amount of agency on our parts, regarding what portions of the "skin" of our identities we reveal, and when. At what point do we pull the scroll of our own lives out a little further? When do we scroll backwards to reflect or reveal; when do we scroll to hide; when do we leave it in the same place? It is where we exist in both time and place, I think, that determines our manipulation of the megillah of our identities. Edith Stein lived during catastrophic times, and their influence on her choices seems clear. Earlier we identified Stein's religious identity as "queer," and we can find some modern parallel to her act in the case of the revelation of "queerness," in the sense of deviant or minority sexuality; in Stein's case, we find it in the sense of a religious identity which has clearly deviated from prevailing norms. The "closeted" part of the scroll would be written in a coded format, apparent or legible only to those who can decipher it by virtue of their be-longing to queer community (either as self-defined queers or as "fluent" allies), while the "out" part of the scroll would be written in a kind of direct language, readable by all, queer or not. From the moment the queer identity is "revealed" in the scroll, the coded references in the past are subject to re-reading and de-coding in light of the revelation. In this way, both her Catholic and her Jewish "readers" are forced to revisit their interpretation of her, based on the deciphering she offers in her (auto)biography.

The whole megillah of Edith Stein's life and sense of identity offers many lessons, but one of the most compelling is that we ourselves need to reconsider our categories of identity, especially in the areas where religion and ethnicity overlap. I have turned to queer theory to untangle her paradoxical expression of religious belonging, and of her *Blutgemeinschaft* – literally, her blood community. Her life poses this question: does one's religious identity necessarily imply allegiance to a particular ethnicity? For Jews, this has always been a critical question, one whose roots are readily found in a study of their history as a people in diaspora, facing continual threats to their existence. Are Jews an ethnic group, a religion, a tribe, a culture? Whole bodies of literature consider this question, and a satisfactory answer to it is likely still far off. Any persuasive one, however, would have to take into account the subtle truths we can learn about identity in the apparent contradictions of Stein's life. Her spirituality and her religious identity are not those of a Jew, but of a devout Carmelite; yet, she still felt her *Blutgemeinschaft* to be Jewish: it transcended her spirituality as a Carmelite, her intellectual identity as a philosopher. The path she found to it was not orthodox; she found her way through her sense of being a woman, through matrilineage; literally through her foremothers' blood legacy.

Chapter 4

REGINA JONAS: FROM CANDIDATE TO RABBINERIN

Regina Jonas, the first woman rabbi in Jewish history, was ordained in the German liberal tradition in 1935 in Offenbach, Germany, under the Nazi regime. She had studied at the Academy for the Science of Judaism in Berlin, and went on to serve her people as a rabbi from 1936 until her deportation to Theresienstadt in November 1942. She served there until her October 12, 1944 deportation to Auschwitz, where she served until her death a little over a month later.

Jonas described what drove her to become a woman rabbi in a response to a survey published in 1938 in the *C. V. Zeitung*, a weekly published by the Central Association of Germans of Jewish Faith. Answering the question "What do you have to say on the theme of WOMAN?" she wrote to the journalist Mala Laaser:

> If I must say what drove me as a woman to become a rabbi, two elements come to mind: My belief in the godly calling and my love for people. God has placed abilities and callings in our hearts without regard to gender. Thus each of us has the duty, whether man or woman, to realize those gifts God has given. If you look at things this way, one takes woman and man for what they are: human beings.[1]

In a subsequent interview with the journalist Annette Löwenthal of Hamburg, she said:

> I came to my profession from a religious conviction that God does not oppress any human being, that therefore the man does not rule the woman or occupy a spiritual position of supremacy over her. *I came to it from the view of the final and complete spiritual equality between the sexes, which were created by a just and merciful God.*[2]

Jonas navigated every aspect of her life based on her burning desire to be a rabbi, which she considered less a choice than a divine calling. Of her joining the rabbinate, she said to Laaser, "actually [the profession] chose me and not the reverse!"[3] It was an imperative in the Rosenzweigian sense: God was calling to her.[4] Moses, in Exodus 3:13, asks God, "Who are you? What is your name? What shall I tell the Israelites, my people?" Jonas felt God was calling out to her to be a leader of her people, and Jonas was calling out to God. Jonas felt that God's divinity was present in human beings, and it was her job as a rabbi to bring this divinity forth, and to remind them that they were human beings who reflected God. Jonas inscribed God's response to Moses, in Exodus 3:14, on the back of her ordination photo in 1936: *"Ehyeh Asher Ehyeh,"* or "I will be what I will be," or "I am who I am."[5]

Just how Jonas followed her calling is told through the story of her ordination and of how she filled the role of rabbi, once ordained. Like Moses, Jonas crossed over many borders. Moses received help and support to become a leader, as did Jonas. Moses did not get to see the promised land, and neither did Jonas. But Jonas was true to her divine calling. Jonas's life in her role as a rabbi lived up to God's calling. In other ways, Jonas was more like Abraham, to whom God called out, "Go forth from your country, And from your relatives, And from your father's house, To the land which I will show you" (Gen. 12:1). God was calling out to Jonas in a similar way, but unlike Abraham she did not leave her father's land; she joined her father in his land and community as a spiritual leader, just as Abraham and men who have been called by God have always done.

Neither did she leave the land of her mother, the land of women; she brought her mother's land to join the land of her father. She brought the geography of women to the male geography of rabbi; she expanded the circle of those who have been called. God was guiding and showing her the way, just as God had shown Abraham and her foremothers Sarah, Rebecca, Rachel, and Leah. Jonas was reclaiming these foremothers along with other women biblical leaders, such as Miriam, Deborah, Esther, and Hulda.

As Jonas scholar Elisa Klapheck notes, Jonas "identified [in] body and soul with the rabbinical role – a preacher or minister, and a legal scholar required to make decisions based on religious law and as a teacher of religion."[6] She ministered to those in spiritual need in their homes, in the hospital, in her own home, and in the community room at the Synagogue, as well as to Jewish women's groups and Jewish cultural groups. She gave sermons as a rabbi in Berlin and later in Theresienstadt. She dressed in the robes of a rabbi – though when she worked at the Jewish hospital, she wore purple robes instead of the black ones that male rabbis wore.

The inspiration that she spread to her community speaks for itself. She inspired people to realize their own humanity, their own sense of the divinity within their humanity. Rabbinerin Jonas was truly, in the Arendtian sense, showing who she was by her speech and action within and for the community.

Her identity as a rabbi is demonstrated by her desire, by her dress, by her speech, by her performance, and most importantly by her deeds.

As more people within the Jewish community came to know her and hear her preach, they demanded that she have the full responsibility of a rabbi. Before Jonas became an ordained rabbi she stated that her new title would be *rabbinerin*, or woman rabbi; the last time Jonas signed her name as a practicing ordained rabbi ministering to her people in Theresienstadt – before she was transported from Theresienstadt to Auschwitz – she signed her sermon "Rabbinerin Regina Jonas, formerly of Berlin."

This chapter tells the story of her queering the woman question and crossing gender borders, as she moved from rabbinical candidate to fully fledged practicing rabbinerin, the first woman to occupy this position. The first part of the chapter explicates her ordination thesis and examines how, from a *Halakhic* perspective, she constructed her argument that women can and should serve as rabbis. The second part of the chapter investigates how Jonas performed the role of rabbi within the Jewish rabbinical and lay communities of Berlin. In the process, it examines the perceptions of Jonas as rabbi – including both her self-perception and her reception by the communities in which she served. The last part of the chapter analyzes the significance of Jonas's identity claims, and her self-identification as a rabbinerin: Jonas named herself before she finally became a woman rabbi.

JONAS'S BIOGRAPHY: A SYNOPSIS

Though many survivors knew of Rabbinerin Regina Jonas, she has largely remained a forgotten enigma because her life and work were almost completely annihilated in the massive destruction of the Holocaust. Few of her male colleagues remembered her, and her papers were presumed lost. Various scholars had mentioned Jonas in passing, but German Christian feminist theologian Katharina von Kellenbach was one of the first to conduct extensive research on the Jonas archives; they were unearthed in 1991 in the former German Democratic Republic following the collapse of that state. Katharina von Kellenbach found to her surprise a treasure chest of Jewish women's history in the archival papers. These include Regina Jonas's *hatarat hora'a* (ordination certificate), her transcripts from the Hochschule (Academy), numerous newspaper articles about her ordination and activities as a rabbi, articles which she wrote herself and published in local and national papers and magazines, her contract with the Jewish community of Berlin, as well as personal letters from congregants, colleagues and friends.[7]

Regina Jonas was born August 3, 1902 in Berlin to Wolf and Sara Jonas. Her family was poor, and lived in an area known as the Scheunenviertel, a Jewish neighborhood consisting of dwellings converted from horse barns, mostly inhabited by impoverished immigrant Jews from Russia and Poland (although Jonas's parents were themselves native to Germany). In 1936, her mother Sara Jonas told newspaper reporter Frieda Valentin that:

> Already as a little girl – her mother tells – did she influence her little peers (all girls) in a school in Berlin which she attended. There was always something of a caretaker in her. From early on her wish was to study theology, and so she studied for six years in the Academy for the Science of Judaism.[8]

Katharina von Kellenbach provides an excellent synopsis of Jonas's teaching life and ministry, worth citing here for its comprehensiveness:

> Jonas graduated from the *Hochschule für die Wissenschaft des Judentums* (the Academy for the Science of Judaism) in Berlin in December 1930. She was ordained privately by Rabbi Max Dienemann in 1935. She worked as a religion teacher in public and private Jewish schools, as hospital chaplain, in senior citizen homes and institutes for the blind, and as guest preacher and lecturer, until she was deported to Theresienstadt in the fall of 1942. She was widely known during this time: she published several newspaper articles on Jewish faith and observances, as well as on her experience as the first female rabbi; she lectured widely in synagogues, schools and various Jewish organizations in Berlin and various other German cities. Her topics ranged from "Women in Bible and Talmud" to "Religious Customs of Jewish Life" to the "Significance of the Revelation on Mount Sinai – Thoughts for Shavuot." She held services in synagogues, Jewish senior homes, the Jewish hospital, as well as in congregations outside Berlin. After her deportation to the ghetto-camp of Theresienstadt on 5 November 1942, she continued working as a *Seelsorger* (or caregiver of the soul), as a member of the staff of Victor Frankl, the well-known psychiatrist. She was assigned to greet newcomers, boost their spirits, and help them adjust to the cruel realities of overcrowding and starvation. She also continued "preaching" there, and was a member of the *Freizeitgestaltung*, a group which organized lectures, concerts and performances to distract people from the daily misery. A list of 23 lecture topics survived, including topics such as women in Jewish history, Halakha, prayer, Sabbath observances and Jewish obligations in the camps. She maintained her contact with Leo Baeck, who supported her throughout her rabbinic activities in Berlin, although he did not publicly endorse her struggle for recognition as a full rabbi. (His correspondence shows, however, that he helped her behind the scenes.)[9]

From this account it is abundantly evident that not only did Jonas preach compassion, she practiced it. In the most extreme of circumstances, Jonas made real the deepest meanings of the Jewish teachings that the way to resistance is through acts of compassion.

ORDINATION THESIS: MANUSCRIPT HISTORY

Regina Jonas had studied for six years, from 1924 to 1930, at the Academy for the Science of Judaism in Berlin (the seminary for Liberal Judaism), in the hopes of becoming ordained as the first woman rabbi. Her *Halakhic* ordination thesis was titled "Can Women Serve as Rabbis?" She turned it in to Talmudic Professor Edward Baneth during the summer of 1930, but he died unexpectedly, just a few days after Jonas handed in her thesis, and could not give her the oral exam in Jewish law that she needed for her rabbinic ordination and diploma. The community was waiting to see if he would give her the ordination, but they would have to wait another five years. She had already passed every other required exam in Jewish studies, which included religious history and education, the philosophy of religion, Jewish history and literature, the science of the Talmud, Hebrew language, and Bible studies. Jonas did not give up her quest for the rabbinate and continued to audit lectures, especially on the Talmud, at the Academy. Meanwhile, she worked as a Jewish Religious studies teacher in the Berlin public schools. Rabbi Ted Alexander fondly remembers how when he was a teenager in Berlin, Regina Jonas often came over after services during Shabbat for the traditional third meal to his family home.[10] Everyone reportedly loved Regina Jonas: she was a very warm, endearing personality, and extremely observant.

Rabbi Ted's father, Hugo Alexander, president of the Liberal Rykestrasse Synagogue, was very supportive of Jonas's ordination, and urged her, with the support of others, to try to get a private ordination since Baneth had passed away. The Liberal Rabbi Leo Baeck was president of the Berlin Jewish *Gemeinde* (community), and would not publicly back Jonas, though he did support her behind the scenes. It was not until December 27, 1935 that she received a private ordination from Talmud professor Rabbi Dr Max Dienemann of the Liberaler Rabbiner-Verband (the Liberal Rabbinic Association), with the help of Rabbi Max Weyl, Rabbi Hugo Alexander, then President of the Liberal Synagogue in Rykestrasse, and possibly also Rabbi Leo Baeck behind the scenes (Rabbi Baeck did sign Jonas's German translation of her ordination certificate in 1941, after Jonas had proved herself and the Jewish community were being deported). Rabbi Dr Dienemann administered her oral examination and give her the *hatarat horaʾa*. It was a historic moment.

The copy of Jonas's ordination thesis that survived the Holocaust did not come to light until after the Berlin Wall fell. Jonas's papers were originally found in the Central Archive of German Jewry (Gesamtarchiv der deutschen

Juden), from where they were sent to the German Central Archive in Pots-
dam in 1958. In 1996 they were moved to the Centrum Judaicum. It is not
known if Jonas gave her papers and thesis to a trusted contact, or if they were
directly given to the remaining Jewish administration a few days before she
was transported to Theresienstadt in November 1942.

It was Rabbi Elisa Klapheck, a German Jewish Renewal rabbi, who published an annotated copy of Jonas's ordination thesis in 2000, seventy years
after Jonas wrote it, and sixty-five years after her ordination as the first female
rabbi in Jewish history.[11] The surviving copy of the thesis is probably not the
final version; it appears to be a working draft, complete with handwritten
notes in the margins. Jonas might have used the surviving copy for feedback
and then revised for the final version that was submitted. Regardless of its
draft state, the discovery and publication of Jonas's ordination thesis, along
with her story, dispelled the claim that Rabbi Sally Preisand of the Reform
movement in America was the first woman to be ordained a rabbi in 1972.
The ordination of the first female rabbi had in fact taken place nearly 40 years
earlier.

THESIS SYNOPSIS

Jonas grew up thinking that there was no reason why women could not
be rabbis – even though she had no role models for this, and was a serious *Halakhic* Jew. She studied at the Academy of Science for Judaism, yet
chose not to seek ordination in Reform Judaism, which theoretically allowed
women to be ordained, because it was not a *Halakhic* Judaism. Liberal
Judaism in Germany was *Halakhic*, and this fitted more into Jonas's serious
practice. Her intent was to prove that it was *Halakhically* possible for women
to be rabbis, and this is just what she accomplished in her thesis.

In it, Jonas argues that one can find in neither the *Halakhic* literature of
the Talmud nor in post-Talmudic literature a statement that women cannot
be rabbis. One of the foundations of her argument is that in Weimar Germany the roles of women had changed, as had the role of the rabbi. Now is
the time, she argues, for women to bring what they have always been doing in
the private sphere into the public realm. She points out that the Weimar-era
"new women" were involved in the professions – not just the teaching professions, to which they had long contributed, but the medical as well.

In the introduction to her ordination thesis Jonas remarks that "the job
of a rabbi as such, according to today's understanding of the role as communal servant, also is not found clearly in the Biblical, Talmudic, and post-
Talmudic texts."[12] Jonas goes on to explicate the new role of the rabbi and the
fact that women now are being called. She distinguishes between the past,
when women did not have public roles and lacked access to the study of the
holy texts, and the present, in which the "new women" of Weimar have access

to them. In the summer of 1932, out of a student body of 155 at the Academy of Science for Judaism, 27 women were enrolled, most of whom were studying for the academic religious teacher certification.[13]

Jonas's thesis goes on to pursue a series of a dozen arguments, which build upon one another. First, she asks and answers the question, "What do we call a woman rabbi?" Next, she explores the role of the rabbi, which she divides into nine tasks. Next, she examines biblical and post-biblical women who served their communities. Next, she presents an examination of Talmudic descriptions of women in general, their religious obligations, and their adaptation of some of the male practices such as *tefillin*. Following this, she dissects the attribute of modesty, proposes how women should practice this today, and discusses how much women rabbis could do to provide an example of this. Next she reviews regulations which would influence women's learning to become rabbis, analyzing the Talmud, Rambam, Tur, and *Shulchan Aruch*. She asks: Can women learn the holy literature? If not, why not? This leads to the rhetorical question, If women can learn, can they teach? And if they can teach, can they make legal decisions? To answer this question, Jonas draws on women's knowledge of *kashrut*. Next, Jonas examines women as preachers in the synagogue, in the process defining just what is a sermon. She discusses pastoral care, asking and answering the question of whether a woman can serve in this role. She uses much of her argumentation from her previous sections on women's abilities to learn, to teach, and to make legal decisions based on their knowledge of *kashrut*. She next examines how a woman rabbi would handle a *get* and marriage, and reviews the question of testimony. Finally, Jonas concludes by arguing why it is necessary for women to become rabbis, since she has proven that there is no *Halakhic* reason why women should not do so.

Jonas demonstrates two major points in her thesis: first, women could become rabbis because the role of rabbi has changed, and second, women could become rabbis because the Jewish legal rulings of the past which bear on this question were made in a different historical context than Weimar Germany, and these rules could be renegotiated. In the next three sections of this chapter, I will explore the key aspects of her dissertation argument in greater detail.

RABBINERIN: A NEW NOMENCLATURE FOR A NEW (WOMAN) RABBI

In order to address the question that forms the title of her thesis – can a woman serve as a rabbi? – Jonas states that we must first "adopt a new term for this position – [asking the question] whether a woman can serve as a *Rabbinerin*."[14] In German there was simply no term for "female rabbi." The German word for "rabbi," *rabbiner*, has a masculine ending; thus it was assumed in Germany and other German-speaking countries that a rabbi was always male. Jonas had to invent a new way of referring to a female rabbi, and so coined the term *rabbinerin*, adding the feminine ending *"in"* to the male term for rabbi.

A new way of talking about a female rabbi, in the gendered German language, represents a revolutionary and critical change. In English, a less overtly gendered language, one would have assumed that the otherwise neutral-sounding word "rabbi" implied a male figure – at least during the time when all rabbis were men. But in the current context, with the prevalence of women rabbis, we do not assume that "rabbi" is always male; instead we imagine such a person can be either male or female, without a consequent variation in the word itself. In German this is not possible: the ending of a word specifies the gender of the noun.

In Weimar Germany, conceptualizing "rabbi" as female would have been impossible unless one specified *Fräulein Rabbiner*. (The term *Fräulein* refers to an unmarried woman, or "Miss.") In newspaper articles Jonas was sometimes referred to as *Fräulein Rabbiner*, but not rabbinerin. This move on Jonas's part to create a new word is bold and novel, since along with it a new concept has to be developed and inserted into the language. This new concept and word, I contend, represents a queering or crossing of a boundary.

Jonas thus begins her ordination thesis by rupturing a two-thousand-year-old wall and crossing over the boundary it maintains. But before she challenges conventional wisdom regarding women in the rabbinate, she notes the challenges inherent in pursuing this question. She writes, "This brings one to the main difficulty ... that if the term *Rabbinerin* is a novelty today, how much more so when relating it to the time of our Jewish sacred texts!"[15] She realizes that she could not explore the full question of women rabbis by surveying and explicating *Halakhic* literature, so she proposes that her ordination thesis be limited to a *Halakhic* investigation of the different roles that a rabbi serves in mid-twentieth century Germany.

The primary argument of Jonas's thesis is that, through careful theological examination, God could be understood to have granted spiritual equality to the sexes. She attempts to demonstrate that one does not have to change Jewish tradition to see this, but rather to regard that tradition in a new light. Women were now fulfilling what God had always assumed. Jonas scholar Rabbi Elisa Klapheck describes Jonas's approach this way: "the equality of woman had to be grounded in Jewish religious law itself. She felt strongly that the female rabbinate should not ring in a new era but rather should strengthen and continue an existing tradition."[16] Jonas's arguments throughout her thesis reflect her contention that God does not oppress any human being. Because she "connected Halacha with the emancipation of women, Jonas was able to achieve a considerable intertwining of the conservative, preservationist approach and modern demands."[17] Jonas explains negative Jewish legal rulings against women as contextual: they did not emerge because women were deemed (by God) to be inferior; they were the result of rabbis' fears regarding the mingling of men and women. As Rabbi Klapheck explains, "it was not the ban itself that was decisive, but rather the reason for the ban."[18]

JONAS'S ARGUMENT FOR WOMEN'S ORDINATION

Before Jonas introduces the role of rabbi, she explains that it is essential to understand why there is no mention of female rabbis in Jewish texts. This is how she phrases the question that launches the *Halakhic* investigation. She outlines in the introduction what she is going to do: first she will look at what has been written about the rabbinic profession, in order to determine the role of rabbi according to Jewish texts. Her next task is to examine if it is *Halakhically* possible for a woman to fulfill this role. In addition to examining *Halakhic* understanding of rabbinical roles, she will explore how Jewish texts have interpreted the actions of Jewish women in the Torah and the Talmud, and how the sages have historically related to the actions of these Jewish women.

Jonas notes that in the holy texts there were few references to women in public roles, apart from an exceptional few. Certainly there is no mention of a woman's role as rabbi. It was inconceivable for the sages and rabbis to imagine that a woman could be a rabbi, since the whole system of the study of Jewish holy texts was set up to educate boys and men. Women were *Halakhically* exempt because of their work in the private sphere taking care of the family. Jonas notes that "not only is the female rabbinate not mentioned in our holy texts, but – with very few exceptions, which will be discussed later – there is virtually no discussion of the female *public* roles."[19] The emphasis on "public" is Jonas's, and for good reason: if the female had a role in public this would be more conducive to serving as a rabbi. The role of a rabbi, after all, is to serve the public and act as a public figure.

Jonas goes on to explain that there are two reasons there are no public roles for women:

> the basic spiritual foundations for such roles were, according to my understanding, less available to the woman, in that the spiritual education of Jewish youth was almost exclusively theological and intended only for Jewish boys. ... A second important reason seems to me to be that *the woman's societal and economic position was completely different from what it is today,* so that there was no need for her to take on a self-affirming profession.[20]

Jonas makes a clear reference here to the *Neue Frau,* or "new woman", of Weimar. Women at this time were pursuing careers in medicine, science, law, and academe, receiving graduate degrees such as doctorates (as did Edith Stein). Women were working in retail, in offices, in manufacturing. Women's roles in Jonas's time had indeed become public; women were no longer restricted to serving in the private sphere.

It is interesting, at the close of the statement above, that Jonas notes there was "no need" for women to "take on a self-affirming profession." What does Jonas mean by "self-affirming?" Is Jonas arguing that the reason women enter into professions is that they want affirmation of their intelligence, talents, and abilities that would otherwise go unrecognized at home in the domestic sphere? Were women in Weimar seeking to unleash their power to demonstrate their roles as more than just *Hausfrauen*? This seems to be the case, for if we examine the cultural context of Jonas's treatise, we see that women were beginning to enjoy choices: they could choose to go to the university to pursue a profession; they had earned the right to vote and become involved in party politics. Whereas up to this point in Jewish history women had never enjoyed an officially sanctioned public role, thanks to women's liberation in Weimar Germany they did, and as a result Jonas was able to consider pursuing the rabbinate.

Jonas concludes this section of her argument thus: we cannot find out about women's public roles in Jewish history and texts because so few were known or written about. So in order to comprehend the skills demanded of a woman in the contemporary rabbinate, we need to explore two things: women's activities and roles in the *private* sphere, and the contemporary understanding of rabbinical roles. We can then ask if the skills and natural or essential qualities upon which women rely for running a home and raising children may be applied to the role of an early-twentieth-century Weimar rabbi.

THE ROLES AND RESPONSIBILITIES OF A WEIMAR RABBI

Upon review of biblical, Talmudic, and post-Talmudic texts, Jonas finds that the description of the rabbinical role, "according to today's understanding of the role as communal servant," did not appear until the late nineteenth and early twentieth centuries. The rabbis of the past were quite different, according to Jonas:

> the heads of communities were *gedolim* [great scholars] in knowledge and in character; they studied and taught after receiving *smicha* [rabbinical ordination] from their teacher and they cared for those who put their trust in them. Today, however, the duties of the rabbis have grown significantly.[21]

What distinguished rabbis of the past, according to Jonas, was their brilliant scholarship, grounded in the holy texts. Rabbis of the past had a full grasp of the intricacies of Jewish law and the laws' application to religious practice. A rabbi was an interpreter and judge, and it was through his knowledge of the Torah and of Jewish legal texts – in essence, his role as learned gatekeeper of the laws – that he could serve his community. In Weimar Germany, however, the role of the rabbi had expanded. No longer a *gadol* who served his community with his knowledge and character, the contemporary rabbi was to play multiple roles and attend to much broader tasks. A rabbi had to prove not only his scholarship, but also his ability to be of service to his people in an all-encompassing way.

Jonas defines nine ways in which a present-day rabbi serves his community. The first five tasks entail the traditional functions of a rabbi, embedded in deep knowledge of Torah and *Halakha*. The last four are service roles, new rabbinical duties. Jonas argues that, first, the rabbi "must be well versed in the most important Jewish writings of both a spiritual and secular nature, particularly the *Torah shebichtav* [Written Torah] and the *Torah sheba'al peh* [the Oral Torah]."[22] The rabbi must have knowledge of traditional Jewish texts, including the Bible, or Tanakh – the five books of Moses (Torah, narrowly speaking), the Prophets (Neviim), and the Writings (Ketuvim). The Oral Torah is the Mishnah and the Gemarah. But what are the writings that are "of secular nature"? She may be referring to the secular texts of the culture in which the rabbi was serving – the local literary, philosophical, and political texts that influence the congregation. In Weimar Germany, this could imply an awareness of Freud, Marx, women's emancipation, and the literary canon that informed German culture, including Goethe, Heine, Kant, and Hegel. Jonas's first definition of the task of a modern rabbi thus speaks to the role that the *gedolim* or rabbis had served up until the twentieth century. Although a woman was capable of studying these texts, she never had access to them.

Second, the rabbi "must teach others, both children and adults."[23] In the past it had usually been a learned teacher known as *melamed* who taught the children, but such a person was not necessarily a rabbi. Rabbis did not have to teach children, but the new role of the rabbi meant society called upon him to be able to teach children. The rabbi became the one who prepared the boy for his *Bar Mitzvah*, and taught adult education and Torah classes.

Third, the contemporary rabbi "must be active as a preacher in the synagogue and in addition must deliver religious addresses for funerals, weddings, and bar mitzvahs."[24] Traditionally, a rabbi would give a *drash* on the weekly Torah reading as well.

Fourth, a rabbi "must fulfill actively the requirements for marriage and for the *get* [divorce decree], the *chalitzah* [taking off the shoe] and the acceptance of *gerim* [converts]."[25] This role had always been part of the rabbi's job in the past, a matter of supervising and administering the *Halakha* in these situations. The ritual of the physical removal of the shoe from the brother-in-law signified that the widowed or infertile sister-in-law was rejecting the levirate marriage to the husband's brother.[26] A rabbi had to know the intricate laws and the legal ramifications of giving a couple a *get* or of freeing women from a levirate marriage.

Fifth, a rabbi "must make *Halakhic* decisions or *pasken*" (legal decisions based on Jewish law). These five tasks of the rabbi made up the role of the *gedolim*. These tasks are the role of an Orthodox, Liberal, or conservative rabbi. A Reform rabbi would not have been obligated to know Jewish law; such was not the premise of Reform Judaism, and Jonas is only considering the roles of traditional rabbis.

The remaining four rabbinical tasks of concern to Jonas represent expanded roles taken on by modern Orthodox and liberal rabbis. The sixth task of the rabbi, Jonas says, is to "deliver talks outside of the synagogue to arouse interest in Jewish subjects among the Jewish community." [27] This represents a novel, public role, beyond the deciding of *Halakhic* matters and officiating at life-cycle events. In this role, the rabbi brings the Jewish community back to the synagogue, back to learning more about Judaism and Jewish texts. Many German Jewish men at this time were secular and did not know as much as Jewish men once did. As Jonas conceptualizes it, the rabbi's role at the time should include a degree of public relations work on behalf of Judaism. A modern rabbi should make Judaism accessible to those who were outside of the synagogue.

The seventh task of the rabbi is to "be available to help congregants with personal matters related to any distress of the soul."[28] Members of the Jewish community in the past usually came to the rabbi not with personal matters of distress of the soul, but with personal matters in need of a *pasken*, or legal decision regarding the action that should be taken. For example, a couple might come to a rabbi asking him if they could use birth control because the doctor had told the wife that it would be detrimental to her health to have more children. The rabbi would then examine the legal code and decide whether or not a couple could use birth control. Usually if the woman's life was in danger he would make the *pasken* that they should. In this case, the couple would not be seeking emotional and spiritual support for their loss as much as a sense of certainty regarding the correct action to take according to Jewish law. The modern rabbi, however, has turned into spiritual counselor. A congregant might come to the rabbi seeking comfort, sharing with him grief over the loss of the loved one. In instances such as this, there is no need for a *Halakhic* decision.

Eighth, Jonas believes the rabbi "must work for social welfare, for youth welfare and for general communal welfare, as well as arbitrate in conflicts between members."[29] This work is much more than what rabbis in the past would have done. The modern German rabbi might be engaged in helping *Ostjuden*, or eastern European Jews, gain access to resources upon immigration to Germany. He might work with the board of the *Kehillah*, or Jewish community, making sure that there were soup kitchens and other resources to help the poor in the local Jewish community. The rabbi might make sure that Jewish youth received a Jewish education, and that youth who were in trouble had access to social workers and resources to support them. He might also be involved in ministering to the sick and elderly in hospitals and old age homes.

Finally, the rabbi "must lead an appropriate lifestyle by following the religious teaching of Judaism and fulfilling the tasks given to him as a leader of the community."[30] This role was expected of both the traditional rabbi and the modern rabbi.

After examining these nine tasks of the rabbi, Jonas poses the questions: What have women always done in their private lives that they can now bring to these nine roles of the rabbinate? Are there examples of Jewish women communal leaders in the holy texts? Have women practiced some of the time-bound *mitzvoth* related to public religious practices, such as praying with *tefillin*, or wearing *tzitzit*? The new role of the rabbi as ministerial – that is, as something more than just a legal arbitrator and explicator of the Torah, but rather as one who would minister to the needs of his people – would speak to Jonas, who was staking some of her claims on a belief in women's innate nurturing qualities (a notion of women similar to Edith Stein's, which we have seen in Chapter 3).

It is the role of the rabbi as minister that speaks to women's unique strength, in Jonas's eyes, for she believed that this very ministerial quality was one that that men did not naturally possess. Jonas's investigation of the Jewish sources later reveals, or reinforces, the conclusion that women always displayed these natural qualities as they raised and taught children, took care of the elderly, and comforted the sick. Further, a woman had to be an authority on Jewish law in order to keep a kosher home, showing she possessed knowledge and intelligence in addition to innate ministerial qualities.

After clarifying the historical and modern roles of a rabbi, Jonas next goes about constructing her argument that women are biblically permitted to serve as rabbis. She does so using two lines of argumentation. First, she compares the different contexts of biblical, post-biblical, and later rabbinic treatises, looking at how their notions of women and women's permissible behavior compare to the current condition of women in Weimar. She draws from rulings and texts of the previous hundred years to demonstrate that times have indeed changed for women; to these she adds social and political texts from the contemporary context of Weimar women's advancement.

Jonas cites nineteenth-century German texts such as Leopold Zur's *On History and Literature*, in which the author dedicates a whole chapter to righteous Jewish women who took on traditional male Jewish practices and were able to make legal decisions, and *Zunz*, published in Berlin in 1845. She draws on Mayer Kayserling's *Jewish Women in History, Literature and Art*, published in Leipzig in 1879, and Rabbi Zvi Elimelach Shapira's *The Path of Your Command*, a rabbinical text from 1874. She cites in her bibliography *Women's Voting Rights*, an unpublished, undated manuscript by Alfred

Freimann Posen; *The Religious Position of the Female Sex in Talmudic Jewry*, by Dr P. Holdheim (Schwerin 1846); and *The Woman in the Jewish People*, by Dr Adolf Kurrein.[31]

It is noteworthy that in the nineteenth century there were a number of male scholars and rabbis who investigated the roles and actions of notable, accomplished women in Judaism. Jonas took advantage of these secular sources outside of the traditional rabbinical texts. The nineteenth-century assessments of Jewish women by these scholars were in turn supported by the ideas in circulation by Jonas's contemporaries in the movement for women's emancipation. It was they who succeeded in winning German women the right to vote, just as Jonas was emerging into her adulthood, in 1919.

Jonas's explication of Talmudic and rabbinical texts becomes the pivot on which her argument for women in the rabbinate turns. She finds in *Halakhic* rulings that it is possible for women to learn sacred texts; to teach the Torah; and to make legal rulings. These three tasks – learning, teaching, and making *paskens* – are an important part of a rabbi's job. Jonas builds her argument on the foundation of learning. If women can learn, then they can teach; if they can learn and teach, then they can come up with legal rulings; for "rabbi" actually means "teacher."

In order to begin to prove that women are capable of entering the rabbinical profession, Jonas provides examples from biblical, post-biblical, and Talmudic texts of women's action in the public realm. She cites Miriam leading the Israelites in song with her timbrel after they crossed the Red Sea; Zelophehad's daughters publicly questioning Moses regarding their right to their father's inheritance; Deborah's leadership as a judge and prophetess of the Israelites; and Queen Esther saving her people from annihilation. Jonas also notes that in the Talmud the rabbis elevated seven women to the title of "prophetess": Sarah, Miriam, Deborah, Hannah, Abigail, Hulda, and Esther. All these women were spiritual leaders of their communities. Most of their contemporaries led private domestic lives, but these women were the exception, and demonstrated their ability to lead their people. Jonas writes:

> a few towered above the rest through some major historical feat that bears witness to the knowledge, abilities, skills, and intelligence for which they worked *for* the *entire* community and also sometimes *in* and *with* the *entire* community – though not in the sense of a profession as would be defined today.[32]

In these examples, Jonas is making it clear that these women were already acting as spiritual and natural leaders, and had demonstrated that they had the skills and abilities to be rabbis. She emphasizes the words "in," "with," and "entire," drawing parallels between this type of leadership and the ways a modern rabbi would lead his community. For how does a rabbi function? He lives "in" his community as a role model of Jewish practice. He works for the social welfare of, and leads, the "entire" community "with" their consent. Today the actions of these women prophets would be recognized as indications of the kinds of leadership qualities which women bring to their professional lives. Jonas demonstrates that even in biblical and post-biblical times women had the ability to be spiritual leaders, before there was even the notion of a rabbi, which was itself a post-biblical development. And she provides commentary to counteract the negative descriptions and characterizations that so many rabbis had made about women.

Jonas writes that these examples

> demonstrate, I believe, that in any era when women *wished* to and were *able* to express themselves, no obstacle was placed in their way as long as their work was valuable and carried out in a solid [true] way. One does not encounter religious immaturity, excessive seclusion, false timidity, or carelessness, frivolity, and ignorance on the part of these women; rather they are graced with salvation, bravery, kindness, and gentleness.[33]

Jonas lists these negative traits in order to demonstrate that women in leadership positions did not fit the stereotypical traits that the rabbis ascribed to women.

As Jonas goes on to make her examination, she makes it clear that earlier rabbinical perspectives on women were based on a context very different from the present. One of the issues that the Talmudic rabbis grappled with was their belief in the uncontrollable attraction that men felt toward women when they saw them in public. It was rare for women to be seen in public, and when they did it was considered provocative. Jonas makes the case that women were now a major part of the public sphere, and that it was no longer shocking for men to see women in professional positions in public. Hence, men's sexual attraction would be negated or more muted than in the times of the Talmudic rabbis. Jonas quotes a recent rabbinical text of Rabbi Zvi Elimelach Shapira from 1874, *Derech Pikudarih* ("The Path of your Command"). The rabbis put an *eruv* (fence) around adultery by prohibiting men from talking to married women, since the rabbis feared that this alone would lead to adultery. Rabbi Shapira notes that in times when there were few economic hardships, women were rarely seen in public. But in times when Jews suffer economic hardship, it was especially necessary for women to help their husbands with their trades, crafts, and shops, and so it was common to see them in public. And in the 1870s Jews were in a time of deep economic crisis.

> But here there is no longer anyone who *fears this* [adultery] ... it would likely no longer be warned today, because women *are accustomed to be among us,* among men, that is, in the trades,

in the crafts, in the shops, and so on, without it coming to sinful fantasies. Her appearance to us is like that of the white geese [an Aramaic expression for "without an erotic attractiveness"].[34]

Rabbi Shapira reasons that economic necessity has brought women into the public realm, and their familiarity there has diminished the power of attraction, Jonas points out in her thesis that the times are very different for women since they have been liberated. Women were no longer home-bound and had taken their professional position in the work place. And now that the role of the rabbi had changed, Jonas emphasizes that women are needed more than ever in the rabbinate profession:

> But if it was important to do so [for a woman to leave the home], then – as we have seen – she became openly active, without inflicting damage on her self-image or that of society. Why should it then be impossible today, *when rabbinic service performed by women gradually becomes a necessity!*[35]

Why is Jonas stating that women's rabbinic services were becoming a necessity? Is it that the role of the rabbi had changed? Is it that there were fewer men available to become rabbis since so many died in World War I? Or perhaps is it that expectations so changed with the increasingly public roles of women, and Jonas is making an emphatic case for change?

ECHO OF THE HOLIDAYS

Jonas gave a sermon/lecture titled "Echo of the Holidays," either at the end of or shortly after the Jewish fall holidays. It could been given at any time between her ordination exams and her deportation; the surviving copy does not have a date. Jonas preaches:

> When our holidays have reached their end, the Jewish individual and Jewish collective must ask itself, what now? What can ripen from all the prescriptions and experiences into deeds? Everyone must come to understand what is sublime and unique about our festivals.[36]

In fall, there are four major Jewish Holidays: the Jewish New Year, the Day of Atonement, the Feast of the Tabernacles, and Simchat HaTorah. Rabbinerin Jonas wants her audience to contemplate what they can bring with them into the coming year and what they can manifest in actions. She points out that each of these major Jewish holidays have powerful symbols associated with them:

The festivals are rich in substantive symbols. The highest ideas are brought, through the eye and the ear in the vestments of symbols, close to the heart of the Jewish people. People, whose hearts had gone astray, away from Judaism, often have found the Ariadne's Thread back to Judaism on the path of Jewish symbols.[37]

One of Rabbinerin Jonas's teachings is that the role of the rabbi was to reach out to the lost souls of the community. The metaphor of Ariadne's thread is an appropriate image. The metaphor points to the multiple paths to assimilation, such as conversion to Christianity or secularization, which many Jews had chosen. The thread connects these "lost souls" all the way back to their ancestors and returns them to the German Jewish community. The symbols are the threads that guide them out of the maze. It is the actual performance, the ritual practice that the symbols evoke. Jews hear the blowing of the *shofar* (Ram's horn) on New Year's. Jews wear white shrouds on the Day of Atonement to remind themselves that they stand before life and death. They need to ask for forgiveness from family, friends, and neighbors. The building of the Tabernacle reminds them of the time the Israelites dwelled in the desert. The shaking of the *lulav*, four species of plants from the Holy Land, is done during the Feast of Tabernacles. Simchat Torah is the celebration of the end and the beginning of the reading cycle of the Torah, when Jews dance joyously with the Torah, both in the synagogue and in the street. Rabbinerin Jonas recognized that the power of actually performing the symbolic ritual inscribes into the lost soul a heart connection to the Jewish community. The symbols provide a powerful impetus to those who had abandoned Judaism and Jewish practice, especially under the Nazis, to return their religious roots.

She reminds her congregants that when Jews encounter these symbols and their souls are receptive to them, they will return home to their mother religion. She also states that it is very important especially to teach the children the Jewish religion when they are young.

> Among we Jews, those who know how to strike the tones bring a long-forgotten sound to a deep ringing in the hearts of the Jewish "lonely ones." But the assets of Jewish thought and Jewish community should also be brought in the most noble form and the purest way to the youth, who offer us a receptive soul. Just as the person in his "I" is formed at the deepest level – even if he is not always conscious of it – by his parents, so is the Jewish person spiritually formed by our ancient honorable mother religion.[38]

She then reminds her congregants that the meaning of Yom Kippur is not just to ask for forgiveness from your neighbor just one day of the year, but that one should do this every day. We should echo the holiday every day because the Talmud teaches we will live a long noble life if we ask for forgiveness from our neighbor every night before we go to bed. The point is that we can practice the teaching of this holiday every day and Jonas views this as Jewish piety.

What we see in this sermon is that Jonas's theology is not dependent on faith but on practice, which is the Jewish theology and teaching. Practice, such as ritual actions that we perform on the holidays, can bring us to faith and connect us to our community. Jewish symbols will bring lost Jews back to the Jewish religion and the ethical practice of asking forgiveness every day will bring rest to our souls. Jonas knew the power of symbols and how the symbols she mentions have a ritual practice.

PERCEPTIONS OF JONAS

Throughout her thesis, Jonas is constantly comparing the actions, qualities, and descriptions of Jewish women from the past to those of her time. She cites historic examples of pious Jewish women carrying out time-bound *mitzvoth* and actually putting on the *tefillin* and *tzitzit* with which every Jewish male adorns himself when he prays. She provides the examples of Michal, the daughter of King Saul, who used to put on *tefillin*; Rashi's daughters, who did the same; and the wife of Jonah the prophet, who would go on pilgrimages for the three-pilgrimage holiday.

An important source for understanding perceptions of Jonas at this time is a manuscript on Jonas's ministry submitted on December 16, 1931. We do not know to whom the article was submitted or whether it was published. Jonas had not yet taken the oral exam at this point, but had written the thesis. The article is called "Chanukah Celebration at Helene Lange 2 City School Middle School for Girls in Berlin." It is not clear who wrote it: it may have been written by Jonas or by a supporter of Jonas, because it is signed "Requesting acceptance in your paper, signed: sincerely, [no signature]." We also do not know to which paper the author was submitting the article; an educated guess would suggest that it was one of the Jewish newsletters or periodicals of the time.[39] Regardless, it is the reference to Jonas as "*Fräulein Rabbiner, candidate*" that is significant: it is a sign of Jonas crossing over the border of the two-thousand-year-old male rabbinate. The article begins with reference to "Miss Rabbi candidate Regina Jonas, a teacher of religion." This appellation is very telling: it reflects what many in the community were likely wondering: Would Regina Jonas ever become a rabbi? Or would she just remain a religious school teacher, which was what most women interested in being Jewish leaders or rabbis could ever hope to do?[40]

We can draw three major points from this article. The first is that Jonas was queering religious boundaries. Second, Jonas states her position about women's education. Third, Jonas demonstrates her pedagogical gift, showing that sermons are not only dry speeches or biblical exegeses delivered from the pulpit; they can also be morality plays or performance pieces enhanced with singing and dancing. To deliver a sermon as a performance piece enhances the student's understanding of the meaning of the Jewish holidays and the Torah. This is creative and brilliant pedagogy on Jonas's part, and under-scores one of what Jonas saw as her God-given talents. It reflects her theo-logical stance that God's gifts, in the form of talents, come without regard to gender. It happened to be that Jonas's talent was her calling to serve her com-munity as a teacher and as a rabbi.

This article also reflects the difficult economic times of the Weimar Repub-lic. Jonas asks herself whether something like the "festivity" of celebrating Chanukah should take place in such hard times. She answers yes, as long as the festivity becomes a significant experience and the children are able to keep it as a memory and take it as an example. She says this not only to an audience made up of families with children, but also to Rabbi Leo Baeck and his wife. Rabbi Baeck was president of the *Gemeinde*, or local Jewish religious community. It is interesting that the author points out his presence at this event. Rabbi Baeck had the power to recommend and support Jonas's ordina-tion, though he never publicly did so. When asked about Rabbinerin Jonas after the war, Rabbi Baeck said that he had gone to Theresienstadt with her; but he had not thought about her passing the ordination exam.

The play that the young women students put on for the celebration addresses the question: Why must we celebrate the Jewish holidays? It also illustrates Jonas's pedagogical gifts and her theological positions. Through the play that she puts on with the children, Jonas shows that a sermon can be delivered via performance. To demonstrate the importance of Jewish ritual and festivals she uses the motif of the four sons from the Passover Haggadah. She includes the different characters of the sons, and the children play each one – the wise, the wicked, the simple-minded, and the one not able to ask a question. The wicked son challenges the wise son, saying that the holiday is boring and useless; one can't go shopping; one can't spend money; the only thing one does on a holy day is pray and contemplate. Rasha, the bad son, questions the use of the holiday, saying the only good thing about it is the food. The wise son then attempts to win over the bad son by demonstrat-ing the meaning and importance of the Jewish holidays, each of which the young women then act out. The bad son repents and decides to celebrate the holiday. Then one of the sons asks, "Where is the celebration for the children among all these solemn festivities?" Eight girls jump up with candles in their hands and announce the joy of Chanukah.

Not only is Jonas demonstrating a new way to present a sermon, she is also demonstrating the potential role of women rabbis. Jonas demonstrates that it is important for her female students to understand the sacred event: "A sacred event should become, especially for the female youth with their new rights and duties, an experience as Hannah once had with her seven sons, Esther, Japhas' daughters, and Deborah."[41] Jonas feels that as an educator she should empower her students, just as if they were biblical women leaders. She brings the examples of Hannah, Esther, and Yiftach's daughters, Bible stories of strong women who demonstrated public leadership by dying for their beliefs: Hannah and her seven sons, saving her people; Esther, challenging Moses on the legal ruling of sole male inheritance rights; Yiftach's daughters, viewed as prophets and a judge. By giving her female students the opportunity to act out the holidays, she was teaching her charges – and presumably also the audience – that women could now be leaders in the Jewish community. Jonas herself was a model for such leaders' new rights and duties.

The gifts that Jonas demonstrated as a teacher were later made full use of in her rabbinate to ignite people's passion to resist and find their humanity during the insane and oppressive times of the Nazi regime. Jonas was able to bring these pedagogical gifts with her into every position she filled in the rabbinate. In the beginning, however, she was denied the right to give services from the official pulpit within the sanctuary. Her first contract as a rabbinerin with the *Gemeinde* was to minister to people in the nursing homes and hospitals. Even then, she could only give "lectures" – which could also be described as sermons – in community centers or the community room. An article describing Jonas's ordination noted that she was teaching children and conducting an *Oneg Shabbat* with them.[42]

The first article to share the news of Jonas's ordination in December 1935 appeared in the Jewish community newspaper, the *Jüdische Allgemeine Zeitung*, on January 22, 1936. It is titled "Bekanntschaft mit einer Rabbinerin," ("Acquaintance with a Rabbinerin"), using the term for a woman rabbi that Jonas had coined in her ordination thesis. The unpublished "Chanukah Celebration at Helene Lange 2 City School Middle School for Girls in Berlin" article about Jonas from 1931 had used the term "Miss Rabbi candidate." Now, in 1936, the crossing had actually taken place. Frieda Valentin, the author of the article, uses Jonas's own term,[43] and subtitles the article "How Regina Jonas took her exam."

Valentin was extremely impressed with Jonas as a spiritual leader. She describes how she came to meet Jonas at the Neue Synagoge[44] on a Sunday morning when she had dropped by to pick up her High Holiday *machzor*, or prayer book, which she had left there during the previous fall of 1935. Valentin ran into the rabbinerin leading the children in an Oneg Shabbat,[45] and was immediately taken by her.

> How strong was my experience when I got the opportunity to participate in the celebration of the "Oneg Shabbat," a celebration for children. The lead was in the hands of a young lady whose noble face in its biblical expression radiated an extraordinary delight that also emanated from her gesture and her words which she not only spoke to the hearts of the children but also to the hearts of the adults.[46]

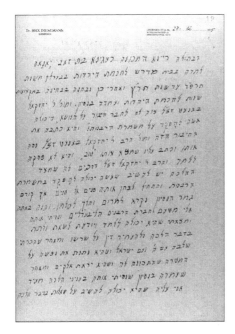
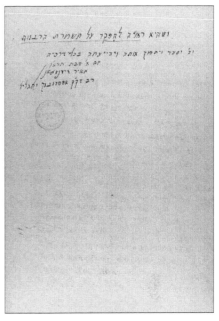

Figure 2 Regina Jonas's signed ordination certificate (©Stiftung Neue Synagoge Berlin–Centrum Judaicum, Archiv CJA 1, 75 D Jo 1, Nr 14, #13356, Bl. 19).

Valentin was perceptive when she noted that Jonas inspired her audience with her gestures and her words: Jonas wrote to journalist Mala Laaser about her reluctance to provide a written answer to Laaser's "question of woman" survey, saying "in a sermon I could say woman to woman what I want to write now. *Tone, gesture, gaze and body posture animate what one will announce.* [I'm concerned about] How what I write down will, in an attempt to express myself, get stuck."[47]

Frieda Valentin's impression and Jonas's own statement demonstrate the notion that one's performance expressed one's identity, and that it was fluid. Jonas states that she felt more comfortable answering a question through a sermon, which is a performance piece, than having to write a response. A written response can never capture the tone, gesture, gaze, and body posture that animate and inspire. People regarded Jonas as such an inspiring rabbi because of what emanated from her when she spoke, from her gestures and words. Part of serving as a rabbi consisted in how one expressed oneself through one's performance of the role. Valentin was smitten with Jonas – as were many people who encountered her – and could not find enough words to describe how engaging and moving she was:

> For me Regina Jonas seems to be born for the pulpit. And apparently there was a possibility; do women exist who are female

rabbis (*rabbinerin*)? Is it not possible that in a woman as well can lie the strength and the calling, inspired by faith, blissful through holiness, to preach God's words? Why can't a woman too, as it is already fact in the Protestant religion, where they have female preachers and priests, take the profession of a rabbi? Mostly to provide pastoral care with womanly instinct, and serve womanly sensitivity? And when God has given to that the language and the word, which captivate people to be led towards God and prayers, he [*sic*] must carry in himself [*sic*] the calling to become a *rabbinerin*.[48]

Figure 3 Ordination photo of Rabbinerin Regina Jonas, probably taken in Berlin in early 1936 (© Stiftung Neue Synagoge Berlin–Centrum Judaicum, Archiv, Nachlass Regina Jonas CJA, 1, 75 D Jo 1, Nr 14 #13356).

Valentin raises the same questions that Jonas did in her ordination thesis. And Valentin answers them: Jonas was a living example of the fact that not only could a woman serve as a rabbi, but some, like Jonas, were born with the gifts to become one. With her words and deeds she brought people back to the word of God, back to the community. Valentin's own story was that she did not feel connected to her Jewish being; it was only the difficult circumstances of the times that had brought her to the synagogue to fetch a forgotten prayer book. She was probably a "High Holiday Jew," observant for but a few occasions each year. But, as Valentin writes at the beginning of the article:

> in the midst of the hardship of current events ... We are brought together with people with whom we would not have crossed paths before, because we behaved indolently and had distanced ourselves carelessly from a place where they are effective, where one can feel the breath of their spirits.[49]

Valentin may have started the article with this thought because of the extremely difficult times Jews were experiencing in 1936 under the Nazi regime. At another time she might not have stayed to listen to Jonas. She did now out of a need to feel connected; she was now willing to linger and encounter Jonas.

Valentin concludes that the wonder of these difficult times is that she is more open to these experiences. Her encounter made her realize that she was looking for something; she has found her humanity, her connectedness to what it means to be a human being within the realm of the Jewish community. She writes at the end of the article, "Wonderful are the experiences of our present time. I came to look for something I had lost, and found a human being."[50] What an amazing statement for a Jewish journalist to make in 1936! Jonas inspired this kind of humanity in people and in their communities. This was the mark of a true spiritual leader. Jonas not only lived up to her own definition of rabbi, she went further: she inspired people to spiritually find their way home, and resist the oppression that they were facing.

A little later that same year, on October 22, 1936, an article appeared by Julie Wolfthorn in the *Israeli Family* newspaper describing a lecture that Jonas gave at the Culture Club in Berlin, entitled "Women in the Bible and the Talmud." The lecture echoed Jonas's basic theology that we are human beings first and above all else. God does not distinguish between the sexes. Wolfthorn writes:

> Miss Jonas lectured us about the astonishing passages from the Talmud i.e. those which supposedly picture the man as the sovereign of his wife, and in contrast passages in which the man refers to advice of a woman: there, the lecturer posits a natural balance,

which in the end already exists in Judaism in the distribution of rights between man and woman because essentially it doesn't distinguish between men's or women's rights but only human rights. The audience responded with heartfelt applause for the interesting and insightful lecture.[51]

What is very telling is how the reporter goes on to *kvetch* about (lament) the behavior of some of the audience members. Wolfthorn's reaction demonstrates how impressive and respected Jonas was among most of her listeners when she writes:

> Certainly it has nothing to do with small mindedness when one asserts that it is beneath the dignity of a lecture hall when a woman enters the room long after the beginning, carrying in one hand a huge hat box, in the other a full shopping bag, and that she felt it necessary not to choose one of the empty chairs in the back row, but to make her way relatively close to the front and to seat herself in the middle of the row. Then, after only a short time she starts looking through her shopping bag – of course not without making noise – until she finds the right bag, and for the remaining time of the lecture occupies herself with eating. And if someone says: "Maybe this is a woman who just came from work and is very hungry," one can only respond: if one comes right from work into the middle of a lecture and is so hungry that one can't wait for an hour, then one could not really benefit from the lecture, and to stay absent would have been better and in the interest of all. And to comment on a second "case": ... shortly after the lecture began two very good-looking and well-dressed "young ladies" shamelessly pulled out of their bags knitted pullovers and began diligently, as if they were sitting at an afternoon coffee, knitting, knitting, knitting. Because the pattern must not have been easy they were helping each other in a whispering tone ... one really doesn't know what kind of comment would be appropriate here.[52]

I found Wolfthorn's complaint extremely telling of the respect that she felt that Jonas demanded as a fully fledged rabbi. The Nuremberg Laws had been implemented in 1935; Jews were banned from many activities and extremely limited in their movements. Wolfthorn clearly felt indignant when she wrote that this woman had insulted Rabbinerin Jonas by showing up late, making noise with her shopping bags, and eating her dinner in the middle of the lecture. Furthermore, other women were treating the lecture as a more relaxed gathering and decided to knit. Wolfthorn felt that this, too, was demeaning. Jonas's presence demanded the same respect as one would give to a rabbi delivering a sermon from the pulpit. Would these women have eaten their dinner or started knitting in the sanctuary? Did women do this in the sanctuary balcony, where they listened to sermons, separated from the men? Was Wolfthorn implying that there is a certain amount of decorum that one expects in a synagogue sanctuary that should also be given to Jonas delivering a rabbinic lecture in the Culture Club?

As a scholar looking back and reviewing these articles in the newspapers, I felt that Wolfthorn's comments brought me back to earth. The post-Holocaust reader is struck with a foreboding feeling, knowing that the situation of the community was only getting worse; nevertheless, these details remind one that people went on living their daily lives to the best of their ability.

THE WOMAN QUESTION

Two articles were written after Jonas's ordination, asking her what she thought about "the woman question." Jonas felt burdened by this question, responding to Mala Laaser:

> After I have, to the best of my ability, resisted sending you a contribution, that is, to write something about me and about my taking the profession of rabbi (actually it took me and not the other way round) as a woman. ... I'd like to say that I hope for us all a time in which questions on the topic "woman" don't exist anymore: because where questions are, there is something wrong.[53]

Jonas wished that she did not have to respond to the woman question, yet the fact is that she was constantly asked the question: What does it mean to be the first woman rabbi? She really just wanted to do what she felt called to do, rather than analyze it. Not only did she feel called as a rabbi, her practice of Judaism was Orthodox, and she could not be ordained as an Orthodox woman rabbi. Jonas was always true to her own spiritual calling: even in her ordination as a Liberal rabbi she felt aligned in spirit with a more *Halakhic* approach to Jewish practice. This trueness to herself emerged in a 1939 article in the Swiss *Frauenzeitung Berna* newsletter by Annette Löwenthal, a German Jewish journalist living in Hamburg at the time:

> I came to my profession from a religious conviction that God does not oppress any human being, that therefore the man does not rule the woman or occupy a spiritual position of supremacy over her; I came to it from a view of the final and complete spiritual equality between the sexes, which were created by a just and merciful God.[54]

Löwenthal notes that Jonas was not politically active in the women's movement – in the same way that Stein had not been a suffragist. Löwenthal comments that:

> although Rabbi Jonas never belonged to a movement [for women]
> or was associated with one, we may count her, because of her
> opinions about gender equality, about women in the work force
> and the matters of women's education, resolutely as one of us. She
> demands that "woman should be permitted everything in equal
> ways." Not gender but diligence, intelligence, and determination
> should be the only deciding factors for one's career.[55]

Löwenthal observes that Jonas was her own person and followed her calling
without being concerned about political affiliations.

THE LINGUISTIC QUEERING OF "WOMAN RABBI"

In her biography of Jonas, *Fräulein Rabbiner Jonas: The Story of the First
Woman Rabbi*, Rabbi Elisa Klapheck notes the fluidity, the uncertainty and
insecurity with which people addressed Jonas in her new role as rabbi.

Among the countless variations of address, however, there was also a slight
undertone of insecurity about Jonas's title and gender in German. One letter
contained four possible modes of address: "*Liebes Fräulein Rabbiner! Liebe
Frau Rabbiner! Liebes Fräulein Regina! Liebe Regina!*" ("Dear Miss Rabbi!
Dear Mrs Rabbi! Dear Miss Regina! Dear Regina"). Felix Singermann, Berlin's
leading Orthodox rabbi, addressed her in his card, written in Hebrew as "*Rabbanit*" (female rabbi). The Orthodox former rector of the religious school in
Annenstrasse, Isidor Bleichrode, who by then had moved to Jerusalem, called
Jonas "*Rav*," Hebrew for rabbi. Her longtime mentor, Max Weyl, addressed
his effusive letter "*An die Rabbinerin Fräulein R. Jonas*" (to the [female] Rabbi
Miss R. Jonas). Some joked in their letters: "Dear Miss Jonas, I congratulate
Mrs. Rebbetzin [the rabbi's wife] … Oh, excuse me! Mrs. Rabbi – because
you alone have earned this awe-inspiring title deserving of respect." Others
honestly took great pains to find a fitting, respectful address for a woman –
such as "*Liebe Frau collega*" ("Dear Mrs Colleague"), "*Sehr geehrte Frau Rabbiner!*" ("Honored Madam Rabbi!"), "*Fräulein Rabbinerin*" ("Miss Rabbi"), or
Fräulein Rabbinerin Jonas ("Miss Rabbi Jonas") – but never as *Frau Rabbiner
Jonas* (Mrs Rabbi), which might refer to the title of a husband.[56]

Jonas had broken down the two-thousand-year-old barrier and received
ordination as a rabbi, crossing over that barrier to a new territory. Her claim
as a rabbi was not that she was a woman trying to be like a man but rather that
her position and role *as* woman enabled her to serve as a rabbi. Women could

serve in their own unique style, she argued; they did not have to pretend to be men or hide behind their male robes.

In the introduction to her thesis, Jonas poses "the question of whether women can serve as rabbis – or – to adopt the new term for this position – whether a Jewish woman can serve as a *Rabbinerin*."[57] The mere fact that Jonas coins a new term for a woman rabbi shows her strong position that women can serve as rabbis without pretending to be a *male* rabbi. These subtle connections between the linguistic possibilities available to Jonas and her deeply held beliefs do not emerge so clearly in English. English is not a gendered language, so to the English-speaking mind, "rabbi" can seem to be gender-neutral. Until women started becoming ordained as rabbis in the 1970s and 1980s, there was an underlying assumption that only men were rabbis, just as mostly men were doctors. In other words, the terms "rabbi" and "doctor" were implicitly male terms. Eventually, the language changed in response to changes in society at large: there was a critical mass of English speakers who did not assume that rabbis, doctors, and engineers were men, and these terms have now come to be understood to refer to both genders.

Both German and Hebrew, on the other hand, are gendered languages, and unless a woman was to disguise her biological gender, she would have to employ a gendered term – a feminine term – for her professional title in these languages. A woman rabbi should be called a rabbinerin, not just "Miss Rabbi." The professional term would be modified to denote the feminine gender in order to reflect that women were rabbis as well.

Jonas herself was ambiguous about how to refer to herself. Sometimes she called herself Rabbiner Regina Jonas and other times Rabbinerin: "Bernhard Burstein, a patient in the Jewish hospital in July 1940, reported that a 'young woman' visited him 'daily,' and she introduced herself as '*Frau Rabbiner Jonas* [Mrs. Rabbi Jonas]'."[58]

As Klapheck remarks:

> Jonas clearly wavered between these possibilities – "*Rabbiner*" in the masculine form, or *Rabbinerin* in the feminine form. She signed a letter to a journalist with "*Ihre (feminine form) Rabbiner (masculine form) Regina Jonas*" [Your Rabbi Regina Jonas]. Even her rubber stamp said "*Rabbiner Regina Jonas*," and from 1939 on, when Jewish women were forced to take on the name "Sara," her stamp said "*Rabbiner Regina Sara Jonas*," using the masculine form. In the archive of the memorial and former ghetto and concentration camp of Theresienstadt was another document signed as "Rabbinerin Regina Jonas," using the feminine form. The most common address, however, was "Fräulein Rabbiner Jonas" [Miss Rabbi Jonas].[59]

Jonas might have been trying on different styles of address during her short-lived rabbinical career between 1936 and 1944. In the beginning she played with using the masculine term Rabbiner; maybe she thought that if she used the term Rabbiner with her full name Regina Jonas it would let people know that she was a woman rabbi. Her final signature on the last document she ever wrote was with the feminine form Rabbinerin Regina Jonas. This suggests that she now wanted it to be known that she was indeed a woman rabbi, that the rabbinical gates excluding women from the rabbinate had opened, and that in the gendered German language there was now a new term: *rabbinerin*.

This was Jonas's political and theological stance: God does not discriminate based on gender, and those professions that had always been male-dominated were now changing to recognize women as members. She was no Yentl, the character in the Isaac Bashevis Singer short story "Yentl the Yeshiva Boy," who felt he had "the soul of a man in the body of a woman," and dressed like a man, passing as one in order to have access to the same knowledge.[60] That story was set in the nineteenth century; as of the early decades of the twentieth century, times had changed. Jonas removed the bricks in the walls keeping women from full participation in society, one by one, opening a doorway in the wall around the rabbinate for future generations of women to cross over.

After Jonas received her ordination, the congratulatory notes and articles about her varied in the forms of address they used. Not surprisingly, each different title of address has a slightly different connotation. It is remarkable that the Orthodox rabbis Singermann and Bleichrode viewed her as a colleague, even though they would not have signed her ordination certificate had they been asked, nor been part of a *Bet Din* or rabbinical court to offer her an official *simcha*. Nevertheless, one addressed her with the Hebrew term *rav*, and the other with *rabbanit*, which is the feminization of *rav*. Does one rabbi's calling Jonas a *rav* mean that she was now, in his eyes, one of them? And does the other's calling her a *rabbanit* imply that she was not *exactly* one of them, but was nonetheless now a part of this two-thousand-year-old profession? There is a categorical difference here: to employ the masculine term is to imply that one is a female in a male role, a *trans-rabbi* of sorts. This is where queer language and definitions can help us.

Similarly, in German the equivalent to *rabbanit* is *rabbinerin*. German is much more formal than Hebrew, and the proper address to an unmarried woman would be *Fräulein*, or Miss, and for a married woman, *Frau*. So reference to Jonas as a *Fräulein Rabbiner* or *Frau Rabbiner*, using the feminine address but the masculine form of rabbi, would imply/connote a hyphenated term to the German ear. On the other hand, reference to Jonas as *Fräulein Rabbinerin* or *Frau Rabbinerin* would signify a double feminization of the term *rabbi*.

Understanding this terminology can help illumine the categorical struggles that Jonas was contending with when she established a name for her new role as rabbi. As we have seen before in Klapheck's account, Jonas's reference to herself was not clear-cut: many times she would introduce herself with the masculine form for rabbi (a form which a number of women journalists used). And yet in the last document that she hand-wrote in Theresienstadt she signed off using the feminine form. We see here fluidity not just in people's perceptions of Jonas but in her own self-perception as well.

The questions this naming brings up are critical to our understanding of what Jonas was doing. Was Jonas crossing over from one category of gender to another and now becoming a male, serving the role and performing *as* a male rabbi, part of a two-thousand-year-old male community? Or was Jonas crossing over, bringing her female gender with her, not trying to hide or pretend that she was male, but practicing as a female rabbi in an all-male rabbinical community? Was Jonas claiming that the role of a rabbi was not limited to gender and that it did not matter if a rabbi was male or female – that a rabbi could be both male and female, and it was irrelevant what gender they were? In our view, this is both true and untrue of Jonas's stance. That is, Jonas argues that female and male rabbis brought *their own special gifts*, the ones to which their gender had a propensity.

When Jonas was addressed as *Rabbiner*, this would imply to me that she had joined a male profession and expressed the same gender as the men in it. If Jonas was addressed as *Fräulein* or *Frau Rabbiner*, I infer that she was a woman who had joined a male profession and male community. But when Jonas was addressed as *Rabbinerin* it was transformative. It achieved what Jonas was claiming: that women could serve as rabbis; that women in the rabbinate broadened the category of rabbi; that rabbinical service was open not only to men but also to women. I do not know what the address for a queer-identified rabbi in German would entail, but I do believe that queer terminology gives us useful insight into the implications and possibilities of these category shifts.[61]

Queer terminology provides names for all sorts of nuanced spaces between male and female, using terms such as transgender, transsexual, transman, transwoman, and transvestite. Someone who is *transgender* is a person who feels at odds, internally, with what their biological sex appears to be, externally. In other words, their genitals do not match their sense of gendered self. A *transgender* person is one who *lives as* their "correct" gender, even when their biological self remains "incorrect" or at odds. Those who reassign or "correct" their sexual characteristics via medical and surgical intervention become *transsexual*. A person born with female genitals but who knows themself as a man and lives as one is a *transman*; a *transwoman* is one born with male genitals who sees their self as a woman and lives as one. A *transvestite* is a person who dresses up in the clothes of the gender opposite their sex, such as a man who dresses up in a woman's clothes. *Transvestites* do not necessarily have any desire for gender reassignment, nor are they necessarily homosexual.

Armed now with a review of the various nuances of "trans," we can see that Jonas was not transgendered, *per se*: she had no desire or feeling that it was necessary to change her gender in order to serve as a rabbi. She had no desire to hide her female gender under the robes of a male rabbi, nor did she feel that she was a woman who really should have been born a man so she could join a male profession as a male. Her whole *Halakhic* thesis, "Can Women Serve as Rabbis?," demonstrates that women *acting as their gender* could serve as rabbis. Furthermore, not only could they serve as rabbis, but the rabbinical profession had changed and was in dire need of women's presence as rabbis. Jonas's argument was that the role of the rabbi had expanded and there was now a demand for women as spiritual and communal leaders and as rabbis, just as they existed as leaders in the Torah. Jonas served as a leader herself, as a female rabbi. I therefore contend that when Jonas states at the beginning of her ordination thesis that a woman rabbi would be a rabbinerin, and when, in the last document she writes in Theresienstadt, she signs herself "Rabbinerin," the term "rabbi" had broken down. "Rabbinerin" defines her crossing, and at the same time creates her new identity on the other side.

Jonas was very aware that becoming an ordained woman rabbi was not simply a novelty, but was very strange; it was queer, even in the context of the Weimar Republic, a period of fervid social change. Before the advent of queer identity politics, the women's movement was calling for the expansion of the role of women in all professions that were once considered the male domain. The liberal strands of the early-twentieth-century First Wave of the women's movement called for legal and social equality of the sexes. Jonas was saying that rather than being "equal" to men, women brought their own unique characteristics and style to their professions. Stein had argued the same thing.

Part III

GOD

Chapter 5

STEIN SUFFERING ON THE CROSS:
THE CALL OF ABRAM LECH LECHA

The Lord said to Abram, "Go Forth from your native land and from your father's house to the land I will show you."

(Genesis 12:1)[1]

"Go Forth," "Go to yourself," i.e., go to your roots to find your potential.   (Hasidic interpretation)[2]

A fugitive brought the news to Abram the Hebrew [ha-Ivri].

(Genesis 14:13)[3]

Rashi "the Hebrew." He crossed over a river [maAvir].[4]

The Torah portion "Lech Lecha," or the story in Genesis 12 – in which God calls to Abram to leave the land of his father, the land he grew up in, the land of the status quo – is a metaphor for the religious journeys and spiritual resistance of Edith Stein and Regina Jonas. For they had literally been called; historical conditions had made their inner spiritual journeys imperative. The imperative call from God follows the Hasidic interpretation of Genesis 12:1. Stein and Jonas did turn inward, and heard God's calling. They returned to their roots as they knew them and found their true potential. They had become Hebrews. After Abram left his fatherland, the Torah refers to him as the "Hebrew" or the "Ivri." In this chapter I argue that Stein and Jonas were "Hebrews" in the literal sense of the word. The word "Hebrew" comes from the root letters Ayin, Vet, Rash; it means to pass, to cross over. Rashi states that the Torah refers to Abram as "the Hebrew" because he had crossed over a river when he left his fatherland. These passages from Genesis speak to the crossings or queerings of Stein and Jonas. Just as Abram was called to go forth and leave his native land to connect to his internal roots and to mani-fest his potential, so Edith Stein and Regina Jonas were connecting to their own internal roots to fulfill their true potential. They were listening to an inner voice that had called out to them through their historical conditions. For them, this was both an internal and external exodus.

When the Nazis took power in 1933, Jonas was a rabbinical candidate and Stein was an instructor at the University of Münster. Stein was then expelled from her job because she was a Jew, despite also being a practicing Catholic. Her expulsion came to her as a divine calling to enter the Carmel. There she returned to what she felt were her innermost roots, becoming Sister Teresa Benedicta of the Cross and embarking on her journey as a contemplative Carmelite in service of God's will. Regina Jonas received her ordination and became a rabbinerin, a woman rabbi – the first one in Jewish history – as the Jews were emigrating and being deported from Berlin. She felt called to serve as a rabbi to the Jewish community, and her role as a rabbinerin expanded because of the suffering being visited on them. At the moment that suffering was inflicted on Germany's Jewish community, the spiritual quests of Stein and Jonas became even stronger. The external circumstances of their people were empowering their internal calling. Abram was called to leave his native land; the Nazis harshly forced deportations and exodus upon the Jews. In both cases, this was as much a spiritual as a physical journey.

Stein and Jonas confronted the impending Nazi Holocaust as a Catholic Jewish Carmelite and a woman rabbi, both of which were queer religious identities. They deviated broadly from the traditional perceptions and roles of nun and rabbi. A Catholic nun was not a Jew, after all, and a rabbi was not a woman. Stein had crossed over from her native land of Judaism to become a Catholic Jew. Jonas had crossed over from traditional womanhood into the unfamiliar land of the male rabbinate. They were both literally Hebrews, just as Genesis 14:13 refers to Abram as the "Hebrew," he who crossed over a river. Yet Stein and Jonas had one foot planted on each side of the crossing, their feet straddling the river. Sister Teresa Benedicta outed herself in her new land at the Carmel as the Jew Edith Stein as well. And Rabbinerin Jonas brought a unique woman's style of spiritual leadership to the male rabbinate.

This chapter and the next demonstrate the connection between Stein and Jonas, and between their deviant religious desires and their spiritual resistance. The spiritual callings of these women manifested themselves as queer religious identities that ruptured the binary categories of the either/or dichotomy. Traditionally, Stein had to be either a Catholic or a Jew, but could not be both. Jonas could be a woman but not a rabbi; only men could be rabbis. Both women resisted the imperative to conform to normative definitions of religion and gender.

Committing these and other forms of spiritual resistance constituted an ethical stance that each took, demonstrating their multiple communities of belonging and their ethics of human uniqueness, therein reflecting the image of the divine. In the first part of this chapter, I show how Edith Stein expressed her spiritual resistance and what it meant for her to be a contemplative Catholic Jew. In the second part, I examine Regina Jonas's spiritual resistance through her calling to serve as a woman rabbi, first in Berlin, and later in Theresienstadt. Both Stein and Jonas were called to by God to go forth and leave their native lands in multiple ways. Their internal exile brought forth the manifestation of the true potential of both women, expressed in a form of spiritual resistance and a form of spiritual leadership.

What do we mean by spiritual resistance in the cases of Edith Stein and Regina Jonas? How did Stein and Jonas resist the crumbling of the external world, the deconstruction of all structures, the disintegration of all forms, which for many people also meant the collapse of their inner worlds? The world around them was being taken apart piece by piece to the ultimate end-point of total annihilation. For Stein and Jonas, this collapse directed them inward and led them to take outward actions.

The war against the Jews occurred in four stages: first, legalized discrimination; second, forced emigration; third, resettlement and ghettoization; and fourth, total annihilation. The first two stages occurred between 1933 and 1939; the final two stages during 1939–45.[5] Stein's and Rabbinerin Jonas's lives followed the Nazi trajectory. Their respective responses as a contemplative and a woman rabbi reflect their internal calling and connectedness to the Divine eternal.

EDITH STEIN: SPIRITUAL RESISTANCE AND PROTEST

The events in Stein's outer world gave her a powerful sense of meaning, and ultimately an experience of divine love and union with God. Stein's reflections in her story "How I Came to the Cologne Carmel," which she wrote just before her forced emigration to the Echt Carmel in Holland on December 18, 1938, point to her inner certainty regarding her spiritual path. From the moment Dr Stein converted to Catholicism in 1922, she had wanted to become a Carmelite contemplative: "For almost twelve years, Carmel had been my goal; since summer 1921, when the *Life* of our Holy Mother Teresa had happened to fall into my hands and had put an end to my long search for true faith."[6] (Stein was only accepted into the Carmel in 1933, after she had lost her job as an instructor because she was a Jew. Under Nazi laws passed that year, no Jews were allowed to hold academic appointments.) On February 16, 1930, Stein wrote a letter to a friend and former philosophy student, Sr Adelgundis Jaegerschmind, with a foreboding sense of her divine mission:

> There is a real difference between being a chosen instrument and being in a state of grace. It is not up to us to pass judgment and we may leave all to God's unfathomable mercy. ... After every encounter in which I am made aware how powerless we are to exercise direct influence *I have a deeper sense of the urgency of my own Holocaustum* ...
>
> However much our present mode of living may appear inadequate to us – what do we really know about it ? *But there can be*

no doubt that we are in the here-and-now out of our salvation and that of those who have been entrusted to our souls. *Let us help one another to learn more and more how to make every day and every hour part of the structure for eternity – shall we?*[7]

Let us note how Stein referred to her sense of urgency in the presence of God. It was uncanny that Stein had such a strong sense of her own self-sacrifice that she used the Latin word *Holocaustum* three years before the Nazi reign of terror. *Holocaustum* comes originally from the Greek, and means "burnt offering." A *holocaustum* was a burnt offering that was totally consumed by flames. What did it mean to Dr Stein to live with a sense of being a burnt offering? If one felt the urgency of sacrifice, then it demanded a total

Figure 4 Edith Stein as Sr Teresa Benedicta of the Cross, December 31, 1938 (© Edith Stein Archiv, Karmel Maria vom Frieden).

presence in the here and now at every single moment. We connect to the eternal through the here and now. We have no control over whether God will choose us or, in other words, if we will receive the gift of God's grace. This means expressing or having an epiphany, a revelation that comes to a mystic. A mystic recognizes her powerlessness before God, but also knows that the only way to be connected to God, to the eternal, is through the here and now. If one can focus on the here and now, one has the potential to be granted grace and truly connect to a state of divine union. Sister Teresa Benedicta of the Cross writes in her 1936 philosophical magnum opus *Finite and Eternal Being*, about the meaning of divine union: "Despite this fleeting being, I am; from moment to moment I am being held in being and in my fleeting being I am fastened to an enduring Being. I know that I am being held and therein I find calm and security."[8]

Stein recognized that being in communion with the enduring Being from moment to moment gave her an inner sense of calm and security that helped her confront the horror of what was happening to her nation, to her own chosen new religion, and to her community of origin, the Jewish people. Stein's awareness of the demand to be present in the here and now gave her an extraordinary perception that most Jews and Catholics or decent Germans were not fully able to share – the impending danger when the Nazis took power on January 30, 1933. It was exactly because of Stein's straddling the two worlds or simultaneously being both from the Jewish community and a devout practicing Catholic, who had lived in and taught in Catholic religious institutions, that she could see the impending Holocaust. This was long before German Jews could even comprehend the looming catastrophe of their situation in Germany. In her urgent sense of "now," she saw the oppressive political situation very clearly; and this enabled her to take a drastic action that became a major form of resistance.

Shortly after the Nazis' rise to power, Stein had a deep insight in a conversation with someone who did not know she had been a Jew. She chose not to reveal herself as one, and their discussion turned to the topic of American newspapers' reports about the precarious situation of Jews in Germany. Stein writes of this conversation: "True, I had heard of rigorous measures against the Jews before. But now a light dawned in my brain *that once again God had put a heavy hand upon His people and that the fate of this people was also mine*."[9] Stein realized even then that being a Catholic was not going to save her from the Nazis. She would share the same fate as her people, a fate she linked to Jesus' own Jewish blood. This epiphany led her to her first act of resistance, outward protest, and to another realization.

In April 1933, she had just visited her spiritual director Archabbot Raphael Walzer (1888–1966) during Passion Week in Beuron. While attending evening services on the Friday of Passion during the first week of April, she was called by her Lord the Savior, just like Abram before her. Stein writes about this calling:

> I talked with the Savior and told Him that I knew that it was His cross that was now being placed upon the Jewish people; that most of them did not understand this, but that those who did would have to take it up willingly in the name of all. I would do that. He should show me how. At the end of the service I was certain that I had been heard. But what this carrying of the cross was to consist in, that I did not yet know.[10]

What did Stein mean by saying that now the cross was being placed upon the Jewish people, who were also her people? Did the Savior's cross represent the suffering of the Jewish people in the same way that Jesus had suffered at the hands of the Romans? Was Stein equating Jesus' suffering with Jewish suffering? Did this mean that someone who was born Jewish like Stein but who recognized the Lord as the Savior, the son of God, had an extra special responsibility because they could see the whole picture from the perspective of the passion of Christ? Did Stein see that the Jewish people were about to go through unbearable agony and suffering and that no one was trying to stop it or intercede on their behalf? Stein had this conversation with her Savior during Passion Week, which commemorates the suffering, death, and resurrection of Christ. Was Stein in a position to do something about the suffering of her people that no one around her was able to because of her unique identity claim of being a Jew, like Jesus, while also realizing that he was the Savior?

Stein clearly saw the suffering of her people, and from a practicing Catholic perspective she could do something that no other Jew would be able to. She could take on the suffering of her people the same way that Jesus did on the cross. The myriad possible meanings of this are fascinating: What was the meaning of the cross itself, to Stein? Did taking the cross also mean repenting for the Jews' refusal to accept Jesus as their Messiah?

Stein states that she was not sure how her bearing of the cross had yet to unfold. Did Stein also have a transcendent, mystical understanding of the cross? Was perhaps one meaning of the cross that the vertical line of the cross represented finite linear time, while the horizontal line meant transcendence of linear time? Did Stein see the suffering of the cross as a way to break out of the linear confined time of historical circumstance and give the Jewish people a way to connect to the Eternal? This might make sense to Stein, although this would never make sense to a Jew or the Jewish community. These possibilities would be an outrage to and show a lack of understanding of Judaism because Jews had always had their own way of connecting to the everlasting God long before Jesus was born and died. The presumptions would be on Stein's part; traditional Jews would view them as antagonistic and a repudiation of Judaism.

We are examining how Stein was anticipating the impending Holocaust and how she had found a way to resist it. It is in these Passion Week remarks that she had identified a form of spiritual resistance that would lead to action and to her being called to be a contemplative, although in a form that Jews had trouble understanding because it was outside the realm of Jewish practice and experience. When Stein had her conversation with Jesus, she was not yet a practicing contemplative; she was still an instructor. In this personal revelation Stein embarked on her journey of resistance and martyrdom. Her first step in carrying the cross was to write a letter to Pope Pius XI. Her second was to be called to Carmel to live the life of a contemplative. Her third was writing a book about what it meant to grow up in a Jewish family. Her fourth was to accept her fate and see her own death in the gas chambers as similar to Jesus' death on the Cross. Jews at the time could not understand Stein's view of her experience, and many viewed it as victim to enemy ideology (indeed, many to this day share that view).

With the support of Archabbot Walzer, Stein decided to write a letter to the Holy Father in Rome to protest the new Nazi government, in the hope that the Holy Father would issue an encyclical. She had not yet lost her job at Münster; this happened soon after she returned from this visit. It was a prophetic letter that only could be written by someone who was able to see clearly the situation around her. I believe she was able to do this because of the two world views she embraced and the gift of grace from God that demanded her full presence and observation of the world, from which she was soon to be cloistered. This letter, released in February 2003 from sealed Vatican archives, was made public seventy years after Stein wrote it. The publication of the letter was controversial in its own right, let alone its content. For years historians and others have questioned why the Catholic Church remained silent. Stein asked this same question in April of 1933. The full 250 words follow:

Holy Father!

As a child of the Jewish people who, by the grace of God, for the past eleven years has also been a child of the Catholic Church, I dare to speak to the Father of Christendom about that which oppresses millions of Germans. For weeks we have seen deeds perpetrated in Germany which mock any sense of justice and humanity, not to mention love of neighbor. For years the leaders of National Socialism have been preaching hatred of the Jews. Now that they have seized the power of government and armed their followers, among them proven criminal elements, this seed of hatred has germinated. The government has only recently admitted that excesses have occurred. To what extent, we cannot tell, because public opinion is being gagged. However, judging by what I have learned from personal relations, it is in no way a matter of singular exceptional cases. *Under pressure from reactions abroad, the government has turned to "milder" methods. It has issued the watchword "no Jew shall have even one hair on his head harmed." But through boycott measures – by robbing people of their livelihood, civic honor and fatherland – it drives many to desperation;* within the last week, through private reports I was informed of five cases of suicide as a consequence of these hostilities. I am convinced that this is a general condition, which will claim many more victims. One may regret that these unhappy people do not have greater inner strength to bear their misfortune. *But the responsibility must fall, after all, on those who brought them to this point and it also falls on those who keep silent in the face of such happenings.*

Everything that happened and continues to happen on a daily basis originates with a government that calls itself "Christian." For weeks not only Jews but also thousands of faithful Catholics in Germany, and, I believe, all over the world, have been waiting and hoping for the Church of Christ to raise its voice to put a stop to this abuse of Christ's name. Is not this idolization of race and governmental power, which is being pounded into the public consciousness by the radio, open heresy? *Isn't the effort to destroy Jewish blood an abuse of the holiest humanity of our Savior, of the most blessed Virgin and the apostles? Is not all this diametrically opposed to the conduct of our Lord and Savior, who, even on the cross, still prayed for his persecutors? And isn't this a black mark on the record of this Holy Year which was intended to be a year of peace and reconciliation?*

We all, who are faithful children of the Church and who see the conditions in Germany with open eyes, fear the worst for the prestige of the Church, if the silence continues any longer. We are convinced that this silence will not be able in the long run to purchase peace with the present German government. *For the time being, the fight against Catholicism will be conducted quietly and less brutally than against Jewry, but no less systematically.* It won't take long before no Catholic will be able to hold office in Germany unless he dedicates himself unconditionally to the new course of action.

At the feet of your Holiness, requesting your apostolic blessing,

Dr Edith Stein, Instructor at the German Institute for Scientific Pedagogy, Munster in Westphalia, Collegium Mariana[11]

In the opening sentence to the Holy Father, Stein states her queer identity claims: she has been first a child of the Jewish people and then through her conversion she has become a child of the Catholic Church. She is signaling that she has a unique, all-encompassing perspective – a *Weltanschauung*. Stein had entered the Catholic community guided by the grace of God. In other words, she saw the light. She had an epiphany and realized that Jesus was indeed the Savior. At the moment she accepted Jesus as the Son of God, she simultaneously understood that Jesus was a Jew just like herself. In 1933, this was a radical perception of Jesus. The church had not yet contextualized Jesus' Jewish heritage. Since Jesus had been born and died a Jew, he was no different than the Jews in the present day worldwide Jewish communities. Jesus never claimed to be anything else but a Jew.

However, Stein made a different claim than Jesus did. She was both a Jew and Catholic. She did not die because she was a Catholic; she died because she was a Jew, like the other six million Jews killed by the Nazis.[12] Jesus was crucified because he was a Jew; he could not have been anything else but a Jew. But Stein did not view her own suffering as that of a Jew. She was a Catholic Jew, identifying with Jesus as one who shared the same Jewish blood. We will see later that she took on Jesus' suffering on the Cross as a Carmelite with this same deep sense of affinity. We should note, however, that many religious Jews can never accept Stein's claim of being both Jewish and Catholic. It goes against Jewish theology, according to which Jesus is not the Messiah. By Jewish definition Stein was an apostate. She held to a supersessionist theology that asserted that Jesus was the Messiah and that his teaching replaced the Old Testament, a notion we will expand on later in the chapter.

Stein's ability to hold on to and embrace what appeared to be two opposing theologies can be traced back to her dissertation on phenomenological empathy, where she asked how one human being can experience another, or have an inter-subjective experience of another person. For Stein, her own self-identification served as an example of the question she was asking about the nature of empathy and inter-subjective experience. The modern Hebrew literature scholar Rachel Brenner was one of the first to correctly demonstrate the connection between Stein's phenomenological philosophy and her ability to embrace both her Jewish and Carmelite identities simultaneously. Brenner views this as an ethical convergence in Stein's personal religious conversion.

Stein's *Weltanschauung* thus seems to denote convergence of religious identities, rather than conversion from one identity into another. She seemed to find no contradiction in claiming her part in Jesus and at the same time asserting her indelible ties with the Jewish people.[13]

Brenner speaks to the inner truth of how Stein understood herself. We can trace Stein's ability to fully hold two world views and merge them back to her dissertation, which she wrote as a self-proclaimed Jewish atheist in 1916. Her definition of empathy in her dissertation carried her to her conversion, which guided her in the religious and historical encounters she faced. The seeds of Stein's internal self-truth that turned her into a phenomenological mystic are found in the following description of phenomenological empathy:

The world I glimpse empathically is an existing world, posited as having being like the one primordially perceived. The perceived world and the world given empathically are the same world differently seen. But it is not only the same one seen from different sides as when I perceive primordially and, traversing continuous varieties of appearances, go from one standpoint to another. *Here each earlier standpoint motivates the later one, each following one severs the preceding one. Of course I accomplish the transition from one standpoint to the others in the same manner, but the new standpoint does not step into the old one's place. I retain both at the same time. The same world is not merely presented now in one way and then in another, but in both ways at the same time.* And not only is it differently presented depending on the momentary standpoint, but also depending on the nature of the observer. This makes appearance of the world dependent on the individual consciousness, but the appearing world – which is the same however and to whomever it appears – is made independent of consciousness. Were I imprisoned within the boundaries of my individuality, I could not go beyond "the world as it appears to me."[14]

The seed of Stein's spiritual journey, her mysticism and embracing of Jesus as a Jew, is stated in the following sentences: "I retain both at the same time. The same world is not merely presented now in one way and then in another, but in both ways at the same time." This was exactly what she meant when she asserted to the Holy Father that she was both a child of the Jewish people and a child of the Catholic Church. Her old standpoint of being a Jew was not entirely replaced by her new standpoint of being a Catholic; she retained both.

However, replacement theology is the worldview that Jews thought Stein had claimed, because of the long and horrible anti-Semitic history of Europe and of the Catholic Church forcing Jews to accept Jesus as the Messiah. The late Bishop of Stockholm Krister Stendhal correctly grasped Jewish views of Christian attempts to force conversion. He, too, called it not just a supersessionist theology, but a replacement theology. Stein did not see it this way, although ultimately she viewed herself as bearing the cross and dying for her people. Stein's phenomenological and empathic lenses enabled her to see beyond the world as it ordinarily appears, lending to her a kind of mysticism, a hybrid identity that few others had written or spoken of. She hoped that by stating her unique perspective outright, her allegiances to both communities would attract the Holy Father's attention.

In her letter Stein clearly explains the danger of the new Nazi government and how its policies went against everything Christianity stood for. Stein gives an accurate description of what was happening around her. The Nazis had implemented a policy of hatred towards Jews by taking away their occupations, denying their citizenship, boycotting their businesses, and ostracizing them. Stein claims that this is not a particular case but a general policy of the Nazi government. This has left Jews in a desperate situation; some Jews in despair have committed suicide, which Stein sees as form of spiritual weakness inherent in Jews. It had, in fact, been one of her reasons for conversion, since she felt that Judaism did not offer an internal spiritual connection to eternity, as she points out in her letter to the Holy Father. Stein later writes about this in her autobiography, *Life in a Jewish Family*, as she was cloistered in Carmel:

> I believe that the inability to face and to accept the collapse of
> one's worldly existence with reasonable calm is closely linked to
> the lack of the prospect of life in eternity. The personal immortal-
> ity of the soul is not considered an article of faith; all of one's effort
> is concentrated on what is temporal. Even the piety of the pious
> is directed toward the sanctification of *this* life. A Jew is able to
> endure severe hardship and untiring labor coupled with extreme
> privations for years on end as long as he sees a goal ahead. ... The
> true believer, of course, is deterred from such a course by his sub-
> mission to the will of God.[15]

Because the Jews seemed unable to bear the misfortune of Nazi persecu-
tion, Stein pleads with the Holy Father to do something. The Church should not remain silent. She points out that world opinion did have an effect, and protest could have an impact on the treatment of the Jews.[16] Stein makes it explicit that the Nazi government claimed to be a so-called Christian govern-
ment. In her plea for the Church to speak out, she asks, "Isn't the effort to destroy Jewish blood an abuse of the holiest humanity of our Savior, of the most blessed Virgin and the apostles?" In her argument she again draws on empathy in two ways. She asks, Is not the call for Jewish blood actually the killing of Jesus the Savior, the Jewish blood of the Holy Mother the Virgin Mary, and the Jewish blood of the apostles like Paul? To kill present-day living German Jews was to kill Jesus himself. This is a very bold statement. For millennia, the Church had persecuted Jews for killing Jesus, and now Stein is turning the argument around. The Nazis, who in their deeds were anti-Christian, were killing Jesus' own community of living Jews. Stein herself was an example of the living Jews who embraced Jesus. It was because of Stein's queer identification that she was able to make this point.

She goes on to prophetically warn that Catholics were not immune to the anti-Christian policies of the Nazis. "For the time being, the fight against Catholicism will be conducted quietly and less brutally than against Jewry, but no less systematically." If Catholics did not speak out against the abusive policies against the Jews, they themselves would eventually be persecuted. Stein asks if all this was not diametrically opposed to the conduct of our Lord and Savior; did he not, even while on the cross, still pray for his persecutors? This implies that the Church policy of not speaking out against the Nazis was the total opposite of the teaching of the Church and Jesus. A good Christian and a strong Church speak out against oppressors and pray for them – this was what Jesus had taught and why he died on the cross. Stein's passionate and moving plea unfortunately remained unanswered. She never received a response from the Vatican, nor was she granted a private audience with the Holy Father.[17]

After Stein wrote this letter, she went back home to her position at Munster – but not for long. She was fired on April 19, 1933 because of the new Nazi race laws banning the employment of Jews. After she lost her job, she did have an opportunity to get out of Germany and go to South America. Interestingly, Regina Jonas would also receive offers to emigrate, possibly to America. Both chose not to leave. Instead, each chose to follow their inner calling to be with their spiritual communities. Stein describes it thus: "I did in fact receive an offer from South America, but by that time a very different path had been revealed to me."[18] The path that was revealed to her was her acceptance into the Cologne Carmel. This was her chance to follow her divine calling; this was the second step in her journey of carrying the cross. The major issue that stood in the way of her divine calling was the intense pain this caused her mother, as we have discussed above in Chapter 4. Stein claims that she had not been admitted into Carmel earlier in her career because her spiritual counselors felt that she could be of greater service in the external world as a teacher, lecturer, scholar, and writer, all of which she had successfully done. However, she longed to be a contemplative. Stein writes:

> Lately, this waiting [to become a Carmelite] had become very hard for me. I had become a stranger in the outside world. Before I began my job in Munster … I had urgently pleaded for permission to enter the order. … *But now the walls that stood in my way had crumbled.* My effectiveness was at an end. And surely my mother would prefer me to be in a convent in Germany rather than a school in South America.[19]

Stein's world had crumbled, as it had for all Jews in Nazi Germany. It was interesting that Stein felt her mother would have preferred her close by in a convent, but the family might in fact have preferred her to go to South America than to enter what was perceived to be a cloister sealed off behind the walls of the enemy. Rachel Brenner perceptively points out the family's misunderstanding.

> It was not surprising that Stein's intention to become a Carmelite was completely misunderstood by her family, who thought she was taking the vows to escape persecution: "What I was planning

seemed [to them] to draw a yet sharper line between me and the Jewish people – at that moment when it was being so oppressed. They could not understand that from my point of view it seemed quite different." Her reason for entering the Carmelite Order was that "it always seemed to me that our Lord was keeping something for me in Carmel which I could find only there." She appeared to reassert her will to take up the cross when she commented on entering the convent: "It is not human activity that can help us but the Passion of Christ. It is a share in that I desire."[20]

Not only did her family not understand her spiritual path, but they also tried very hard to persuade her not to follow it. Her brother-in-law Hans Biberstein said that he would support her if money were an issue since she had lost her job. Susanne Batzdorff remembers that her father also tried to persuade her Aunt Edith not to go by reminding her of the anti-Semitic history of Breslau. In 1453, 41 Jews in Breslau had been burned at the stake because the Franciscan Friar John of Capistrano accused them of desecrating the Host. This was why the Stein family believed – and many Jews, both then and now, would agree – that Stein was joining the enemy. It was a feeling of complete betrayal. It appeared that Stein was running from one enemy, the Nazis, to join another, the Catholic Church. Christians in general and Catholics in particular had persecuted Jews for being Christ-killers.[21] For Stein, however, her call was similar to Abram's.

Just before Stein entered the Carmel, she began her memoir, *Life in the Jewish Family*, in her mother's house. This was also a form of protest and resistance. The introduction echoes what she had put in her letter to the Pope. She wrote the Foreword five months after her letter to the Pope in September 1933:

> Recent months have catapulted the German Jews out of the peaceful existence they had come to take for granted. *They have been forced to reflect upon themselves, upon their being, and their destiny*, but today events have also impelled many others, hitherto non-partisan, to take up the Jewish question.[22]

German Jews had tried to fit into German society with the reform of Jewish practices and notions of *Bildung*.[23] Stein understood this history, yet accurately realized their situation. Many Jews in 1933 still had high hopes that the Fatherland would come to its senses. They had proudly fought in World War I, and they were no less German then their Christian brethren. To them, the Nazis were not true Germans; Nazi ascendancy was just a temporary situation.

Stein had already sensed the urgency of the situation back in April when she sent a letter to the Pope. Now she felt that writing about what it meant to grow up in a Jewish family from the perspective of someone who had become a Catholic might help Germans empathize with the Jewish plight. She wanted to dispel the misconceptions that regular Germans might have about Jews and the propaganda that the Nazis were broadcasting on the radio and in newspapers:

> Is Judaism represented by ... powerful capitalists, insolent liter-
> ati, or those restless heads who had led the revolutionary move-
> ments of the past decades? Persons who reply to that question
> in the negative can be found in every stratum of the German
> nation. These persons who have associated with Jewish families as
> employees, neighbors or fellow students, have found in them such
> goodness of heart, understanding, warm empathy and so consist-
> ently helpful an attitude that their sense of justice is *outraged by
> the condemnation of this people to a pariah's existence.*
> But many others lacked this kind of experience. The opportu-
> nity to attain it has been denied primarily to the young, who these
> days are being reared in racial hatred from the earliest childhood.
> To all those who have been deprived, we who grew up in Judaism
> have an obligation to give our testimony ... It is intended as infor-
> mation for anyone wishing to pursue an unprejudiced view.[24]

It was through a personal connection to Jews that non-Jews and Germans could empathize with them as ordinary human beings, such as they themselves were. We only get to know someone through the particular, through the personal, where we can have empathy for another. Stein acknowledges that there were good people who did not buy into the Nazi racist stereotype. Stein had come to the same conclusion as Hannah Arendt, ten years before Arendt would claim that Jewish existence in Germany and Europe had always been one of a "pariah people." Instead, Stein saw this condition as a result of the Nazis' rise to power.

Hannah Arendt wrote two articles, "We Refugees" (January 1943) and "The Jew as Pariah: A Hidden Tradition" (April 1944), after she escaped from Europe to New York in 1941. Arendt argues in these reflective articles that Jewish existence had always been a pariah existence. Those Jews who thought that they could fit into German and European society, or, in Arendt's words, "ape the gentiles,"[25] were seen as parvenus, upstarts, mistaken. They were deluding themselves. They had argued that it was their duty to serve the Fatherland. Arendt argues that it was the job of "conscious pariahs" – meaning those Jews who already knew that they would never really gain full emancipation and equality – to awaken the rest of Jewry. Ironically, Stein's foreword to *Life in a Jewish Family* fits with Arendt's definition of a conscious pariah. Stein states that German Jews were being awakened from what they had taken for granted, meaning that they had thought that they were fully emancipated German citizens. It would appear that Stein herself then was a conscious pariah. She was a Jew who saw that Jews did not fit in. However, this was only a part of Stein's identity. Arendt argues that Jews were always Jews in Europe and could not be anything else. Stein felt that she was something else. From one perspective, Stein was a radical conscious pariah because she recognized the pariah existence of German Jews. From another perspective, Stein would appear to be an assimilationist, fitting into German and European society as a Catholic, and could be viewed as parvenu. She was neither pariah nor parvenu but something Arendt had not imagined – a Catholic Jew.

This would have been Arendt's view of Stein, even though Stein saw the coming end of Jewry. Nevertheless, this was not Stein's truth; she was neither fully a conscious pariah nor an assimilationist Jew. Hers was a profound spiritual faith that very few, either mainstream Jews or Catholics, can truly comprehend, even today. It was exactly because of Stein's unique perspective of being a Jew like Jesus, but having faith that he was the Savior, that she could see the coming Holocaust. She held two worldviews at the same time, and this illuminated for her the impending doom. This way of seeing, this *Weltanschauung*, was very difficult for most people to grasp; her claim to be a daughter of Jewish people and a daughter of the Catholic Church was prohibitively queer. Stein saw the end of German Jewry, but instead of escaping she went deeper into her unique practice of faith, which led her to Carmel.

SPIRITUAL RESISTANCE IN CARMEL: THE WAY OF THE CROSS

Stein entered the Carmel two days after her 42nd birthday, on October 14, 1933. She was finally able to serve her Savior. What did it mean for her to be a Carmelite? Sister Teresa Benedicta of the Cross gave the answer in a newspaper article titled "Before the Face of God: On the History and Spirit of Carmel," published in March 1935 in the *Augsburger Post*: "To stand before the face of the living God, that is our vocation. The holy prophet [Elijah] set us an example. He stood before God's face because this was the eternal treasure for whose sake he gave up all earthly goods."[26] A Carmelite takes three vows upon entering the order, of poverty, obedience, and chastity. Stein explains that "The vow of poverty opens one's hands so that they let go of everything ... [It] is intended to make us carefree as the sparrows and the lilies so that our spirit and hearts may be free for God."[27] Once we let go of desire and wanting things in the material world, it frees the soul to receive from God. The vow of obedience was to make one free to follow the will of God: not one's own personal will that was ruled by emotion and reason, but God's will. The vows of obedience mean self-denial in order to serve and obey the Lord:

> Therefore the obedient person ... recognizes ... how many small sacrifices are available daily and hourly as opportunities to advance in self-denial ... because doing so deepens the burden, the conviction of being closely bound to the Lord, who was obedient to death on the cross.[28]

Obedience was another way to bind one to the cross and to the Lord. Finally, the vow of chastity "intends to release human beings from all the bounds of natural common life, to fasten them to the cross high above the bustle and to free their hearts for the union with the Crucified."[29]

The practice of these vows and the willingness to freely choose suffering was the meaning of the cross, the very way to take it up. This was exactly what Stein wanted to do, for she saw this as the way to spiritually resist the evil going on around her and as an action that could transmute the evil. For when Christ died on the cross for the sins of humanity, he was transmuting evil and offering himself up as a sacrifice to God. Christ's suffering on the cross showed humanity the path back to God. Those who were accepted into a life of contemplative practice were taking the path of Christ for the sake of the sins of humanity. This was the way to prepare oneself to be open for receiving and uniting in God's divine love.

These vows guided the sisters of Carmel to experience the love of the cross, the face of God, and atonement. As Stein explains, these three vows lead to what the Prophet Elijah experienced:

> Elijah stands before God's face because all his love belongs to the Lord. He lives outside of all natural human relationships. His "relatives" are those who do the will of the Father ... Glorifying God in his joy. His zeal to serve God tears him apart: "I am filled with jealous zeal for the Lord, the God of hosts." ... By living penitentially he atones for the sins of his time.[30]

Stein clearly recognized when she entered the Carmel of Cologne in 1933 that there were intense sins in her time that needed to be atoned for. These sins were clearly those of National Socialism, which she called the Antichrist, and those of the Jews who did not accept Christ as the Savior. Stein fled to the Carmel of Echt in Holland in 1938, and preached to her new Carmel community about the renewal of their vows on September 14, 1939. "The world is in flames," she said, "the battle between the Christ and the Antichrist has broken out into the open. If you decide for Christ, it could cost you your life."[31] Carrying the cross did cost some sisters their lives. Sister Teresa Benedicta's life, however, would have been taken regardless of whether she was carrying the cross or not. Sister Teresa Benedicta knew Catholicism was not going to save her, but that her faith was a way of resisting the Holocaust.

Sister Teresa Benedicta understood that she did not have to live in the world, for behind cloistered walls one could take on spiritual suffering even more intensely. She explains exactly why she was offering herself up to Christ:

> The world is in flames. The conflagration can also reach our house. But high above all flames towers the cross. They cannot consume it. It is the path from earth to heaven. It will lift one who embraces it in faith, love and hope into the bosom of the Trinity.
>
> The world is in flames. Are you impelled to put them out? Look at the cross. From the open heart gushes the blood of the Savior. This extinguishes the flames of hell. Make your heart free by the faithful fulfillment of your vows: then the flood of the Divine love will be poured into your heart until it overflows and becomes fruitful to all the ends of the earth. ... *You can be at all fronts, wherever there is grief, in the power of the cross. Your compassionate love takes you everywhere, this love from the divine heart. Its precious blood is poured everywhere – soothing, healing, saving.*[32]

The blood with which Sister Teresa Benedicta identified so intensely as a Jew was the precious blood pouring from the Jewish body of Christ – divine love that flowed everywhere and soothed, healed and saved souls. In her description of it extinguishing the flames of hell, we can grasp why being both a daughter of the Jewish community and a daughter of the Church had so much personal meaning for Stein. It gave Sister Teresa Benedicta's suffering double meaning. Christ's blood was her blood; she was the same as Christ when she bound herself to him with her Carmelite vows. The Jews' precarious state was similar to Christ's suffering, and now she, one of Christ's own flesh and blood, was able to suffer as he did. In contrast, Melissa Raphael has demonstrated that the majority of Jewish art depicting the cross during the Nazi period was of Holocaust Passions, demonstrating Jewish suffering on a cross that does not bring redemption or end the suffering, but illustrates the ongoing suffering. A prime example is the artist Marc Chagall's painting "White Crucifixition" of 1938.[33] Stein's contemplative practice showed her the way of the cross as a form messianic redemption for herself, her fellow Jews and the Germans.

CARRYING THE CROSS FOR ATONEMENT AND REDEMPTION

Lucy Gelber explains the interior religious life of Edith Stein, which guided her in becoming a contemplative, and what the love of the cross and atonement meant for her:

> One of these is *love of the cross*, which gives our being, unstable because of change and transience, an ultimate security in the

constant primal Ground of eternal Being. The other is *atonement,* which breaks the disastrous and endless cycle of our own and others' debt of shame in the face of God's goodness and justice and so achieves reconciliation and peace.[34]

When Stein was deported, her behavior did in fact demonstrate her inner primal grounding in eternal Being. Stein saw that her ultimate act of bearing the cross and suffering would lead her to be able to see the face of God, achieve peace, and advance justice. Stein felt that if she could take this on personally as a contemplative she was literally offering herself up as a *holocaustum* to somehow assuage the madness of the Nazi war against the Jews and against all of humanity.

Stein explicitly states that the way of the cross, which was Stein's atonement and reason for dying, addressed the sin of the Jews who did not accept Christ. Similarly, her dying was an atonement for the Germans; she was offering her life up on the cross for world peace and all humanity. This was Stein's way of resisting oppression. And more than offering herself up on the cross, it was a way to let divine love flow into the world through this suffering. She expressed this intention in her last will and testament, and in her recurring image of Queen Esther redeeming her people for the Lord.

The first place Stein wrote about the meaning of her future death was in her last will and testament, composed on June 9, 1939: "I pray to the Lord that he may accept my living and dying ... *as an atonement for the Jewish people's unbelief and so that the Lord may be accepted by his own* and that his reign may come in glory, that Germany may be saved and that there be peace in the world."[35]

Sister Teresa Benedicta was atoning for the Jews, praying for them to accept their own fellow Jew, Jesus, as the Messiah, so that he might return again and bring world peace in with his reign. By this means, Germany would be saved. Sister Teresa Benedicta repeated these sentiments again in a dialogue she wrote entitled "Conversation in the Night." On June 13, 1941, Stein wrote the dialogue in honor of the Celebrations of Mother Antonia's birthday, honoring a *Spiritu Sanctus* and prioress of the Carmel in Echt. It is the vision of a mystic, but reiterates Stein's reason for suffering and atonement. Stein again views herself as Queen Esther.

We may note that Catholics have a different Queen Esther story than the one in the Hebrew Bible. In the Catholic version, God is present in the story and the Jews are redeemed by God as a savior, not in the form of the Son of God. The Catholic Church version is sixteen chapters long, while the Jewish one is ten chapters. The Catholic Church merged the late Greek translation with the Hebrew one.[36] In the Hebrew Bible, the story is part of the only book of the Torah not to mention God. The Jews were saved by human interception, not by a redeeming God. In Chapter 4, we explored the notion of Sister Teresa Benedicta of the Cross coming out of hiding with the Queen Esther motif. Sister Teresa Benedicta had referred to herself as Queen Esther in a letter in 1938. She now returns to this image in the dialogue entitled "Conversation in the Night." A year before the end of her life Stein had an image of herself as Queen Esther delivering her people to the Savior. What she said in this conversation was very clear. Queen Esther was delivering the Jewish people to her redeeming God, the Lord Jesus, and this would bring about His second coming. Sister Teresa Benedicta was Esther; and she was having a conversation with the Mother, who was Mother Antonia. In this dialogue we can see Sister Teresa Benedicta's deep sense of her mission as a contemplative and the meaning of her offering up her life on the cross while the world was in flames. This was the way she resisted and made sense of the suffering of her people. Sister Teresa Benedicta reinterpreted the Esther story and put it in the context of a Catholic story of the redemption of her people through conversion and acceptance of the Lord. In the "Conversation in the Night," Sister Teresa Benedicta reveals that she is Esther, reappearing this time to save her people. The Mother asks Esther, "And today another Haman has sworn to annihilate them in bitter hatred. Is this, in fact, why Esther has returned?"[37] This Haman was of course the Nazi Hitler in particular, who was in the process of annihilating the Jews with his Final Solution. In June 1941, the Mother may not have known how literally true her statement was to become.

In June 1941 the Nazis had just invaded the Soviet Union, and the special SS units called *Einsatzgruppen* had followed the German army during the invasion. The *Einsatzgruppen*'s job was to exterminate complete Jewish populations, along with Gypsies and communists, in the towns of the Ukraine. The SS first attempted to do this by group massacres, using firing squads on Jewish communities; later in 1941, they used mobile gas units. In the winter of 1942, the major concentration camps, such as Auschwitz, were in full operation, systematically gassing the Jews and carrying out the Final Solution. Jews from all over Europe were concentrated in ghettos or interim prison camps, then directly deported to the extermination camps. When she was deported, Edith Stein was first taken to the holding camp at Westerbork, only to meet her fate in the summer of 1942 at Auschwitz.

Queen Esther explains why she has returned to Earth. She tells the Mother that she has died a normal death: "To the place of peace I found rest in Abraham's bosom with its ancestors." Queen Esther was also received into the heart of Jesus. Once she had entered there, she had seen the Holy Mother, the virgin Mary. Queen Esther explains to the Mother:

> I saw the church grow out of my people ... The unblemished pure shoot of David. ... I saw flowing down from Jesus' heart, the fullness of grace into the Virgin's heart. From there it flows to the members as a stream of life. ... *But now I know that I was bound to her. From eternity in accordance with God's direction – forever. My life was only a beam of hers.*[38]

Sister Teresa Benedicta was in a state of divine union with the Holy Mother and God. She knew that she was a beam of light coming from the source of light. She had literally seen the face of God and was now returning to save her people. Queen Esther had been sent as an emissary of the Holy Mother to gather up her people like a shepherd and bring them back to her and to the Son of the Lord: "The Mother ceaselessly pleads for her people. She seeks souls to help her pray. Only then when Israel has found the Lord, only then when He has received His own, will He come in manifest glory, and we must pray for the second coming."[39]

We see the Mother with a capital M, meaning the Holy Mother, trying to rescue her people, the Jewish people, with the help of prayers from the ones who are bound to the Lord and know that he is the Redeemer. Queen Esther states that once Jews have found the Lord, they can return to earth at the second coming, and all suffering will end. The reason Queen Esther has appeared to the Mother prioress at this moment is to ask for help and prayers for the redemption of Jews, to return to the Lord so that they can be saved from annihilation through the Lord's redemption. The hearts of those cloistered in a contemplative order offered the best chance for the prayers of Queen Esther to be heard. The Mother responds to Queen Esther:

> Where else was she [Holy Mother Mary] to find hearts prepared if not in her quiet sanctuary? Her people [the Jewish people], which are yours, your Israel, I take up into the lodgings of my heart. Praying secretly and sacrificing secretly, I will take it home to my Savior's heart.[40]

This was Stein's way of asking help from the spiritually strong to pray for redemption. Stein shows that the task at hand was to pray for the Jews to come to Jesus the Savior. As Queen Esther, she conveys the message that this work is to be done contemplatively and secretly within the heart through prayer and sacrifice. It was truly a way for Stein to show mystical resistance. After the Mother responds that she understands why Queen Esther has appeared to her, Queen Esther replies:

> You have understood and so I can depart. ... We will meet again on the great day, the day of manifest glory. When the head of the Queen of Carmel [Holy Mother Mary] is loved, the crown of stars will gleam brilliantly because the twelve tribes will have found their Lord.[41]

From this dialogue we see the synthesis of Stein's true spiritual sense of being. The German feminist theologian Dorothee Sölle notes that Stein's suffering and sacrifice were a form of mystical resistance:

Edith Stein understood the fate of the Jewish people as participation in the cross of Christ ... It is a mystical approach to the reality that comes from a passive experience of being overwhelmed to accept voluntarily the suffering of the downtrodden and insulted.[42]

Sölle points out that Roman Catholics use the word "sacrifice," which Stein has indeed used in her dialogue. Stein, in an overwhelming situation, had an opportunity through suffering or sacrifice to become an active participating subject in her fate, not just an object of it. Sölle explains clearly the meaning of Stein's suffering, and suggests that bearing the cross was a form of mystical acceptance of God's Love.

In what others call "fate," acceptance finds the suffering God and calls her/him "love." Acceptance deprives icy meaninglessness of its [fate's] power because it clings to God's warmth even in suffering. ... Rather that *concept expresses the participation of humans who do not acquiesce but who, in mystical defiance, insist through their suffering that nothing becomes lost.*[43]

Stein had found a way to end her suffering. She was not going to acquiesce in her fate. She had found a way to be the subject of her fate, not the object. If she atoned for the Jews and the Jews accepted their Lord, then He would come and end their suffering and bring world peace. Stein affirms this in the dialogue between Esther and the Mother prioress and in her last will and testament. This was Stein's interpretation of the horror around her, and her way to spiritually resist the destruction of the Jews in Germany. This was Stein's spiritual truth – she was a contemplative mystic with the unique world view that came from being a daughter both of the Jewish people and of the Catholic Church. This gave her a dual insight and a demanding urgency to take on the suffering of her own people. Stein's sense of urgency goes back to her 1930 statement that she sensed her own *holocaustum*. In light of Stein's writings, we can comprehend the meaning of her interior life. Stein saw herself as a burnt offering who gave herself up in the presence of God and to Christ the Savior on the Cross. As a burnt offering, she was consumed by the flames of Auschwitz.

Just before the Gestapo came to arrest all the Catholic Jews in Holland, Sister Teresa Benedicta completed her last manuscript entitled "The Science of the Cross," which examined the writings of St John of the Cross. She had drawn an illustration, a cross with flames all around it. On July 26, 1942, a protest letter against the deportation of the Jews was read from the pulpit in the Catholic Dutch and Dutch Orthodox branch of the Protestant Church during Sunday morning services. Following this, all Catholic Jews, including monks and nuns living in cloistered convents and monasteries, were rounded up on August 2, 1942. Sister Teresa Benedicta and her sister Rose were among them. Stein's predictions, going all the way back to 1930 and 1933, were being fulfilled. In her internal sense of who she was, Stein died on a cross as a burnt offering. Externally, she died no differently than any other Jew, identified by the Nazis and recognized by fellow Jews. In these circumstances, no one Jewish life was greater than another. Susanne Batzdorff, Stein's niece, writes:

> It was a fact that Edith Stein died in solidarity "with her people." Even though she had left the Jewish fold, she was finally, in an ironic twist, reunited with them in death. She was resigned to that fate, but she had no control over it. It was rather due to the Nazi definition of who was a Jew. It was because she was born Jewish, of Jewish parentage that she became a martyr in Auschwitz.[44]

Chapter 6

RABBINERIN REGINA JONAS:
SEEING THE FACE OF THE *SHEKHINAH*

Stein died "for" her people, while Jonas served and suffered "with" her people. These are two very different forms of spiritual resistance. Stein's resistance was that of a Catholic nun; Jonas's was that of a Jewish rabbi.

When Sister Teresa Benedicta was arrested in the summer of 1942 and deported to the east, Jonas was working as a slave laborer in an armament factory and as a rabbinerin in Berlin to communities that had lost their rabbis. In 1942, Berlin Jews were being deported at a rate of a thousand a day to Theresienstadt and to ghettos in Riga and Lodz, but more and more they were sent directly to Auschwitz. Rabbinerin Jonas ministered to local congregations who had lost their rabbis due to deportation or emigration. She worked at the Jewish hospital and the Jewish old age home, and consoled and taught people in her home when there were few other places for the Jews of Berlin to meet. Jonas's calling was to be "with" and "among" her community. She had correctly argued in her ordination thesis that Israelite and Jewish spiritual leaders "worked *for* the *entire* community and also sometimes *in* and *with* the *entire* community.[1]

Jewish practice reaffirms community and does not have contemplative orders. Jews do not need to leave the hustle and bustle of everyday life in order to have a direct experience of God. The practice of Judaism, especially the observance of Jewish *Halakha*, the study of Torah, and acts of good deeds, draws God close. For God is reflected in each human being, and Jewish practice makes Jews recognize the holy in every moment and in everyone.

Stein's inner calling had guided her to contemplate the interior life at Carmel.[2] Stein had been called to see the face of God, just as the prophet Elijah had. Stein did this by taking the vows of a contemplative and giving up all earthly possessions and desires as a Carmelite. In her suffering on the cross "for" her people, Stein saw the face of God, but this God bore the face of the Savior. This was a form of Catholic mystical resistance. Stein was suffering and dying "for" her people by offering herself as burnt sacrifice. According to the biography by the Carmelite Waltraud Herbstrith, a neighbor recalled that Stein said to her sister as they were being deported, "Come Rosa, we are going for our people."[3]

Jewish suffering and spiritual resistance is very different. Judaism does not have a theological concept of someone dying for others' sins. Jews are personally responsible for their own actions before God and in relationship to others, and there is no savior. Jewish spiritual leaders suffered with their community, with their people, along with their people.

This notion of Jewish spiritual leadership and Jewish spiritual resistance became even more pronounced during the years of the Nazi Holocaust. For Jonas, being a Rabbinerin meant being with her people in their suffering, supporting them and inspiring them to care for one another, to study, learn, and defy the destruction around them through the Jewish teaching of Pirkei Avot 1:2: "Three things the world stands on are the study of Torah, service to God, and acts of loving kindness." Jonas's rabbinate embodied the essence of these teachings.

Rabbinerin Jonas, along with many rabbis of Europe, demonstrated spiritual leadership and support of their communities by being with them and not abandoning them. This was the Jewish path of spiritual resistance. It was embedded within the concept of Jewish religious practice. Those rabbis who were not immediately deported, forced to emigrate, or did not choose to emigrate, followed the words of Rabbi Hillel: *"Do not separate yourself from the community"* (Pirkei Avot 2:5). There is a Midrash that the reason that Moshe Rabbenu was not allowed into the promised land was because he separated himself from his community. He had spent almost twenty-four hours a day meditating on the name of God and was not there, was not present, when his community, the Israelites, needed him. Likewise, Moses had lost his ability to be a leader. Martin Buber had a similar realization regarding mystical contemplation.[4] This refusal to separate from the community is one reason why there are no contemplative orders in Judaism.

So Rabbinerin Jonas, along with a number of others of her friends and colleagues of the German rabbinate, including Rabbi Leo Baeck, Rabbi Siegfried Alexander, Rabbi Max Weyl and Rabbi Joseph Norden, stayed with her people. As the scholar Rabbi Elisa Klapheck points out, numerous people had encouraged Jonas to leave Germany after *Kristallnacht*, but Jonas rejected the notion. Fellow Berlin Jew and survivor Gad Beck worked in the same forced labor factory as Jonas. He remembered that Jonas "wanted to stay where her people were, just like Leo Baeck."[5] Her former pupil, Rita Nagler, recalled, "One sensed that for her it meant more to serve those who trusted in her than to save herself."[6] In the same light, Rabbi Ted Alexander explained why his uncle, Orthodox Rabbi Siegfried Alexander, did not escape from Berlin. His Uncle Siegfried had not wanted to abandon his orthodox Jewish community in Berlin; he wanted to be with them and serve them.[7] Rabbi Siegfried Alexander was deported with the rest of the Jewish community of Berlin and did not come back. The elder Rabbi Joseph Norden came out of retirement to serve the Hamburg community after *Kristallnacht*, when Rabbi Bruno Italiener of Hamburg was forced to emigrate. Rabbi Norden remained behind to serve the Israelitscher Tempel in Hamburg. Thirty-two years her senior, and a widower, he and Rabbinerin Jonas developed a close relationship, and were engaged to be married before he was deported to Theresienstadt in the summer of 1942. Like the Liberal Rabbis Jonas and Baeck, and the Orthodox Rabbi Alexander, he had chosen not to escape with his children. Such loyalty to their communities was not only true for German rabbis but for rabbis throughout Europe. Some of the rabbis who were heads of Hasidic communities stayed with their people. Rabbi Israel Spira (1890–1989), head of the Bluzhov Hasidim in Poland, was deported with his community to forced labor and concentration camps.[8] The Hasidic Rabbi Kalonymus Kalman Shapira, the *Rebbe* of the Warsaw Ghetto, stayed and died with his community.[9]

Jonas's rabbinate reminded the Jewish community of the exiled *Shekhinah*, which meant affirming to her community that God was always with them, especially in their exiled and oppressed circumstances. This was what guided rabbis and other Jewish spiritual leaders. This concept came through Jonas's teaching, ministering, lecturing, and then working as a rabbi and spiritual counselor at Theresienstadt. Rabbinerin Jonas was a woman rabbi who brought with her the particular qualities of a woman – caring, compassion, and orientation towards relationships. Through the acts of care and learning, one can see the face of God in the other.

Jonas and Stein's approach were two very different ways of spiritually resisting oppression in the external world. Melissa Raphael, in *The Female Face of God in Auschwitz: A Jewish Feminist Theology of the Holocaust*, clearly identifies the meaning and way of Jewish spiritual suffering and a kind of resistance that is radically different than Stein's Catholic way of suffering: "In Jewish understanding, the suffering of the *Shekhinah* is that of one who, being among us, suffers with us, but does not suffer vicariously *for* us."[10] Raphael demonstrates that the face of God in the form of the *Shekhinah* is seen in the faces of those women who cared for each other in the concentration camps. It could be the simple gesture of trying to clean a dirty face, or putting a torn blanket around a shivering, starving friend. In these acts of care for the other, that divine spark of God is seen.

The word *Shekhinah*, which is feminine in gender, comes from the root letters shin, kaph, nun, meaning "to dwell." In the Torah, the word for the portable tent that Israelites carried with them was *mishkan*. God dwelled inside this *mishkan*. After God gave the Torah to the Israelites, God commanded that they build a tent so "I can dwell among you" (Exod. 25:8). Then God appeared as a cloud of light that traveled with the Israelites. The presence of God was literally within the community of Israel and even more so when they were exiled. Raphael explains:

Rabbinic literature has an unshakeable belief in the indwelling presence of God in the daily life of the people of Israel. Even when Israel is unclean, the Shekhinah is with them (Yoma 56b) and although it drives her away, she watches over the sick (Shabbat 12b). When a human being is in pain, the Shekhinah's head and arms ache (Sanhedrein 46b). ... The Shekhinah is a symbol of God's self-revelation and immanence in the everyday world; rabbinic theology is also a mystical theology. ... The Shekhinah denotes less God's presence in a particular place than the presence of God among the exiled community of Israel, and the body of Israel was God's dwelling place. ... The Shekhinah [reaffirms] God's closeness to the suffering of Israel and her sharing its exile.[11]

The Talmudic rabbis noted that when the Jews were exiled from the Holy Land, it was then that God went into exile with the community of Israel, and it was the *Shekhinah* that went with them. The *Shekhinah* became known as the feminine face of God, and whenever Jews study the Torah or do good deeds, they experience God's feminine presence among themselves. Each mitzvah draws God's face closer, which could be seen in the face of the other in the camps. It is through our relationship and care of the other that we see God. In Jewish mystical tradition, the feminine face of God is known as the *Shekhinah*. It is the tenth and last sphere of the kabbalistic spheres, and the *Shekhinah* is the intermediary between the earthly realm and the higher realm.

The Jewish communities of Europe lived in a double exile under the Nazis. First, they lived in exile from the Holy Land because of the diaspora. Second, they were forcibly exiled by the Nazis from lands they had lived in for hundreds of years. The *Shekhinah* went with them into ghettos and concentration camps. Rabbinerin Jonas showed her people that God was indeed with the community of Israel and that God was reflected in their individual faces. As Gad Beck observed about Jonas, "Her synagogue was everywhere."[12] Beck's statement truly reflects the two theological names for God: one of the *Shekhinah* and the other *Ha-Makom*,[13] which literally means "the place and omnipresent." As Beck has observed, everywhere Rabbinerin Jonas went she created a place for God's dwelling. From the moment she received her ordination in December 27, 1935, about a month after the Nuremberg Laws stripped German Jews of their citizenship, Jonas showed her people that God did dwell among them, no matter what place they were living in. The laws severely restricted Jews in their movements and in the spaces where they could congregate, especially in identified Jewish spaces, such as synagogues.

In the beginning of her career, when she was a Fräulein Rabbinate Candidate, Jonas worked as a teacher in the Elisabeth Lyceum in Berlin Charlottenburg, The Helene Lange Städtische Mittelschule, and the Auguste Viktoria Schule, and taught Hebrew at the Jüdische Schule. When Jonas lost her job in the public schools, she taught at Jewish private schools. In 1937, her role as a rabbi expanded and her contract with the *Gemeinde* let her minister to and console the elderly and sick. This was what Jonas had envisioned in her ordination thesis, that a woman rabbi would have a unique capacity to teach youth and take care of the sick and elderly. She worked at the Jewish home for the elderly and in Jewish and non-Jewish hospitals – the Jüdisches Kranken-haus, the Lazarus Krankenhaus, the Städtisches Krankenhaus Pankow, and the Erwin Lieck Krankenhaus. Jonas describes one of the many roles of the rabbi: "He must work for social welfare, for youth welfare, and for general communal welfare ... [and] he must be available to help congregants with per-sonal matters related to the distress of the soul."[14] Now that the Jewish com-munity was in despair, Jonas's role as a spiritual counselor and caretaker of the community was especially needed. This was one of the meanings of serving her community and being with her community. It was when the community fell upon difficult times and more and more Rabbis were deported that Jonas actually crossed over and started to serve as a fully fledged woman rabbi.

Jonas gave lectures on the meaning of Judaism, including the meaning of liturgy, the Bible, and the Talmud. Jonas demanded that her community understand that they were chosen and blessed, not in the arrogant sense of being chosen, but in an enlightened sense that they were called to shine the light of God's presence in the world through acts of kindness. Prayer and study led to acts of kindness and compassion. Her audiences consistently reported how inspired they were and how they found new meaning in Juda-ism and in being drawn closer to God. These lectures were a tremendous source of spiritual sustenance for an oppressed community. Her messages were the same: we are a blessed people; we are a good people; it is our duty to bring good into the world and to treat each other with care, especially those less fortunate. These messages inspired resistance and gave Jews a sense of self-worth and pride in their heritage and in their community when the Nazis were treating them as less than animals.

One place where German Jews were allowed to gather was the synagogue. In her January 1936 article in *Jüdische Allgemeine Zeitung*, Frieda Valentin explains that her experience of meeting Jonas brought back her humanity and her feeling of connection. As noted earlier, Valentin concludes: "And when God has given the language and the word, which captivate people to be led towards God and prayers, he must carry in himself the calling to become a rabbinerin."[15]

In 1937, a 16-year-old pupil heard Rabbinerin Jonas's lecture in Hermsdorf Synagogue, where hundreds had gathered to hear her teaching. The unnamed 16-year-old left a manuscript describing what she learned from Rabbinerin Jonas's lecture:

> [Jonas] gave examples of biblical figures from the five books
> of Moses as models for our deeds and actions. ... And Jews in

particular are chosen to fight for the good, in order to bring it to the people. Jews are people of religion ... but the Jewish role in life is above all to plant the belief [faith] in God in all humanity.[16]

Jonas gave another lecture in Berlin at the Ohel Jizchok Synagogue, entitled "Current Religious Problems of the Jewish Community," on June 9, 1938. In the *Jüdisches Gemeindeblatt für Berlin* (Jewish community newsletter of Berlin) of June 26, 1938, reporter Karl Kloppholz comments on Jonas's lecture and its message:

> Many people in the world have thought about the origin of being. But the Jews ask categorically about the meaning of being. For the Jewish view of the world, the first sentence in the Bible is essential: "In the beginning God created heaven and earth." Here, belief becomes a demand, a demand on humankind to preserve the world and to strengthen the supremacy of God in this world. The task of Judaism arises out of this inner talent as a religious and cultural people. The becoming of the body of the Jewish community found completion in the destiny of the spirit of the people and therefore its national tradition. To be the chosen people does not mean for the Jewish people to be arrogant on the basis of a higher worth, but is a demand to complete the original religious–cultural task of community. Fate is above fatalism; fate is God-sent which humankind has to create positively for his life. Jews have always lived a life of solitude. Never did this solitude mean an escape from this world; it was always a way of humankind coming back to itself.
>
> Many ways lead to religion: prayers, learning and observance in daily life. Prayers have to shake man; the purpose of prayer is to transform man. Learning is a commandment that men and women have to obey equally. But learning is not just theory. The end of learning has to be the act.[17]

In this report of Jonas's lecture, we learn that Judaism does not care about ontology in the way Edith Stein, the philosopher, cared. Jonas's statement on ontology sheds light on why Jewish philosophers such as Rosenzweig, Buber, and Levinas may have developed an ethic and a philosophy of the divine relationship to the Other. (Buber was running *Lehrhaus Judaica* in Frankfurt until he escaped to Palestine in late 1937.) Jews care about meaning and relationship. The duty of Jews is to reveal God's presence in the world and to be stewards over the earth to protect it. This is not done through a contemplative practice of cutting oneself off from the world, but by revealing the face of God in the world through praying, learning, and observance of the *Halakha* in everyday life. Jews should follow the saying of the fathers: *on three things the world stands – on the Torah, on service to God, and on acts of kindness.* Jonas states that prayer transforms human beings and that learning guides humans to act in the world.

Observance of Jewish laws makes people recognize the sacredness in every day, every moment. Jewish laws such as keeping kosher make one conscious that a living being gave up its life for yours. Another law, observing the Sabbath, helps quiet the mind and brings people together in the synagogue and at home with family and the community of Israel in order to recognize the presence of God in the world. Jonas did not give specific examples of the meaning of these particular Jewish observances (at least in the documents that have been preserved), but the meaning of observance leads to a higher level of consciousness if observance is imbued with true intention. Blessings remind Jews of the sacredness of each moment.

Jonas lectured on and wrote an important commentary about the Yizkor service, which was the memorial service for the dead recited on Yom Kippur, the last day of Passover, the last day of Shavout, and the last day of the Feast of Tabernacles. The Yizkor service is traditionally recited at the end of the prayer service. It includes three distinct prayers. One is the Yizkor prayer itself, which is the prayer to ask God to remember the departed soul; the deceased's name is mentioned. The second prayer is El Male Rachamim, which carries the soul on the wings of the *Shekhinah* to eternal rest and asks God to grant eternal peace to the departed soul. The deceased's name is again mentioned. The last prayer is Av HaRachamim, which asks God to remember the Jewish communities that have been destroyed through the ages. In all three prayers the person reciting the prayer promises to give charity in the name of the deceased so that they may be remembered. The living person performs acts of kindness in the name of the dead. It was a custom among some Ashkanazic synagogues for Jews not reciting Yizkor to leave and only the mourners to stay.[18] Jonas thought differently. On May 24, 1939, Rabbinerin Jonas wrote a rabbinical commentary on the Yizkor for the *Jüdisches Nachrichtenblatt*, entitled "Above all the Celebration of Our Souls" ("Über alles die Seelen-Feier"):

> In recent times a rather *aggravating misbehavior* has developed. The Yizkor has begun when the youth (not only the children), as well as adults who still are fortunate to have their parents at their sides, leave the house of God and entertain themselves *outside* or in the courtyard with *leisurely gossip*. While on *sacred* ground solemn services take place, there are people who out of a wrong sentiment exclude themselves from the truly *impressive* part of our service.[19]

Klapheck points out that Jonas's commentary came at a very sad moment, six months after *Kristallnacht*. "It referred not only to the shock of the pogrom but also emphasized that once again time had put the Jews to the test."[20] Jonas shows that this test was for the Jewish community to realize that *Yizkor* was not a mourning of the souls of the deceased, but a celebration of our souls. In this article and later sermons Jonas teaches that we are not the *objects* of our fate but the *subjects* of fate, and the Yizkor service was one way that Jews could honor their destiny and have hopes for a future:

> We are living today in a time of trial by fire, testing the strength of our love for children, gratitude, the mutual support of family and friends in these alien conditions. Many people wanted, in spite of all obstacles, to preserve a true sense of Jewish family and people-hood. Our sages say that the Torah was only given to Israel when the people presented guarantees and only after they offered their children as guarantees to God. If worry and despondency seek our undoing, then we should think about *Yizkor* in such a way that we identify ourselves as *arevim tovim* [good guarantees], standing up for Israel, carrying on the work of our ancestors from Sinai: in that we today are truly their children and in that we are the par-ents of the future generations, then the chain does not break and we gain the strength to carry out nobly these historical responsi-bilities and to thank God that *Yizkor* has become the celebration of our souls.[21]

Jonas, like Stein, uses the image of fire, for the Jewish community was being tested by fire. Jewish families were being torn apart as men were deported to Dachau; children were being shipped off to distant lands. It did not look like the Jewish community had any hope of a future, any hope of seeing its children or families again. Jonas reminds the community that we have a past history that guarantees a future. When God gave the children of Israel the Torah, God wanted a promise of good guarantees for the life of the Torah in the future. The community responded that their children were the good guarantees. They were the future generation who were going to carry the Torah forward. Today's Jewish community represents the children going all the way back to Mt. Sinai, and they were the future. Jonas demands that the community understand the meaning of the Yizkor service: it connects Jewish heritage from Mount Sinai to the future. In the moment that one recites the Yizkor, one connects oneself with the past and guarantees the future. Jonas admonishes those not reciting Yizkor not to leave, for the Yizkor service honors all deceased parents and souls going back to Mt. Sinai. The present-day mourners are at once the children and guarantors of the future. By recit-ing prayers or being present as a community with those remembering their parents, we become the children of the past and the parents of the future of the Jewish community. Jonas shows how through these prayers we simul-taneously link ourselves to the past and future in the present moment by remembering that we are both child and parent. There is hope for the future, and this act of witnessing or reciting Yizkor was, as Jonas put, it "a celebration of our souls."

This sermon, which Jonas may have repeated at a Yizkor service on the last day of Passover, on April 8, 1942, gave one woman, Ruth Cronheim, a way to defy the Nazis. She had been comforted by Jonas's sermon, and it supported her in her decision to become pregnant with a second child even though others would think of her pregnancy as ridiculous under such horrible conditions. German–American feminist theologian Katharina von Kellenbach suggests that Ruth Cronheim might have decided to confide in Rabbinerin Jonas because she was a woman and because her desire to have a child was an act of defiance and resistance. Cronheim wrote Jonas a letter dated April 8, 1942, the last day of Passover, about the meaning of the comforting words that she heard during Rabbinerin Jonas's sermon. It "confirmed what I feel very strongly during these days – the miracle of life itself, and that one has much to be thankful to God for, even during the most difficult of times."[22] She explains to Rabbinerin Jonas that she was almost 32 years old, married to a good man, and had a four-year-old son. They had put off having a second child because of the political situation, and had let reason guide them as opposed to their feelings. Cronheim's parents had already been evacuated to the east and she had been in deep anguish and despair over her parents' deportation. She was working as a slave laborer. Ruth Cronheim and her husband made the decision for her to become pregnant. She wrote in her letter to Jonas:

> The thought of my [older] child and the ardent hope for a better future, however, helped me to recover. And now comes what most people will not understand. With every day of increasing improvement, the wish, yea, the determination to have another child grew ever stronger in me, to experience this joy one more time and to give our boy the longed for sister or brother. My husband, who just like myself had completely rejected this idea for "rational reasons" ... all of a sudden agreed that a second child can only bring happiness, because of the external circumstances. We have not taken this decision lightly but in faith in God and thus in our future.[23]

Perhaps after Cronheim heard Jonas's Yizkor sermon similar to the commentary she had presented earlier, Cronheim felt that her pregnancy was a good guarantee for the future, just as Israelites had given God their promise of their children as good guarantees for the Torah on Mount Sinai. Ruth Cronheim's pregnancy gave her hope for the future. She did give birth to a baby boy on December 13, 1942. Not three months later, on March 2, 1943, she, her two sons (Joel and Wolf), and her husband (Alfred) were deported to Auschwitz. They did not return.[24]

Cronheim gave birth to her younger son after Rabbinerin Jonas herself was deported to Theresienstadt with her mother, 68-year-old Sara Jonas, on November 6, 1942. Jonas had made arrangements to have her ordination thesis and other materials, including her ordination photo and sermon notes, deposited with the Jewish community archives that the Nazis were going to use as a museum once the world was *judenfrei* (free of all Jews). Some of these pictures can be seen in the reproductions printed earlier in this book.

SPIRITUAL RESISTANCE IN THERESIENSTADT

After her deportation, Regina Jonas continued her ministry, serving as a rabbi, spiritual counselor, and lecturer. She continued to bring the *Shekhinah* into Theresienstadt through her rabbinate. She demonstrated to her followers how to resist spiritually; she reminded them that they were blessed and meant to take care of each other. She worked for the Department for Psychological Hygiene, where Victor Frankl,[25] the famous psychiatrist from Vienna, was her boss. He wrote the well-known book *Man's Search for Meaning* based on his experiences in the camps, but never did mention Jonas in any of his writings.[26] Katharina von Kellenbach phoned Victor Frankl in 1991 and asked him about Regina Jonas. Did he remember her? He told von Kellenbach that he put Jonas on his staff because "she was a gifted preacher and speaker" and in addition was a "personality with energy" on whom one could depend.[27] One of her roles was to meet the transports from Germany at the train station, which was then a two-kilometer hike from the ghetto. The people arrived in total shock, having been told they were being resettled at a European spa or nice old-age community. "According to Frankl, this welcoming committee was crucial to soften the first shock, for people who had been deceived by the Nazis with tales of homes for the elderly in the East."[28] The Jews had used all their savings on their resettlement. Jonas guided them to their sleeping quarters, where usually 24 people slept in a room on some straw; many elderly Jews died of the shock. Frankl also told von Kellenbach about a lecture he remembered that Jonas gave:

> She [Jonas] was invited to lecture to the staff of the *Psycho-hygienisches Institut* [Mental Health Institute] about the theological connotations of this psychological work. She said that in the Jewish tradition, the mentally handicapped, the senile, and the degenerate's human dignity remains completely intact. By way of analogy, she told the story of Exodus when Moses received the stone tablets on Mount Sinai, which were carried along when the people of Israel wandered through the desert together with the old and the sick. *Carrying the Torah and carrying those who*

cannot walk by themselves are equivalent. The weak and aged must be treated with the same dignity as members of the community.[29]

Rabbinerin Jonas again reminds her fellow counselors and Jews that the *Shekhinah* is with them. God asked for a *mishkan* to be built so that the children of Israel could carry the tablets and so that God would dwell among them. They carried the *mishkan* with the tablets and God's presence with them at all times through their 40 years of wandering in the desert. Rabbinerin Jonas was demonstrating that the presence of God was especially evident among the mentally handicapped, the senile, and the elderly, and that the Jewish community must carry their more vulnerable members, just like the tablets. When the people of Israel carried the *mishkan* with them everywhere in the desert, they were carrying God's divine presence among them. When the Jews of Theresienstadt took care of the most helpless of the community of Israel, they were literally bringing God's divine presence with them into the concentration camp. This was a very powerful theology of resistance. What could be more sacred, more holy than to know that carrying the most helpless was carrying God's presence? Rabbinerin Jonas explained the true meaning of caring. This was the work that one did in a concentration camp. It was the work of bringing and carrying God's presence and seeing the divine spark in the faces of the neediest, for the most helpless brought it as a gift to be revealed by the suffering community of Israel. Nothing can be more holy: *Kodesh, Kodesh, Kodesh Hashem* – "Holy, Holy, Holy is thy Name."[30]

Rabbinerin Jonas took her rabbinate everywhere, just like the *mishkan*. Klapheck writes that one survivor remembered that the "Head Rabbi" did not recognize Jonas's rabbinical authority in any way because she was a woman:

> but this did not stop her from going to the women's quarters and talking about Jewish history, holidays and customs. The women always were pleased to see the *Rabbinerin*. Often they gave her a crust of bread as thanks, which Jonas always gave to her mother.[31]

Rabbinerin Jonas also gave lectures in Theresienstadt, and left a list with the Administration for Spiritual and Leisure Activities in Theresienstadt with the title "Lectures by the Only Female Rabbi, Regina Jonas." The topics included "From the World of the Talmud," "From the Saying and the Words," "Humor in the Talmud," "Figures in The First Book of Moses: an Encounter with God," "From Egypt to Sinai," "The Basic Idea of Judaism through Celebration," "Jewish Religion and the Modern Jew," "The Jewish Source of Strength," "The Content and Meaning of Prayer," "The Power of Prayer," "Jewish Youth and Judaism," "Father and Mother Problems in the Bible," "Woman in the Bible," "Woman in the Talmud," "The Position of Woman in Jewish History," "Rights and Duties of Jewish Women in Jewish Law," "The Jewish Woman as Bearer of Culture and of Jewish Salvation," and "What is a Mitzvah?"[32]

We can see from Jonas's lecture titles that they cover much of what she had written, taught, and preached before her deportation. We can only speculate what exactly she said in Theresienstadt. The lectures on woman in the Bible and the Talmud and the position of woman go back to her ordination thesis and to the lectures she gave to the Berlin Jewish community. The lecture on "The Jewish Woman as Bearer of Culture and of Jewish Salvation" may have addressed the importance of Jewish women learning Jewish texts and Hebrew liturgy. We saw in Chapter 4 that Jonas made a very strong argument for Jewish women to learn Jewish text and liturgy just like Jewish men, so that they could relate the spirit of Judaism to their children. Jonas made the point that Jewish children had a greater chance of turning away from Judaism if their mothers were not educated and could not understand the struggle that the child was going through living in a secular culture.

Another point Jonas might have made in these lectures on woman is noted in a lecture she gave at a "World International Zionist Organization Afternoon" in *the Jüdisches Gemeindeblatt für Berlin* on June 26, 1938. Rabbinerin Jonas declared: "the duty of woman to be, just like the female prophets, custodians and upholders of compassion and justice of all that is good and right of love and courtesy: *Where women enter, hate and enmity fall silent.*"[33] The lectures on "The Content and Meaning of Prayer" and "The Power of Prayer" could possibly reflect what Rabbinerin Jonas had said in the Yizkor commentary and sermon. The act of prayer has the power to transform human beings.

It is interesting that she had a lecture titled "Humor in the Talmud." Humor was one way of keeping people's minds off their horrific circumstances and of keeping up their spirits. Von Kellenbach notes that the Theresienstadt diary of Richard Ehrlich contains the following entry: "On June 4th, 1942 we heard a lecture by Rabbi Jonas in the attic of the home of the blind at Badhausgasse 19: 'From Egypt to Sinai.' The subject was treated very interestingly by the lecturer and especially interested us."[34] Rabbinerin Jonas left a powerful impression on those who heard her preach.

On the last page of the handwritten documents of Jonas's list and notes of lectures that she left in the Theresienstadt archive was a sermon that she gave. At the beginning of the sermon Rabbinerin Jonas writes a Hebrew verse from the story of Balaam, the soothsayer. King Balak of the Moabites engages the soothsayer Balaam to curse the Israelites so that he could beat them in battle and throw them off the land. Instead of Balaam cursing the Jews for King Balak he ends up blessing them. Jonas starts the sermon off with part of a verse from this part of the Torah, Numbers 22:12: "You must not curse the people for they are blessed." Then she starts to explain the meaning of the verse:

> Our Jewish people has been defined in history by God as being blessed. To be "blessed" by God means to bless, to do good and be loyal to others wherever one goes and in every situation. Humility

before God, selfless devoted love to his creatures preserves the world. It is the task of all Israel to build these foundations for the world – man and woman, woman and man are obligated as Jews to carry out this duty in equal measure. This ideal is served by our grave work at Theresienstadt, which puts us to the test as servants of God, and as such we turn from the earthly to the celestial sphere – May all our work be for the blessing of the future of Israel (and of humanity). ... Upright "J. men" and "brave noble women" were always the pillars of our people. May we be found worthy by God to be counted in the circle of these women and men.[35]

She signs the last page of the document at the end of this paragraph "Rabbinerin Jonas, formerly of Berlin."

King Balak of the Moabites is a metaphor for the Nazis. Rabbinerin Jonas is stating that every time the Nazis try to curse the Jews, to dehumanize the Jews, the Jews were blessed. They had been stripped of their citizenship; they had been stripped of their homes and all their possessions; their families had been shattered, torn apart, and gassed; there was nothing left for the Nazis to destroy except their bodies, but they could not destroy their souls or God's presence in their faces and among the community of Israel. God dwells in them and among them. To be blessed means that we take care of each other: We have "selfless devoted love to his [God] creatures [that] preserves the world."[36] It is the duty of every Jew, both male and female, to bring this selfless devoted love of God into the world.

This is the meaning of being a chosen people – that Jews were blessed in taking care of each other and taking care of all of the creatures of the world. In the act of caring and in the act of love is the face of God, living in the faces of those the Jews cared for. This is the deep meaning of the Jewish community's work in Theresienstadt, to evoke the presence of God dwelling in them and among them through selfless acts of love. It is within the community, not away from it, that God dwells. As Cantor Rita Glassman has reflected with regard to Jonas's rabbinate, Rabbinerin Jonas truly embodied God's name, "The Place," *Ha Makom*. The *Shekhinah* was with Israel and showed her face through these acts. Rabbinerin Jonas's teaching was spiritual resistance at the core, at the root. She had gone forth out of the land to the roots of her being, which was God's Being, and this brought her back to her community.

Rabbinerin Jonas, along with her mother Sara, was on the second to last deportation from Theresienstadt to Auschwitz. She was deported on October 12, 1944, the date that would have been Edith Stein's 53rd birthday. Stein had perished two years earlier. She had been taken by the Gestapo from her cloistered Carmel on August 2, 1942, the day before Rabbinerin Jonas's 40th birthday. Stein was brought back to the community of Israel to die with them. Rabbinerin Jonas had brought the presence of *Shekhinah* to the community of Israel and helped them to understand the inner meaning of their suffering,

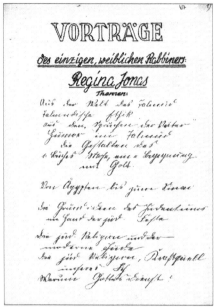

Figure 5 Regina Jonas's sermon notes from Theresienstadt (PT 4142/4, Terezin Memorial, Herman's Collection © Zuzana Dvorakova).

as she indicated in her notes and in the sermons she gave: "This ideal is served by our grave work at Theresienstadt, which puts us to the test as servants of God, and as such we turn from the earthly to the celestial sphere." The acts of selfless love were where God was present.

CONCLUSION

Rabbinerin Jonas and Sister Teresa Benedicta of the Cross were Hebrews, *Ivrim*. They had "crossed over" a river, just as their forefather Abram and foremother Sara had. Leaving their external conditions, the cultural territories of gender and religion in which they had grown up, drove them inward to their callings, to their true being. Both their paths were highly controversial and seemed at the time strange, queer, inconceivable. A woman could not be a rabbi; a Jewish woman who converted to Catholicism could not be a Jewish nun.

Both Jonas and Stein heeded the call of their paths, their deviant religious desires, and, no matter how outlandish their actions were perceived to be, they figured out a way to "become who they would become." The crumbling of the walls around them made their queer religious callings more obvious, and gave them a way to achieve and manifest spiritual resistance. Rabbinerin Jonas was probably able to break the barriers of the two-thousand-year-old rabbinate exactly because of the oppressive political conditions of her lifetime. A woman rabbi, a rabbinerin, could meet a vital need. Stein's inner truth was that of a Catholic Jew; this meant she identified with Jesus as a Jew. When conditions became unimaginable, Jonas and Stein did what they thought would redeem suffering for the community of Israel. Stein went to the Carmel and suffered on the cross for her people; Jonas brought her woman rabbinate to them, reminding Jews how each one had a responsibility to bring God's presence into the world. Rabbinerin Jonas stayed with her people and died with them. Sister Teresa died for them, but with them too, at the end, which was her way of ending suffering, a way to fill the world with God's love, a way to quench the flames of hell.

Sister Teresa Benedicta's offering herself up on the cross for the sins of her own people was highly controversial within the Jewish community of her time and will likely always remain so, for it expresses the nature of Catholic eschatology in the pre-Vatican II era. From the Jewish perspective, to die for the sin of your people's not accepting the Savior is to deny their voice, their existence. Many other Catholic and Protestant priests and nuns who had been put to death by the Nazis and who had not been born Jews never mentioned in their last wills and testaments or in their letters that they were suffering and dying for the sins of the Jews.[37]

However, Stein was not the only Jewish nun who understood her sacrifice this way. A Trappist nun, Sister M. Magdalena Dominica, also known as

Dr Meirowsky, was rounded up with Stein. She wrote a letter to her Father confessor in Tilburg just before deportation from Westerbork to Auschwitz on August 6, 1942:

> We go as children of our mother, the holy Church; we want to join our sufferings to the sufferings of our King, Savior, and Bridegroom and to offer them in sacrifice for the conversion of many souls, for the Jews, for those who persecute us, and thus before all else for peace in the kingdom of Christ.[38]

How do we explain Stein's personal interpretation of her suffering and the Jewish community's suffering? Stein was a Catholic Jew, not a Jewish Catholic. To be a Catholic Jew means that one has become enlightened by the new covenant and accepts that Jesus was the Redeemer, who came from the same Jewish community that Jews still belong to and are a living part of. Jews do not see Jesus as the Redeemer, and they will not be redeemed by accepting Him as the Savior. This is not the Jewish path. Stein's acceptance of this truth redeemed her and gave her life meaning and a way to resist. If she had been a Jewish Catholic she would have accepted that the Jewish community did not need to be saved by her suffering for their sin of not accepting Jesus as the Messiah. She would see this suffering as her own personal suffering, having meaning only to and for her. The Jewish Jesus was not the Savior of the Jewish community, but he was hers.

One Catholic scholar described how Stein appeared from the window of the train of cattle cars traveling east:

> The woman in the window, small but by no means tiny or fragile-looking, was dressed in the dark clothes that immediately identified her as a Carmelite nun. Her large, warm, intelligent eyes and her small, sad mouth were framed by a white coif and black veil that hung down over a brown tunic and scapular. Fastened incongruously to the scapular was a yellow cloth star of David in the center of which was printed the word *Jood,* Dutch for "Jew," which by law all Jews in the Reich and conquered provinces were forced to wear.[39]

We now have a way of understanding this strange sight; the dress and performance of Stein did speak to her inner truth. She was a nun who in her interior life did see herself as a Jew suffering for the Jewish community by offering herself as a burnt sacrifice on a cross. This was her truth, regardless of how the Jewish community perceived it. The nun embraced the Jewish star as Jesus' Jewish star. What the Jewish nun showed us was that through her suffering, divine love did flow from the wounded Jew on the cross into her heart, where it gave her inner serenity and peace in the face of her impending death.

What about Rabbinerin Jonas, a woman rabbi wearing the traditional male rabbinical robes and rabbi cap without a *tallit* (prayer shawl)? She demonstrated through her rabbinate the presence of God in the acts of love which the community of Israel had been chosen to perform. Her role as woman rabbi broadened the membership of the rabbinate and reminded the rabbinate and the community that women had obligations equal to those of their male counterparts and that women brought a special intuitive role to the rabbinate, with compassion and understanding.

We have used queer theory to unravel these women's religious desires and practices. We have shown through the comparison of Edith Stein queering religion and Regina Jonas queering gender that their cases simultaneously demonstrate an allegiance to their multiple communities of belonging and a disruption of normative cultural boundaries, creating a new, multifaceted, mixed identity that is both an ethical stance and a form of spiritual resistance.

I have described their messages of spiritual resistance – of being true to oneself, of being true to one's calling, and of not letting oppression stand in the way of one's spiritual truth. These women stood up for and demonstrated divine love, and inspired compassion for the divinity in every human being. They showed that one gender, one religion, one so-called "race" will not limit this message. Compassion and divine love break down the limits of binary discourse. They teach us that it is our job to align ourselves with our true beings, and that when we do, we broaden – not just for ourselves – the notion of gender, religion, and humanity within a system that seeks to reduce the concept of humanity to either/or. What Stein and Jonas have demonstrated is that each one of us is like a snowflake with our own unique beauty and gifts, which no binary understanding of identity can melt.

Chapter 7

A THEOLOGY OF RESISTANCE AS
LIBERATION IN THE DEATH CAMPS

I discovered Edith Stein and Regina Jonas as the culmination of my journey to still the heart palpitations and cold sweats caused by my nightmares of the Holocaust. Along the way, I discovered a book, *Hasidic Tales of the Holocaust*, which had one story, "Jew, Go Back to the Grave," which speaks to me even today. This story shows a further example of crossing over and a double-take as integral to stories of spiritual resistance and liberation. It is the story of Zvi, the sixteen-year-old son of Reb Michalowsky, who survived a mass execution organized by the *Einsatzgruppen* and carried out by local Lithuanians. After the execution, Zvi miraculously managed to crawl out of a mass grave of hundreds of dead and dying bodies. He was naked, with blood dripping down him, and went to seek help among the local Christians:

> Near the forest lived a widow whom Zvi knew too. He decided to knock on her door. The old widow opened the door. She was holding in her hand a small, burning piece of wood. "Let me in!" begged Zvi. "Jew, go back to the grave at the old cemetery!" She chased Zvi away with the burning piece of wood as if exorcising an evil spirit, a dybbuk.
> "I am your lord, Jesus Christ. I came down from the cross. Look at me – the blood, the pain, the suffering of the innocent. Let me in," said Zvi Michalowsky. The widow crossed herself and fell at his blood-stained feet. "*Boże moj, Boże moj* (my God, my God)," she kept crossing herself and praying. The door was opened.
> Zvi walked in. He promised her that he would bless her children, her farm, and her, but only if she would keep his visit a secret for three days and three nights and not reveal it to a living soul, not even the priest. She gave Zvi food and clothing and warm water to wash himself. Before leaving the house, he once more reminded her that the Lord's visit must remain a secret, because of his special mission on earth.

Dressed in a farmer's clothing, with a supply of food for a few days, Zvi made his way to the nearby forest. Thus, the Jewish partisan movement was born in the vicinity of Eisysky.[1]

Zvi, in a brilliant survival tactic, literally realizes that what would save him is to awaken compassion in his enemy. He makes the Lithuanian woman see his humanity. He uses her own theology to save himself. He instinctively knew that Jesus' blood was his own blood. At first, Zvi was a dirty Jew, with dirty blood. On the double-take, he is the Savior with holy blood. The new meaning to his physical blood from the bullet wound rescues him from being slaughtered. Zvi demonstrates a spiritual resistance that liberated him, as well as liberating the Lithuanian widow to help him survive.

I begin and end the book with "the double-take." The book opened up with images of Stein, a Catholic Jewish Carmelite nun in her black habit with a Jewish star on her scapular, in Westerbork, a round-up camp. Regina Jonas wore the robes of a male rabbi, which she claimed as a rabbinerin, a woman rabbi. The tale of Zvi Michalowsky's survival based on the meaning of his physical blood pouring out of his body is a crossing over. At first he is a dirty Jew, and then he crosses over to being a God. For Zvi, turning himself into Jesus Christ the Savior saves his life. Stein believed she died "for" her people. Even though she thought she was dying for her people, she was also dying for herself. She needed to suffer and experience grace in order to experience God's eternal love. Regina Jonas did not have to suffer in the same way; for her it was apparent. We create the space to receive God's love when we perform acts of *mitzvoth.*

Even for those who did not survive, spiritual resistance was possible. Although they both died in the gas chambers, Stein and Jonas did not go back to the grave. They died with powerful voices that gave their community strength and dignity. I grew up hearing that the Jews who did not join the resistance were simply lambs who went to the slaughter. Stein's and Jonas's spiritual resistance gives us a different way of looking at Jewish agency during the Holocaust. This is not sheep going to the slaughter, it is preserving your human dignity, your humanity, your compassion. This is liberation and resistance at the same time.

Ultimately Stein and Jonas show us a liberation theology[2] of resistance in the time of the death camps.

GLOSSARY

Gemarah. *See* Talmud.

Halakha. Deriving from the word "to walk" or "the way," it is the law or legal code. A *Halakhic* Jew is one who observes the legal code.

Hasidic. Derived from Hasidism, which is a populous movement begun in the eighteenth century by the Baal Shem Tov in eastern Europe. 'Hasid' means loving-kindness or piety. The Baal Shem Tov taught that one can worship God through joy, and it was a response to the dry legalistic approach of strictly studying the Talmud and observing the legal code without embracing the joy. It appealed to the poor Jews of eastern Europe to follow the *Halakha* from a place of feeling God's loving kindness. There are many different sects of Hasidim, with Lubavitch being the most well known.

Kabbalah. The Jewish mystical tradition. Specifically, the term Kabbalah means "to receive." The teachings of the esoteric tradition were "received" by one rabbi from another within in these circles. Usually Kabbalah deals with a particular set of Jewish medieval mystical texts and teachings written between the thirteenth and sixteenth centuries. These texts contemplate and explicate the emanations of God as the ten *sephirort* and four levels of the soul and the four levels of creation.

Mishkan. God's dwelling place or tabernacle, originally carried in the desert for forty years.

Mishnah. *See* Talmud.

Phenomenology. The study of the essence of phenomena as it appears to our consciousness. It is an examination of things of themselves, developed by early-twentieth-century philosopher Edmund Husserl. He developed a method known as the epoché, which is the bracketing of everything that would stand in the way of our experience and consciousness of the essence of thing it itself.

Rambam. Hebrew acronym for Rabbi Moses Maimonides (1135–1204). He was a preeminent Jewish philosopher, rabbi, and doctor. He was born in Spain and emigrated to Cairo. He wrote many philosophical and legal treatises.

Scapular. Part of the habit of the Catholic monastic orders. It is from the word scapula, meaning shoulder, and goes from shoulder to shoulder over the habit. Long ones go down to the feet, short ones are half the size.

Shulchan Aruch. A compendium of Jewish observant laws put together by Rabbi Joseph Karo (1488–1575) in the sixteenth century. It literally means "long table."

Talmud. Oral law of the Jewish tradition. The Talmud was redacted by the Rabbis between the second century BCE to the sixth century CE in Palestine and Babylonia. The first part is the Mishnah, the second part is the Gemarah. The Mishnah codified into 63 tractates the 613 laws that are found in the Torah. The Mishnah are divided into six volumes.

Tefillin. (English: Phylactery). Two small black leather boxes with leather straps that are wrapped around the arm and around the head. Traditionally, male Jews wear them on weekday mornings when they pray. It goes back to the biblical commandment (Deut. 6:5-8) known as the VeHavat, "Thou shall love the lord thy God with all thy soul with all thy might."

Tikkun Olam. ("To repair the world"). Our duties as human beings are to repair the broken vessels, which shattered by the light when the world was created. Our acts of doing good deeds – *mitzvoth* – help repair the world. This concept is explicated in sixteenth-century Lurianic Kabbalah.

Tzitzit. Tassels that hang down from the four corners of a shawl traditionally worn by men during times of prayer. Orthodox and Hasidic Jewish men wear small *tzitzit* under their garments during the day. It is a reminder to perform *mitzvoth* to bring us closer to God.

Torah. The five books of Moses, made up of Genesis, Exodus, Leviticus, Numbers, and Deuteronomy. The Jews are commanded to study Torah, which in a broad sense can comprise the entire Tanakh, which includes the Torah, the Prophets, and the Writings.

Tur. Acronym for the treatise Arba Turim for Rabbi Jacob ben Asher (1269–1340). The treatise dealt with the laws that were used after the destruction of the Temple. It was the basis for the Shulchan Aruch.

NOTES

1. WHY EDITH STEIN? WHY REGINA JONAS?

1. "KL" meant Konzentrations lager, a concentration camp, as I learned later when I researched the Holocaust.
2. Gershom Scholem, *Major Trends in Jewish Mysticism* (New York: Schocken Books, 1961).
3. Hannah Arendt, *Eichmann in Jerusalem: A Report on The Banality of Evil* (New York: Viking, 1963).
4. Claude Lanzmann (dir.), *Shoah* (New York: New Yorker Films, 1985).
5. Yaffa Eliach, *Hasidic Tales of the Holocaust* (New York: Oxford University Press, 1982).
6. Ruth Callmann, life-long Board Member of Congregation Bani Emunah, San Francisco. May her memory be for a blessing. Born in Berlin, 1918, died in San Francisco, 2011. Rabbinerin Jonas showed up at her mother's house once concerned about the lack of Ruthie's interest in Judaism.
7. Edith Stein, *Self-Portrait in Letters, 1916–1942*, ed. L. Gelber & Romanus Leuven, trans. Josephine Koeppel (Washington, DC: Institute of Carmelite Studies [ICS] Publications, 1993), 54, letter dated February 12, 1928.
8. I thank Dirk von der Horst, PhD for this insight into Jonas and Stein.
9. Lukas Rügenberg & Carla Junges, *Edith Stein: Ein Bilderbuch von Lukas Ruegenberg, erzählt von Carla Jungels* (Kevelaer: Butzon & Berker, 1997).
10. Joyce Averch Berkman, "The German-Jewish Symbiosis in Flux," in *Contemplating Edith Stein*, ed. Joyce Averch Berkman (Notre Dame, IN: University of Notre Dame, 2006), 286–7.
11. Rachel Feldhay Brenner, *Writing As Resistance: Four Women Confronting the Holocaust, Edith Stein, Simone Weil, Anne Frank, Etty Hillesium* (University Park, PA: Pennsylvania State University Press, 1997), 63.
12. I thank my colleague, Sr Susan Maloney, for pointing this out when I presented a paper on Edith Stein. Arizona State University AAR Western Region, 2010.
13. P. O. Kempen, "Eyewitness in Westerbork," in *Never Forget: Christian and Jewish Perspective on Edith Stein*, ed. Waltraud Herbstrith, trans. Susanne Batzdorff (Washington, DC: ICS Publications, 1998), 278.
14. Katrina von Kellenbach, "'God Does Not Oppress Any Human Being': The Life and Thought of Rabbi Regina Jonas," *Leo Baeck Institute: Yearbook* 39 (1994), 13–225.
15. Sara Ahmed, *Queer Phenomenology: Orientations, Objects, Others* (Durham, NC: Duke University Press, 2006), 161.
16. See Charles Taylor, *Sources of the Self: The Making of the Modern Identity* (Cambridge, MA: Harvard University Press, 1989). See also Cressida Heyes, "Identity Politics,"

Stanford Encyclopedia of Philosophy, Edward N. Zalta (ed.), http://plato.stanford.edu/ entries/identity-politics (accessed June 6, 2007).

17. Hannah Arendt, *The Human Condition* (Chicago, IL: University of Chicago Press, 1958), 178.
18. *Ibid.*, 179 (emphasis added).
19. Franz Fanon, *Black Skin White Masks*, trans. Charles Lam Markam (New York: Grove Press, 1967), 4.
20. Hannah Arendt, *The Jew as Pariah: Jewish Identity and Politics in the Modern Age*, ed. Ron H. Feldman (New York: Grove Press, 1978), 246.

2. STEIN'S AND JONAS'S VIEWS OF WOMEN: THE PHILOSOPHY STUDENT AND THE RABBINICAL STUDENT

1. Stein had women friends who were also studying philosophy and doing PhDs not only in philosophy but in mathematics. Nellie Courant *née* Neumann received her PhD in mathematics. Grete Henschel dropped out. There were a number of women who enrolled in Hochschule to become religious school teachers. We do not know how many of them would have pursued the rabbinate had not World War II broken out.
2. Harriet Pass Freidenreich, *Female, Jewish, Educated: The Lives of Central European University Women* (Bloomington, IN: Indiana University Press, 2002).
3. See Marion A. Kaplan, *The Jewish Feminist Movement in Germany: The Campaigns of the Jüdischer Frauenbund, 1904–1938* (Westport, CT: Greenwood Press, 1979); and Pamela Susan Nadell, *Women Who Would be Rabbis: A History of Women's Ordination, 1889–1985* (Boston, MA: Beacon Press, 1998).
4. Nellie Courant divorced Richard Courant. She managed to get her PhD in mathematics and taught in Essen in the 1930s, but was later sent away and killed in Minsk in 1942. Edith Stein, *Life in a Jewish Family: Her Unfinished Autobiographical Account*, ed. Dr. L. Gelber & Romaeus Leuven, trans. Josephine Koeppel (Washington, DC: ICS Publications, 1986), 502, n.182.
5. See Kaplan, *The Jewish Feminist Movement in Germany*.
6. *Ibid.*, 7.
7. Edith Stein, "The Ethos of Women's Professions," in *Essays on Woman*, trans. Frieda Mary Oben (Washington, DC: ICS Publications, 1987), 45.
8. Renate Bridenthal, Atina Grossman, and Marion Kaplan, *When Biology Became Destiny: Women in Weimar and Nazi Germany* (New York: Monthly Review Press, 1984), 13.
9. Stein, *Life in a Jewish Family*, 396.
10. Preserved in the Archive of the Stiftung Neue Synagoge Berlin–Centrum Judaicum.
11. Jonas's diploma is preserved in the Archive of the Stiftung Neue Synagoge Berlin–Centrum Judaicum.
12. Scott Edgar, "Hermann Cohen," *Stanford Encyclopedia of Philosophy*, ed. Edward N. Zalta, http://plato.stanford.edu/entries/cohen (accessed September 22, 2012).
13. Stein, *Life in a Jewish Family*, 218.
14. Max Scheler, *The Nature of Sympathy*, trans. Peter Heath (London: Routledge, 1954).
15. *Ibid.*, 376.
16. Edith Stein, "On The Problem of Empathy," in *On the Problem of Empathy*, trans. Waltraut Stein (Washington, DC: ICS Publications, 1989), 3.
17. *Ibid.*, 5.
18. Alisdair MacIntyre, *Edith Stein: A Philosophical Prologue, 1913–1922* (Lanham, MD: Rowman & Littlefield, 2006), 77.
19. For a fuller explication of Stein's theory of empathy, see Joseph Redfield Palmisano, SJ, *Beyond the Walls: Abraham Joshua Heschel and Edith Stein on the Significance of Empathy for Jewish-Christian Dialogue* (Oxford: Oxford University Press, 2012), 68–9.

20. *Ibid.*, 64.
21. For more on the difference between Kant and Husserl, see MacIntyre, *Edith Stein*, which gives an excellent explication of phenomenology and Edith Stein.
22. Stein, "On the Problem of Empathy," 19 (emphasis added).
23. *Ibid.*
24. *Ibid.*, 117.
25. *Ibid.*, 118.
26. Stein, *Life in a Jewish Family*, 397.
27. Marianne Sawicki, *Body, Text, Science: The Literacy of Investigative Practices and the Phenomenology of Edith Stein* (Dordrecht: Kluwer, 1997), 188.
28. Edith Stein, "Letter 36," from *Self-Portrait in Letters*, 44.
29. Edith Stein, "Problems of Women's Education," in *Essays on Woman*, 147.
30. *Ibid.*, 149–50.
31. Stein, *Life in a Jewish Family*, 191.
32. Stein, "Problems of Women's Education," 173.
33. *Ibid.*
34. *Ibid.*, 174 (emphasis added).
35. *Ibid.*
36. *Ibid.*, 182.
37. *Ibid.* Stein was probably not aware of a prayer that is usually sung at the end of a Jewish service, "Adon O'lom" ("Lord of the World"), which states that God has no beginning and no end; God has no form. Stein did not know Hebrew, but she must have heard it sung in synagogue, since she went with her mother to services. Stein claims she is not taking a theological stance here, but the philosophy of Being and Non-Being goes back to the early pre-Socratic Greeks in Western philosophy.
38. *Ibid* (emphasis original).
39. *Ibid.*, 174.
40. *Ibid.*, 184.
41. *Ibid.*, 187.
42. *Ibid.*
43. *Ibid.*
44. *Ibid.*, 187–8.
45. *Ibid.*, 188.
46. *Ibid.*, 188–9.
47. *Ibid.*, 186 (emphasis original).
48. *Ibid.*, 198.
49. *Ibid.*
50. *Ibid.*
51. *Ibid.* When Stein states that Mary is "against the tradition" of her people, she is also indirectly referencing herself and her community of descent and origin as a Jew. Stein's identification that the Son of God was born a Jew and died as a Jew shows up in her personal writing, as does Stein's personally identifying with Jesus' Jewish identity.
52. *Ibid.*, 199 (emphasis added).
53. Stein, "Ethos of Women's Professions," 54. See also Arlie Hochschild's *The Second Shift* (New York: Viking, 1989).
54. *Ibid.*
55. *Ibid.* Although Stein never became a mother, she had much experience with observing her sisters and mother managing work life and family. Just finding the time to write this dissertation, I experience this stress that Stein is talking about. The women who have been helping me in the process of finishing my work – from copy-editing to baby-sitting my children to cleaning my house – themselves are parenting children, and I know they feel this same angst. My husband has taken on the double burden that most women go

through, so that I can finish writing. I constantly feel the guilt as I take the time to finish up this project.

56. *Ibid.*, 50–51.
57. *Ibid.*, 49 (emphasis original).
58. *Ibid.*
59. *Ibid.*
60. *Ibid.*
61. *Ibid.*, 50.
62. Mala Laaser, *Frauenblatt C. V. Zeitung*, June 23, 1938 (trans. Dagmar Theison, 2007).
63. Regina Jonas, "Halachic Treatise: Can Women Serve as Rabbis?" in Elisa Klapheck, *Fräulein Rabbiner Jonas: The Story of the First Woman Rabbi* (San Francisco, CA: Jossey-Bass), 161.
64. Anon., "Enough is Enough! Against the Masculinization of Women," in *The Weimar Republic Sourcebook*, ed. Anton Kaes, Martin Jay & Edward Dimendberg (Berkeley, CA: University of California Press, 1994), 659.
65. Jonas, "Can Women Serve as Rabbis?," 161 (emphasis original).
66. Anon., "Enough is Enough!," 659.
67. *Ibid.*
68. *Ibid.*
69. Jonas, "Can Women Serve as Rabbis?," 123.
70. *Ibid.*, 133 (emphasis original).
71. Rabbi Ted Alexander, interview by author, Danville, CA, July 19, 2007; Kaplan, *The Jewish Feminist Movement in Germany*, 81.
72. Laaser, *C. V. Zeitung*, June 23, 1938.
73. Jonas, "Can Women Serve as Rabbis?," 161 (emphasis original).
74. Klapheck, *Fräulein Rabbiner Jonas*, 33.
75. Moses Maimonides (1135–1204) lived in Spain and then Cairo. He was a revered Rabbinical Sage and philosopher who codified Jewish law from Talmud into a book, *Mishneh Torah*, and wrote a philosophical treatise known as *The Guide for the Perplexed*.
76. Joseph M. Malham, *By Fire into Light: Four Catholic Martyrs of the Nazi Camps* (Leuven: Peeters, 2002), 198.
77. Ultra-Orthodox and Hasidic women today may not wear habits, but they do wear wigs or scarves that fully cover every strand of hair; beneath are long dresses or skirts with white or black stockings. Every body part is covered, up to their chin.
78. Jonas's ordination thesis might have been the first attempt to explicate women and *Halakha* from a woman's perspective. Jonas would have been impressed with the scholarship of the following ground-breaking feminist scholars and their work: Rachel Biale's *Women and Jewish Law: An Exploration of Women's Issues in Halakhic Sources* (New York: Schocken Books, 1984); Judith Romeny Wegner's *Chattel or Person?: The Status of Women in the Mishnah* (New York: Oxford University Press, 1988); and Judith Hauptman's *Rereading the Rabbis: A Woman's Voice* (Boulder, CO: Westview Press, 1997).
79. Jonas, "Can Women Serve as Rabbis?," 104.
80. These holy texts to which Jonas refers include *Mishnah Torah* by Moses Maimonides (1135–1204), *The Tur* by Jacob ben Asher (*c.*1270–*c.*1340) and *Shulchan Aruch* by Joseph Karo (1488–1575). All three of these texts explicate Jewish laws.
81. Liberal Jews did not believe in divine revelation, but that *Halakha* evolved and was shaped by time and culture.
82. See Biale, *Women and Jewish Law*. She does an excellent job of explaining all these laws.
83. I once commented to the late Amos Funkenstein that after I became a mother I finally understood why women were not obligated to time-bound *mitzvoth*. I had always thought these laws to be so sexist, but then I realized that parenting is demanding

enough to be prohibitive of time-bound *mitzvoth*. Amos responded that he, as a single father who raised two children by himself, also identified with the rabbis' ruling that women were not obligated to fulfill time-bound *mitzvoth*. Amos said that he thought it should apply to any parent staying home and raising children.

84. These were *shomer niddah*, the baking and separating of the challah, and the lighting of the Sabbath candles on Friday evening to welcome the Sabbath. *Shomer niddah* refers to the laws of family purity: at the end of a woman's menstrual cycle, she is to go to the ritual bath known as the *Mikvah* to purify herself for her husband. During the time she is menstruating she cannot have sexual relations with her husband until after the *Mikvah*. This is still practiced in the Orthodox communities. The second law dictates that each week, when she bakes challah for the Shabbat meals, she must separate a piece of the challah to be put aside in recognition of the tithing that was offered to the high priest during the time of the Temple. The third law governs the lighting of the Sabbath candles.

85. Jonas, "Can Women Serve as Rabbis?," 141 (emphasis original).

86. In America, Ray Frank was a lay preacher. In 1903, Henrietta Szold became the first woman to study at the Jewish Theological Seminary. Szold was also learned in philosophy and wrote academic articles as a teenager for the Jewish paper. For more on Szold, see the biography by Irving Fineman, *Woman of Valor: The Life of Henrietta Szold* (New York: Simon & Schuster, 1961). In spite of her erudition, Szold was forbidden to become a Rabbi. In 1922, Martha Neumark sought ordination in the Reform movement. In England, Lily Montague was the founder of the Liberal Jewish movement (see Klapheck, *Fräulein Rabbiner Jonas*). See also Nadell, *Women Who Would be Rabbis*.

87. Noted Jewish feminist theologian Judith Plaskow states that "feminism is the process of coming to affirm ourselves as women/persons and seeing that affirmation mirrored in religious and social institutions." See Plaskow's *Standing at Sinai Alone: Judaism from a Feminist Perspective* (San Francisco, CA: Harper San Francisco, 1991). Traditional Judaism has been defined by the male normative experience as men have named and defined for women their own experiences. The images of women, God, ritual, and law have been constructed from heterosexual male perspectives throughout Jewish history. There has been no room in the past for the voices of women and others. Feminism is the movement within Judaism that reclaims and reconstructs the voices of women (and, increasingly, those of gays and lesbians). Key works by Jewish feminists include Susannah Heschel's *On Being a Jewish Feminist* (New York: Schocken Books, 1983) and Rachel Adler's *Engendering Judaism: An Inclusive Theology and Ethics* (Philadelphia, PA: Jewish Publication Society, 1997).

Modern Orthodox feminists such as Blu Greenberg have called for women's voices to be heard, and for women to have access to the texts. Blu Greenberg's views in *On Women and Judaism: A View from Tradition* (Philadelphia, PA: Jewish Publication Society of America, 1998) would overlap with Jonas's, with the exception that Jonas called for female ordination.

88. Jonas, "Can Women Serve as Rabbis?," 108.

89. *Ibid.*

90. See Proverbs 31:10.

91. Jonas, "Can Women Serve as Rabbis?," 109–10.

92. *Ibid.*, 108. The Hebrew word *binah* – understanding, insight – is derived from *bana*, to build. *Binah* is also the name of the third of the kabbalistic spheres, known as the Divine Mother. This sphere is the opposite of the second sphere, *hokmah*, which is a male quality known as Wisdom. I would interpret *binah* as feminine intelligence and intuition.

93. *Ibid.*, 110.

94. *Ibid.*, 189.

95. Marcus Jastrow & Henrietta Szold, "Beruriah," www.jewishencyclopedia.com/view.

jsp?artid=940&letter=B (accessed April 15, 2008). Jonas, "Can Women Serve as Rabbis?," 112.

96. Jonas, "Can Women Serve as Rabbis?," 112. Jewish feminists today still lament the harsh blow that the Talmud deals against the brilliant woman sage Beruriah. See Rachel Adler's "The Virgin in the Brothel and the Other Anomalies of Character and Context in the Legend of Beruria," *Tikkun* (November/December 1988), 28–32, 102–5.
97. Jonas, "Can Women Serve as Rabbis?," 111.
98. *Ibid.*
99. *Ibid.*, 133.
100. *Ibid.*, 111.
101. *Ibid.*, 142–3.
102. Susanne M. Batzdorff, *Aunt Edith: The Jewish Heritage of a Catholic Saint* (Springfield, IL: Templegate,1998), 188 (emphasis original).
103. Stein, *Life in a Jewish Family*, 195.
104. Susanne and Adolf Batzdorff, interview by author, Santa Rosa, CA, 17 July 2007. Susanne showed me the very same prayer book, passed down to her by her aunt.
105. Jonas, "Can Women Serve as Rabbis?," 141 (emphasis original).
106. Batzdorff, *Aunt Edith*, 197.
107. *Ibid.*
108. Jonas, "Can Women Serve as Rabbis?," 141.
109. *Ibid.*
110. Batzdorff, *Aunt Edith*, 191.
111. Julius Guttmann, *Philosophies of Judaism: The History of Jewish Philosophy from Biblical Times to Franz Rosenzweig* (New York: Holt, Rinehart, & Winston, 1964).
112. Stein, *Life in a Jewish Family*, 213.
113. See my essay, Emily Leah Silverman, "On the Frontiers of Faith: Edith Stein Offers Herself as a Burnt Offering," *Hebrew Studies* 51 (2010), 375–8, for a closer examination of the difference between a Jewish understanding of Stein's conversion and her own perception.
114. Stein, "Ethos of Women's Professions," 55.

3. ST TERESA BENEDICTA OF THE CROSS REVEALS THE WHOLE MEGILLAH AS EDITH STEIN

1. Edith Stein, *The Hidden Life: Hagiographic Essays, Meditations, Spiritual Texts*, ed. Lucy Gelber & Michael Linssen, trans. Waltraut Stein (Washington, DC: ICS Publications, 1992), vii.
2. Stein, *Self-Portrait in Letters*, 291.
3. Stein "married" Christ when she joined the Carmelite order.
4. I take the term from the title of Hannah Arendt's book. She states that "even in the darkest of times we have the right to expect some illumination, and that such illumination may well come less from theories and concepts than from the uncertain, flickering, and often weak light that some men and women, in their lives and their works, will kindle under almost all circumstances and shed over the time span that was given them on earth." Hannah Arendt, *Men in Dark Times* (New York: Harcourt Brace Jovanovich, 1968), ix. Esther's and Stein's stories shed some of this light by virtue of their attempts to save the Jewish people.
5. The name Esther comes from the Aramaic "I am Hiding."
6. I use an amalgam of both terms – autobiography and biography – to describe *Life in a Jewish Family* because while she claims in the foreword that she is writing a biography of her mother, she later switches to focus on her own personal development. As we will

see, this slippage is of no mean consequence to our analysis of Stein's self-concept as a Jew.

7. I use this contemporary model deliberately: the compelling parallels between the "outing" or revelation of queer identity and the "outing" of her religious identity will be illuminated in the final section of the paper.

8. The Carmelites found it significant that she was gassed on Tisha B'av; as we will see later, her birthday was on Yom Kippur.

9. Here I use Jean-Francois Lyotard's term "postmodern" to describe our current condition, in which we no longer think in grand, universal totalities. He says: "Let us wage war on totality; let us be witness to the unpresentable; let us activate the differing and save the honor of the name." Jean-Francois Lyotard, *The Postmodern Condition: A Report on Knowledge*, trans. Geoff Bennington & Brian Massumi (Minneapolis, MN: University of Minnesota Press, 1984), 82.

10. Stein, *Self-Portrait in Letters*, 144.

11. Waltraud Herbstrith, *Edith Stein: A Biography*, trans. Father Bernard Bonowitz (San Francisco, CA: Ignatius Press, 1985), 120.

12. Stein, *Self-Portrait in Letters*, 160.

13. In Stein, *Life in a Jewish Family*, 18. Erna Biberstein, *née* Stein, followed her husband to America in 1939 and survived the war; she wrote these reminiscences in 1949.

14. *Ibid.*

15. We should note that Stein's use of this imagery stems directly from her Carmelite theology, and conveys a great deal. The image of the cross and who carries it is critical: in every room of the convent nuns see the *empty* cross; it is above their beds, in their dining hall, even on their bedcovers. The omnipresence of the cross is meant to continually remind the sisters that it is *they* who bear the responsibility to carry on Christ's work; his martyrdom did not end a process of human duty but rather begins one. Caroline LaLande, formerly Sister Clemencia of the Los Angeles Carmel, personal interview, July 4, 1998.

16. Herbstrith, *Edith Stein*, 119.

17. *Ibid.*, 122.

18. Stein, *Life in a Jewish Family*, 23.

19. Indeed, at other points in her (auto)biography Stein notes that there were prejudices against Jews in certain career paths.)

20. *Ibid.*

21. *Ibid.* (emphasis added).

22. Susanne Batzdorff, "Witnessing My Aunt's Beatification," in *The Unnecessary Problem of Edith Stein*, ed. Henry James Cargas (New York: University Press of America, 1994), 31.

23. In his introduction to Herbstrith's biography of Stein, Jan Nota says that "prior to 1933, Edith Stein was one of the few who recognized the catastrophe threatening the Jewish people." Herbstrith, *Edith Stein*, 11.

24. Stein, *Life in a Jewish Family*, 23.

25. *Ibid.*

26. *Ibid.*, 24 (emphasis added).

27. *Ibid.*

28. Had she wished to study Jewish texts further or become a rabbi, she would have been prohibited on the basis of her gender, as we will see in greater detail in the following chapter on Regina Jonas's journey.

29. Stein, *Life in a Jewish Family*, 24 (emphasis added).

30. Emphasis added.

31. Susanne Batzdorff, "Watching Tante Edith Become Teresa, Blessed Martyr of the Church," *Moment* (September, 1987), 50.

32. Glückel of Hameln, *The Memoirs of Glückel of Hameln*, trans. Marvin Lowenthal (New

York: Schoken Books, 1977); Pauline Wengeroff, "Memoirs of a Russian Grandmother," in *The Golden Tradition: Jewish Life and Thought in Eastern Europe*, ed. Lucy Dawidowitcz (New York: Holt, Rhinehart & Winston, 1967).

33. According to David Biale, ethical wills (or *tzavaahs*) are "documents, typically written by a father for his children, [which] might merge details of autobiography with moralistic pronouncement." David Biale, "Eros and Enlightenment," in *Eros and the Jews: From Biblical Israel to Contemporary America* (New York: Basic Books, 1992), 277, n.4. As a feminist scholar I think it is time we gave Glückel her due. For a number of generations, male translators have deleted large portions from her text, assuming that it was not serious scholarship.

34. Glückel of Hameln, *Memoirs*, 1.

35. Wengeroff, "Memoirs of a Russian Grandmother," 168.

36. Stein, *Self-Portrait in Letters*, 252.

37. In her study of women's autobiography, Heilbrun argues that "a woman's 'identity' is grounded through relation to the chosen other. Without such relation, women do not feel able to openly write about themselves." Carolyn Heilbrun, *Writing A Woman's Life* (New York: Ballantine Books, 1989), 24.

38. Stein, *Life in a Jewish Family*, 24–5.

39. *Ibid.*, 73.

40. *Ibid.*, 72.

41. When she made the leap from biography to autobiography she made a literary move. Susan Bell and Marilyn Yalom explain that "the boundaries between autobiography and biography are not always distinct as their definitions imply. Biography is generally defined as 'the story of one's personal life written by another' and autobiography as 'the story of one's life written by oneself.' It becomes apparent then for biographers that all choices are autobiographical." Susan Bell & Marilyn Yalom, *Revealing Lives: Autobiography: Biography and Gender*, (Albany, NY: SUNY Press, 1990), 3.

42. We will see that her feminism for the time is radical and essentialist, a view which she applies to all areas of a woman's professional and domestic life. In particular, she railed against recent Nazi laws relegating women and their bodies to the narrowly proscribed role of reproduction; she advocated for women's political role in the public sphere, speaking to Catholic groups as her audience.

43. Brenner, *Writing as Resistance*, 155.

44. Stein, "Ethos of Women's Professions," 43 (emphasis original).

45. As I see it, Orthodox Judaism emphasizes the importance of these qualities, but as a rationale to keep women from playing active roles in religious life.

46. Rachel Brenner, "Ethical Convergence in Religious Conversion," in Cargas, *The Unnecessary Problem of Edith Stein*, 83. See also Stein's dissertation "On the Problem of Empathy."

47. Stein, *Life in a Jewish Family*, 69.

48. *Ibid.*, 71.

49. *Ibid.*

50. From 1923 to 1927, for example, the suicide rate of Jews in Prussia was over four times that of Catholics and twice that of Protestants. Mary Lowenthal Felsteiner, setting the historical context for her study of the painter Charlotte Salomon, who died in Auschwitz, describes the "suicide epidemic" of the time in detail. Mary Lowenthal Felsteiner, *To Paint Her Life: Charlotte Salomon in the Nazi Era* (New York: HarperCollins, 1995), 15–16.

51. Stein, *Life in a Jewish Family*, 82 (emphasis added). I am curious as to whether Stein had access to Jewish mystical texts. If she had, she would have found that Judaism does include concepts of eternity and reincarnation, such as those in Chaim Vital's sixteenth-century text *Sefer HaGilgul*.

52. Brenner, "Ethical Convergence in Religious Conversion," 95.
53. Judith Butler, *Gender Trouble* (New York: Routledge, 1990).
54. Nazis' recourse was to prove Jewishness using history (i.e., if one could be proved to have had a Jewish grandparent).
55. Timothy K. Beal, *The Book of Hiding: Gender, Ethnicity, Annihilation, and Esther* (London: Routledge, 1997), 120 (emphasis original).
56. Jews who converted to Christianity under the Spanish Inquisition were known as the "new Christians," or *conversos*; they continued to practice Judaism underground.
57. Elspeth Probyn, *Outside Belongings* (London: Routledge, 1996), 41 (emphasis original).
58. This is noted implicitly in the title of a recent book by Jewish scholars on the matter, *The Unnecessary Problem of Edith Stein* (ed. Cargas).
59. Probyn, *Outside Belongings*, 19.
60. Butler, *Gender Trouble*, 144.
61. Brenner, *Writing as Resistance*, 72.
62. Stein, *Life in a Jewish Family*, 23.
63. Probyn, *Outside Belongings*, 12. She goes further: "Basically [the sociology of the skin] comes down to a heightened sensitivity to the sensibilities, to being captured by other manners of being and desires for becoming-other that I call belonging" (*ibid.*, 5). Whereas Butler describes *what* gender *is*, Probyn goes one step further to describe *how* gender *is spoken*, or the process we use to articulate what she would call the gender we desire.
64. *Ibid.*, 34.

4. REGINA JONAS: FROM CANDIDATE TO RABBINERIN

1. Laaser, *C. V. Zeitung*, June 23, 1938, cited in Klapheck, *Fräulein Rabbiner Jonas*, 59.
2. Annette Löwenthal, "The Woman Rabbi," *Frauenzeitung Berna*, February 10, 1939. (emphasis added).
3. Laaser, *C. V. Zeitung*, June 23, 1938, cited in Klapheck, *Fräulein Rabbiner Jonas*, 59.
4. I refer here to Jewish theologian Franz Rosenzweig's mystical experience at Yom Kippur services in Kassel, Germany in 1913, in which he reconfirms his authentic connection to the Jewish faith.
5. Another translation of the phrase is "I am what I am." God/YHVH encompasses the past, present and the future embedded in total in the present. This was the truth of both Stein and Jonas.
6. Klapheck, *Fräulein Rabbiner Jonas*, 10.
7. Katharina von Kellenbach, "Rabbi Regina Jonas (1902–1944)," http://faculty.smcm.edu/kvonkellenbach/jonas.htm (accessed September 23, 2008).
8. Frieda Valentin, "Bekanntschaft mit einer Rabbinerin," *Jüdische Allgemeine Zeitung*, January 22, 1936 ("Acquaintance with a Rabbi," trans. Dagmar Theison, 2007).
9. Von Kellenbach, "Rabbi Regina Jonas (1902–1944)."
10. Rabbi Ted Alexander, interview by author, Danville, CA, July 19, 2007.
11. Jonas's thesis was entitled *Kann die Frau das rabbinische Amt bekleiden? Eine Streitschrift*. Rabbi Elisa Klapheck decided to become a rabbi because of Rabbinerin Jonas. She was ordained privately through the Aleph Alliance; Rabbi Ted Alexander, whose father Hugo Alexander helped ordain Jonas, was on her ordination committee.
12. Jonas, "Can Women Serve as Rabbis?," 101.
13. Von Kellenbach, "'God Does Not Oppress Any Human Being'," 213.
14. Jonas, "Can Women Serve as Rabbis?," 100.
15. *Ibid.*
16. Klapheck, *Fräulein Rabbiner Jonas*, 32.
17. *Ibid.*

18. *Ibid.*
19. Jonas, "Can Women Serve as Rabbis?," 101.
20. *Ibid.* (emphasis added).
21. *Ibid.*
22. *Ibid.*
23. *Ibid.*
24. *Ibid.*
25. *Ibid.*, 102.
26. A levirate marriage is one in which the widow marries the brother of her deceased husband.
27. Jonas, "Can Women Serve as Rabbis?," 102.
28. *Ibid.*
29. *Ibid.*
30. *Ibid.*
31. English translations have been substituted for these texts' titles, which are in German.
32. Jonas, "Can Women Serve as Rabbis?," 104 (emphasis original).
33. *Ibid.*, 108 (emphasis original).
34. *Ibid.*, 123–4 (emphasis original).
35. *Ibid.*, 124 (emphasis added).
36. Regina Jonas, "Echo of the Holidays," typewritten manuscript now in the archives of the Stiftung Neue Synagoge Berlin–Centrum Judaicum, unpaginated (trans. Dirk von der Horst).
37. *Ibid.*
38. *Ibid.*
39. Anon., "Chanukahfeier in der Helene Lange 2 städtische Mädchen-Mittel-Schule zu Berlin," copy of a typewritten manuscript in the archives of the Stiftung Neue Synagoge Berlin–Centrum Judaicum.
40. Pam Nadell's book *Women Who Would Be Rabbis* demonstrates how women in pursuit of the rabbinate in the US could hope to be no more than religious school teachers. There was no path to ordination for women. The best they could hope for was being a religious school principal.
41. Anon., "Chanukahfeier in der Helene Lange 2."
42. Valentin, "Bekanntschaft mit einer Rabbinerin."
43. Most of the contemporary journalism by women about Jonas – such as by Frieda Valentin, Mala Laaser, and Annette Löwenthal – refers to Jonas as a rabbinerin. By contrast, the articles written by men use the term "Miss Rabbi Jonas," and not "Rabbinerin."
44. The Neue Synagoge in present-day Berlin houses the Jewish community archives and contains the archives of Regina Jonas.
45. *Oneg Shabbat* is usually a time when Kiddush is said after the services on Shabbat (Friday evening). The congregants bless the bread and wine with the rabbi and cantor, and then have a snack together, such as herring and schnapps. I was a little confused as to why the article gave the event as taking place on a Sunday. Either Jonas was teaching Sunday school or it is a mistake and it was a Saturday.
46. Valentin, "Bekanntschaft mit einer Rabbinerin."
47. Regina Jonas, letter to Mala Laaser, no date, now in the archives of the Stiftung Neue Synagoge Berlin–Centrum Judaicum (emphasis added).
48. *Ibid.*
49. *Ibid.*
50. *Ibid.*
51. Julie Wolfthorn, *Israeli Family*, October 22, 1936 (trans. Dagmar Theison, 2007).
52. *Ibid.*
53. Laaser, *C. V. Zeitung*, June 23, 1938.

54. Annette Löwenthal, "The Woman Rabbi." Unlike the previous journals in which Jonas's story appeared, the *Frauenzeitung Berna: Organ des Bernischen Frauenbundes, (Women's Newsletter Berna: The Voice of the Bern Women's Association)* was not a Jewish women's newsletter.

55. Löwenthal, "The Woman Rabbi." The *Frauenzeitung Berna* was published in Switzerland and therefore was not under Nazi jurisdiction. Consequently, Jonas was not referred to as Regina Sara Jonas, although at this time all female Jews in Nazi Germany had to use Sara as their middle name, and male Jews had to use Israel. In German articles issued in 1939, Sara was inserted into Jonas's name, as was required.

56. Klapheck, *Fräulein Rabbiner Jonas*, 39.

57. Jonas, "Can Women Serve as Rabbis?," 100.

58. Klapheck, *Fräulein Rabbiner Jonas*, 39.

59. *Ibid.*

60. Isaac Bashevis Singer, "Yentl the Yeshiva Boy," in *The Collected Stories of Isaac Bashevis Singer* (New York: Farrar, Straus and Giroux, 1996).

61. German has changed since the women's movement, to now provide the feminine ending "*in*" (and its plural "*innen*") with a capital I, right in the middle of the words it qualifies, in order to be inclusive. So the new inclusive term for a rabbi would be RabbinerIn (or plural RabbinerInnen). Interestingly, this change is visible, but not audible – which clearly benefits women, since you now hear the feminine ending on all collective nouns.

5. STEIN SUFFERING ON THE CROSS: THE CALL OF ABRAM LECH LECHA

1. W. Gunther Plaut (ed.), *The Torah: A Modern Commentary* (New York: Union of the American Hebrew Congregations, 1981), 91.

2. *Ibid.*, 95.

3. *Ibid.*, 104.

4. *HaHomash HaManukad Bereshit* (Jerusalem: Horev Publishing, 1999), 104 (my own translation).

5. Klaus P. Fischer, *Nazi Germany: A New History* (London: Continuum Press, 2004), 390.

6. Edith Stein, "How I Came to the Cologne Carmel," in *Selected Writings* (Springfield, IL: Templegate, 1990), 17.

7. Stein, *Self-Portrait in Letters*, 60 (letter 52 to Sr. Adelgundis Jaegerschmind, OSB, Freiburg-Gunterstal, St Magdalena Speyer, February 16, 1930; emphasis added).

8. Edith Stein, *Endliches und ewiges Sein: Versuch eines Aufstiegs zum Sinn des Seins; Anhang, Martin Heideggers Existenzphilosophie, Die Seelenburg*, ed. Andreas Uwe Müller (Freiburg im Breisgau: Herder, 2006), cited by Antonio Calcagno, *The Philosophy of Edith Stein* (Pittsburgh, PA: Duquesne University Press, 2007), dedication page.

9. Stein, "How I Came to the Cologne Carmel," 16 (emphasis added).

10. *Ibid.*, 17.

11. "Letter of Saint Edith Stein to Pope Pius XI in 1933," www.baltimorecarmel.org/saints/Stein/letter%20to%20pope.htm (accessed July 4, 2013; emphasis added).

12. See Batzdorff, *Aunt Edith*. Batzdorff explains this point clearly. As a practicing Jew, I agree with Batzdorff that this was the reason that the Nazis killed Stein.

13. See Brenner, "Ethical Convergence in Religious Conversion," 78–9. Also see Rachel Brenner's ground-breaking book *Writing As Resistance*. Brenner's study of Stein was released before Stein's letter to the Pope was made available, but Brenner's point confirms Stein's identity claims.

14. Stein, *On The Problem of Empathy*, 63–4 (emphasis added).

15. Stein, *Life in a Jewish Family*, 82 (emphasis original). This statement from Stein reflects what happens (as Jonas and Batzdorff lamented) when a Jewish woman did not have

a Jewish education. I think Stein's statement shows a lack of understanding of Jewish practice and belief, for Jewish practice does acknowledge that we return to eternal rest and eternal life. The prayer that Jews recite for our dead, El Male Rachnim, describes the soul's return to God, to an eternal resting place. She seems also unaware of Maimonides' thirteenth principle of faith. Jewish practice is very much about *tikkun olam* co-creators, as opposed to surrender in the Catholic sense. I found it upsetting as a practicing Jew that Stein did not know enough about – or was not able to grasp the core of – Jewish faith and practice. At the same time, I understand it was not her path. There was no place in Judaism for a contemplative like Stein. The Jewish understanding she did have helped her to embrace Jesus as a Jew in a way no others in her time could.

I am curious as to whether Stein had access to Jewish mystical texts. If she had, she would have found that Judaism does include concepts of eternity and reincarnation, such as those in Chaim Vital's sixteenth-century text *Sefer HaGilgul*. I think Stein's statement shows a lack of understanding of Jewish practice and belief, especially Maimonides's thirteenth principle of faith.

16. Individual Catholic bishops did protest the Nazi policies. A Catholic priest was able to halt the Nazi euthanasia program that was carried out on mentally ill and retarded Germans. The famous Rosenstrasse protest of German Aryan wives married to Jewish men prevented their deportation to Auschwitz. See Nathan Stoltzfus's *Resistance of the Heart: Intermarriage and The Rosenstrasse Protest in Nazi Germany* (New York: W. W. Norton 1996). Stein called for the Church to speak out because it was one of the few institutions that was powerful enough to intervene.
17. The history of this controversy falls outside the purview of this thesis, but it is an extremely compelling one.
18. Stein, "How I Came to the Cologne Carmel," 18.
19. *Ibid.*, 19 (emphasis added).
20. Brenner, *Writing As Resistance*, 76–7.
21. When I told my beloved Rabbi Ted Alexander and my late father that I was working on Edith Stein, they were outraged. "How could you work on her?" they demanded. A Jew who converts to Catholicism was an apostate, especially in Nazi Germany. "Why waste your time on her?" I can still hear my father's words about anti-Semitism. He said, "Anti-Semites grow up with Jews being Christ-killers in their mother's milk." It was one thing to live like a *converso* to survive, another thing to actually believe in Jesus as Savior. Rabbi Ted feels that my whole project comparing Stein to Rabbi Jonas was an insult to the latter. He had loved and grown up with her. My father came around, but to many older Jews of Rabbi Ted's and my father's generation, it was incomprehensible that I should spend my time on an apostate. My father did make attempts to grasp what I was doing. For his part, Rabbi Ted is waiting to see how this project turns out.
22. Stein, *Life in a Jewish Family*, 23 (emphasis added).
23. See Marion Kaplan, *The Making of the Jewish Middle Class: Women, Family, and Identity in Imperial Germany* (New York: Oxford University Press, 1991) for more on *Bildung* in German Jewish culture. *Bildung* refers to educational attainment and attendant virtues.
24. *Ibid.*, 23–4 (emphasis added).
25. Hannah Arendt, "The Jew as Pariah: A Hidden Tradition," in *The Jew as Pariah*, 68.
26. Stein, *Hidden Life*, 1.
27. Edith Stein, "The Marriage of the Lamb," September 14, 1940, in *Hidden Life*, 99.
28. *Ibid.*, 100.
29. *Ibid.*, 101.
30. *Ibid.*, 2.
31. Edith Stein, "Elevation of the Cross, September 14, 1939: Ave Crux, Only Hope," in *Hidden Life*, 94.
32. *Ibid.*, 95 (emphasis added).

33. Melissa Raphael, *Judaism and the Visual Image: A Jewish Theology of Art* (London: Continuum, 2009), 138–40.
34. Stein, "Elevation of the Cross," xiv (emphasis original).
35. Dorothee Sölle, *The Silent Cry: Mysticism and Resistance* (Minneapolis, MN: Fortress Press, 2001), 148 (emphasis added).
36. See Carey A. Moore, *Esther: Introduction, Translation, and Notes*. Anchor Bible. (Garden City, NY: Doubleday, 1971), for basic issues in text, transmission, and difference in canonical status of the text among Jews and Christians.
37. Stein, "Conversation in the Night," in *Hidden Life*, 131.
38. *Ibid.*, 132 (emphasis added).
39. *Ibid.*, 133.
40. *Ibid.*
41. *Ibid.*
42. Sölle, *The Silent Cry*, 148.
43. *Ibid.*, 148–9 (emphasis added).
44. Batzdorff, *Aunt Edith*, 205.

6. RABBINERIN REGINA JONAS: SEEING THE FACE OF THE *SHEKHINAH*

1. Jonas, "Can Women Serve as Rabbis?," 104 (emphasis added).
2. The Carmelites preserved everything of Edith Stein's so that she is today accessible to scholars. Regina Jonas was not part of a contemplative order, and her work was not preserved by a community of nuns. Jonas's work had to be literally rescued from the ashes.
3. Herbstrith, *Edith Stein*, 180. In my interview with Batzdorff, she said that she doubted the authenticity of this incident.
4. A young man named Mehe came to visit Martin Buber in 1914 for some advice. On the day of the visit, Buber, who was a student of Hasidic mysticism, had been engaged in meditative practices that put him into a state of mystical rapture. Therefore, during this meeting with another in the person of Mehe, Buber was not as engaged in the present as he could have been, as he was still feeling the effects of his otherworldly mystical journey. Buber gave Mehe the best attention he could at the time, but Buber felt that he had not been fully present to the young man with his mind and body. A few months later, one of Mehe's friends came to see Buber and told him that Mehe had died at the front. He further told Buber that Mehe's visit to Buber had been prompted by the kind of despair that may be defined partially as "no longer opposing one's own death." Buber's guilt over his failure to help the young man, which he attributed to his not being fully present with his whole being in his dialogue with Mehe, served as a conversion experience for Buber. Henceforth he redirected himself to being in the world as opposed to being apart from the world, which is where mystical rapture leads." From Maurice Friedman, *Martin Buber's Life and Work: The Early Years 1878–1923* (New York: E. P. Dutton, 1981), 188–90.
5. Klapheck, *Fräulein Rabbiner Jonas*, 63–4.
6. *Ibid.*
7. Rabbi Ted Alexander, personal interview, 2007. I had a copy of the *Jüdisches Nachrichtenblatt from* October 2, 1942. Rabbi Siegfried was listed as offering services. Both Rabbi Ted and his wife Gertrude were shocked to see that the Nazis still let the Jews print a paper, let alone still hold services in Berlin in 1942. It was profound for Rabbi Ted to see the name of his Orthodox rabbi Uncle Siegfried listed. Rabbi Ted had to say goodbye to him in 1939 when the family escaped to Shanghai.
8. Rabbi Israel Shapira survived, and stories of his and parts of his community's survival in the concentration camps are told in Eliach, *Hasidic Tales of the Holocaust*.

9. See Nehemia Polin, *The Holy Fire: The Teachings of the Rabbi Kalonymus Kalman Shapira, the Rebbe of the Warsaw Ghetto* (Northvale, NJ: Jason Aronson, 1994).
10. Melissa Raphael, *The Female Face of God in Auschwitz: A Jewish Feminist Theology of the Holocaust* (London: Routledge, 2003), 55 (emphasis original).
11. *Ibid.*
12. Klapheck, *Fräulein Rabbiner Jonas*, 74.
13. Cantor Rita Glassman once told me that Jonas's rabbinate reminds us of one of the names for God, *Ha-Makom*, which means "the place." Then I remembered the blessings that we had just said at Passover. One of the blessings is called "Bless the Place": "*Baruch Ha-Makom Baruch who Baruch SheNatan Torah La'Amo Israel*" ("[God's name] bless Him, bless that He gave the Torah to the nation of Israel"). It is an interesting name for God. I see both God's immanence and transcendence within this name. God is greater than the universe, but the universe rests within God, and we are dependent on God in the universe that rests within God. "One Hasidic interpretation of God's name, 'The Place' beyond all places, is in accordance with the Hasidic comment that God is in no particular place *in* the world but rather the place *of* the world. It is especially interesting that the Name appears in the *Haggadah*, which is concerned with how the people of Israel may move from place to place." New Jewish Agenda, *The Shalom Seders: Three Haggadah* (New York: Adama Books, 1984), 35.
14. Jonas, "Can Women Serve as Rabbis?," 102.
15. Valentin, "Bekanntschaft mit einer Rabbinerin."
16. Klapheck, *Fräulein Rabbiner Jonas*, 62.
17. Karl Kloppholz, *Jüdisches Gemeindeblatt für Berlin*, June 26, 1938 (trans. Dagmar Theison, Department of German, University of California, Berkeley, August 2007).
18. Ariela Pelaia, "What is Yizkor?," http://judaism.about.com/od/deathandmournin1/f/yizkor.htm (accessed May 6, 2008).
19. Regina Jonas, "Über alles die Seelen-Feier," *Jüdisches Nachrichtenblatt*, May 24, 1939 (trans. Dagmar Theison, Department of German, University of California, Berkeley, August 2007; emphasis original).
20. Klapheck, *Fräulein Rabbiner Jonas*, 63. The second paragraph of the newspaper article was translated by Klapheck's translator Toby Axelrod.
21. Jonas, "Über alles die Seelen-Feier."
22. Katharina von Kellenbach, "Reproduction and Resistance during the Holocaust," in *Women and the Holocaust*, ed. Esther Fuchs (Lanham, MD: University of America Press, 1999), 23.
23. *Ibid.*
24. As von Kellenbach notes in "Reproduction and Resistance during the Holocaust," it is extremely difficult, as both a scholar and human being, to read Ruth Cronheim's letter "in full knowledge of the cynical brutality of the future."
25. My great cousin, Frau Doktor Alma Tannenbaum (1904–97), went to medical school with Victor Frankl at the University of Vienna. She was in the class of 1929; her degree was in infectious diseases. Alma survived Transnistra, a horrendous (though not well-known) concentration camp, where Romanian and Bukovinian Jews were deported. Frankl was in the class of 1930. She did not seem to care for Frankl when I asked about him during my last conversation and visit with her in Vienna in 1990.
26. Women scholars and rabbis have been very upset that Jonas has been almost written out of history. I have to thank Rabbi Ted Alexander for never forgetting her and for always telling me about Rabbinerin Jonas. Ruthie Callman, whom I served with on the board of Bnai Emunah, was one of Jonas's students and always liked to tell me how her teacher, Regina Jonas, came over once to her mother's house to tell her that Ruthie was not taking her Hebrew and Jewish studies seriously. In fact, Ruthie was not a good student. At the time she was much more interested in going to her sports clubs and hanging

out with friends. Ruthie often said, "If Regina Jonas could see me now, she would be so proud of me because I am a *Gabbait*, the first female member of the board of a synagogue. I have the right to vote. I am such a good Jew now." Ruthie still loves to party, and I hope to be able to party with her very soon. I have promised her a girls' night out.

27. Klapheck, *Fräulein Rabbiner Jonas*, 78.
28. Von Kellenbach, "'God Does Not Oppress Any Human Being'," 224.
29. *Ibid.*, 224, n. 38 (emphasis added).
30. I personally have a new understanding of these sacred words: Rabbinerin Jonas is transforming this scholar as she writes.
31. Klapheck, *Fräulein Rabbiner Jonas*, 78.
32. I want to thank Rabbi Elisa Klapheck for sending me a copy of Jonas's Theresienstadt documents, which she copied from the Theresienstadt Archives. I want also to thank Dagmar Theison, PhD student in the German Department at UC Berkeley for translating these lecture titles in December of 2007. The source was written in a very difficult, choppy handwriting, and she was working from a copy of a copy of the original document.
33. Klapheck, *Fräulein Rabbiner Jonas*, 50 (emphasis added).
34. Von Kellenbach, "'God Does Not Oppress Any Human Being'," 224–5.
35. Klapheck, *Fräulein Rabbiner Jonas*, 79.
36. *Ibid.*
37. See Helmut Gollwitzer, Reinhold Schneider & Käthe Kuhn (eds), *Dying We Live: The Final Messages and Records of the Victims and Martyrs, 1933–1945* (New York: Pantheon Books, 1956). This is a collection of letters written by Germans who resisted the Nazis and were murdered. Some were Catholic priests and nuns, some Protestant ministers and members of the resistance.
38. *Ibid.*, 233.
39. Malham, *By Fire into Light*, 197–8. We will never know for sure whether this was actually Edith Stein, but it is probable that it was her.

7. A THEOLOGY OF RESISTANCE AS LIBERATION IN THE DEATH CAMPS

1. Eliach, *Hasidic Tales of the Holocaust*, 53–5. The historical veracity of this story is beside the point. For further information about this massacre, see the Holocaust Atlas of Lithuania at http://holocaustatlas.lt/EN.
2. A theology of liberation has multiple meanings. This is not the traditional liberation theology of the 1960s to 1990s from Latin America and developing countries elsewhere. This is not necessarily about changing political structures. I am taking the term "liberation theology" out of its original context, because this is likewise a form of liberating one's humanity. When one is oppressed one can choose how to respond to the oppression that is heaped upon one: one can either view oneself as a victim or not. One is forced to ask what the response to this situation of oppression is, so that one is not a victim of it. Stein and Jonas teach us that even in the most unimaginably horrific conditions, one still has a choice. These women chose to respond in a sacred, holy way.

BIBLIOGRAPHY

STEIN PRIMARY SOURCES

Stein, Edith 1917. "Zum Problem der Einfuhlung." Thesis (doctoral), Albert-Ludwigs-Universitat, Freiburg im Breisgau.

Stein, Edith 1950–. *Werke*. Louvain: Nauwelaerts.

Stein, Edith 1956. *Writings*. Westminster, MD: Newman Press.

Stein, Edith 1959. *Die Frau: ihre Aufgabe nach Natur und Gnade*. Louvain: Nauwelaerts.

Stein, Edith 1960. *The Science of the Cross*. Chicago, IL: Regnery.

Stein, Edith & Hedwig Conrad-Martius 1960. *Briefe an Hedwig Conrad-Martius*. Munich: Kösel-Verlag.

Stein, Edith 1963. *Die Frau in Ehe und Beruf: Bildungsfragen heute*. Freiburg im Breisgau: Herder-Bücherei.

Stein, Edith 1964. *On the Problem of Empathy*, Waltraut Stein (trans.). The Hague: Martinus Nijhoff.

Stein, Edith 1967. *Briefauslese 1917–1942, Mit einem Dokumentenanhang zu ihrem Tode*. Freiburg im Breisgau: Herder.

Stein, Edith 1970. *Beiträge zur philosophischen Begründung der Psychologie und der Geisteswissenschaften*. Tübingen: M. Niemeyer.

Stein, Edith 1970. *On the Problem of Empathy*, 2nd edn, Waltraut Stein (trans.). The Hague: Martinus Nijhoff.

Stein, Edith 1979. *Wege der Gotteserkenntnis: Dionysius d. Areopagit u. sein symbol. Theologie*. Munich: Kaffke.

Stein, Edith 1980. *Zum Problem der Einfühlung*. Munich: Verlagsgesellschaft Gerhard Kaffke.

Stein, Edith 1980. *A Celebration and Thanksgiving for Edith Stein: Thoughts from Her Writings with Meditative Responses from the New Testament*, Paul T. Coke (ed.). Monterey, CA: Hilleary & Petko.

Stein, Edith 1983. *Edith Stein: Ein neues Lebensbild in Zeugnissen und Selbstzeugnissen* Waltraud Herbstrith (ed.). Freiburg im Breisgau: Herder.

Stein, Edith 1986. *Life in a Jewish Family: Her Unfinished Autobiographical Account; The Collected Works of Edith Stein, vol. 1*, Lucy Gelber, Romaeus Leuven & Josephine Koeppel (eds). Washington, DC: ICS Publications.

Stein, Edith 1987. *Essays on Woman; The Collected Works of Edith Stein, vol. 2*, Lucy Gelber & Romaeus Leuven (eds). Washington, DC: ICS Publications.

Stein, Edith 1987. *Edith Stein zum Gedenken*, Kurt Keller & Kloster St. Magdalena (eds). Speyer: Das Kloster.

Stein, Edith 1989. *On the Problem of Empathy; The Collected Works of Edith Stein, vol. 3*. Washington, DC: ICS Publications.

Stein, Edith 1990. *Selected Writings.* Springfield, IL: Templegate.

Stein, Edith 1992. *The Hidden Life: Hagiographic Essays, Meditations, Spiritual Texts; The Collected Works of Edith Stein, vol. 4*, Lucy Gelber & Michael Linssen (eds). Washington, DC: ICS Publications.

Stein, Edith 1993. *Self-Portrait in Letters, 1916–1942; The Collected Works of Edith Stein, vol. 5*, Josephine Koeppel (trans.). Washington, DC: ICS Publications.

Stein, Edith 1998. *Le Secret de la Croix, Cahiers de l'Ecole Cathédrale.* Paris: Parole et silence; Coopérative de l'enseignement religieux de Paris.

Stein, Edith 2000. *Die Frau: Fragestellungen und Reflexionen*, Sophie Binggeli & Maria Amata Neyer (eds). Freiburg im Breisgau: Herder.

Stein, Edith 2000. *Selbstbildnis in Briefen*, 3 vols, Roman Ingarden, Hanna Gerl-Falkovitz & Maria Amata Neyer (eds). Freiburg im Breisgau: Herder.

Stein, Edith 2000. *Gesamtausgabe*, Michael Linssen, Hanna Gerl-Falkovitz & Internationales Edith Stein Institut (eds). Freiburg im Breisgau: Herder.

Stein, Edith 2000. *Philosophy of Psychology and the Humanities; The Collected Works of Edith Stein, vol. 7.* Washington, DC: ICS Publications.

Stein, Edith 2000. *Knowledge and Faith; The Collected Works of Edith Stein, vol. 8.* Washington, DC: ICS Publications.

Stein, Edith 2001. *Bildung und Entfaltung der Individualität: Beiträge zum christlichen Erziehungsauftrag*, Maria Amata Neyer & Beate Beckmann (eds). Freiburg im Breisgau: Herder.

Stein, Edith 2002. *The Science of the Cross; The Collected Works of Edith Stein, vol. 6.* Washington, DC: ICS Publications.

Stein, Edith 2002. *Finite and Eternal Being: An Attempt at an Ascent to the Meaning of Being; The Collected Works of Edith Stein, vol. 9.* Washington, DC: ICS Publications.

Stein, Edith 2002. *Aus dem Leben Einer Jüdischen Familie: und weitere autobiographische Beiträge*, Maria Amata Neyer & Hanna Gerl-Falkovitz (eds). Freiburg im Breisgau: Herder.

Stein, Edith 2002. *Edith Stein (St. Teresa Benedicta of the Cross, OCD): Essential Writings*, John Sullivan (ed.). Maryknoll, NY: Orbis Books.

Stein, Edith 2002. *Edith Stein: Essential Writings*, Modern Spiritual Masters Series. New York: Orbis Books.

Stein, Edith 2003. *Wege der Gotteserkenntnis: Studie zu Dionysius Areopagita und Übersetzung seiner Werke*, Beate Beckmann, Viki Ranff & Dionysius Pseudo (eds). Freiburg im Breisgau: Herder.

Stein, Edith 2003. *Kreuzeswissenschaft: Studie über Johannes vom Kreuz*, Ulrich Dobhan (ed.). Freiburg im Breisgau: Herder.

Stein, Edith 2004. *Der Aufbau der menschlichen Person: Vorlesung zur philosophischen Anthropologie*, Beate Beckmann-Zöller (ed.). Freiburg im Breisgau: Herder.

Stein, Edith 2004. *Einführung in die Philosophie*, Claudia Mariéle Wulf (ed.). Freiburg im Breisgau: Herder.

Stein, Edith 2005. *Was ist der Mensch?: Eine theologische Anthropologie.* Freiburg im Breisgau: Herder.

Stein, Edith 2005. *Potenz und Akt: Studien zu einer Philosophie des Seins*, Hans Rainer Sepp (ed.). Freiburg im Breisgau: Herder.

Stein, Edith 2006. *Endliches und ewiges Sein: Versuch eines Aufstiegs zum Sinn des Seins; Anhang, Martin Heideggers Existenzphilosophie, Die Seelenburg*, Andreas Uwe Müller (ed.). Freiburg im Breisgau: Herder.

Stein, Edith 2006. *Eine Untersuchung über den Staat*, Ilona Riedel-Spangenberger (ed.). Freiburg im Breisgau: Herder.

Stein, Edith 2007. *Geistliche Texte*, Sophie Binggeli (ed.). Freiburg im Breisgau: Herder.

Stein, Edith 2008. *Übersetzung: Des Hl. Thomas von Aquino Untersuchungen über die Wahrheit, Quaestiones disputatae de veritate 2.* Freiburg im Breisgau: Herder.

STEIN SECONDARY SOURCES

Albert, Karl 1994. *Philosophie im Schatten von Auschwitz: Edith Stein, Theodor Lessing, Walter Benjamin, Paul Ludwig Landsberg*. Dettelbach: J. H. Röll.

Aucante, Vincent & Edith Stein 2003. *Le Discernement Selon Edith Stein: Que Faire de sa Vie?* Paris: Parole et silence.

Baseheart, Mary Catharine 1997. *Person in the World: Introduction to the Philosophy of Edith Stein; Contributions to Phenomenology, vol. 27*. Dordrecht: Kluwer Academic.

Batzdorff, Susanne 1994. "Witnessing My Aunt's Beatification." In *The Unnecessary Problem of Edith Stein*, H. J. Cargas (ed.), 33–42. Lanham, MD: University Press of America.

Batzdorff, Susanne 1998. *Aunt Edith: the Jewish Heritage of a Catholic Saint*. Springfield, IL: Templegate.

Beckmann-Zöller, Beate & Hanna Gerl-Falkovitz 2006. *Die unbekannte Edith Stein: Phänomenologie und Sozialphilosophie*. Frankfurt am Main: Peter Lang.

Berkman, Joyce Avrech 2006. *Contemplating Edith Stein*. Notre Dame, IN: University of Notre Dame Press.

Borden, Sarah R. 2003. *Edith Stein*. London: Continuum.

Brenner, Rachel Feldhay 1997. *Writing as Resistance: Four Women Confronting the Holocaust; Edith Stein, Simone Weil, Anne Frank, Etty Hillesum*. University Park, PA: Pennsylvania State University Press.

Calcagno, Antonio 2007. *The Philosophy of Edith Stein*. Pittsburgh, PA: Duquesne University Press.

Cargas, Harry J. 1994. *The Unnecessary Problem of Edith Stein*. Lanham, MD: University Press of America.

Courtine-Denamy, Sylvie 2000. *Three Women in Dark Times: Edith Stein, Hannah Arendt, Simone Weil, or Amor Fati, Amor Mundi*. Ithaca, NY: Cornell University Press.

Duran, Jane 2006. *Eight Women Philosophers: Theory, Politics, and Feminism*. Urbana, IL: University of Illinois Press.

Elders, Leo & Edith Stein 1991. *Edith Stein: Leben, Philosophie, Vollendung*. Würzburg: Naumann.

Gerl-Falkovitz, Hanna 1991. *Unerbittliches Licht: Edith Stein; Philosophie, Mystik, Leben*. Mainz: Grünewald.

Guilead, Reuben 1974. *De la phénoménologie à la science de la croix: l'itinéraire d'Edith Stein*. Louvain: Nauwelaerts.

Gur-Klein, Thalia 2000. "Some Like Them Iconised: Edith Stein, the Ambiguity of Jewish Female Sainthood in WWII." *Labyrinth* 2 (Winter), http://labyrinth.iaf.ac.at/2000/gur-klein.html (accessed June 18, 2013).

Herbstrith, Waltraud 1963. *Edith Stein: auf der Suche nach Gott*. Kevelaer: Butzon.

Herbstrith, Waltraud 1971. *Das wahre Gesicht Edith Steins*. Bergen-Enkheim: G. Kaffke.

Herbstrith, Waltraud 1971. *Teresa von Ávila: Die erste Kirchenlehrerin*. Bergen-Enkheim: Kaffke.

Herbstrith, Waltraud 1982. *Edith Stein, Bilder des Lebens*. Munich: G. Kaffke.

Herbstrith, Waltraud 1983. *Das wahre Gesicht Edith Steins*. Munich: G. Kaffke.

Herbstrith, Waltraud 1985. *Edith Stein, a Biography*. San Francisco, CA: Harper & Row.

Herbstrith, Waltraud 1990. *Erinnere dich, vergiss es nicht: Edith Stein, christlich-jüdische Perspektiven*. Annweiler: Plöger Verlag.

Herbstrith, Waltraud 1991. *Denken im Dialog: zur Philosophie Edith Steins*. Tübingen: Attempto.

Herbstrith, Waltraud 1992. *Edith Stein, a Biography*, 2nd English edn. San Francisco, CA: Ignatius Press.

Herbstrith, Waltraud 1995. *Edith Stein: Jüdin und Christin*. Munich: Verlag Neue Stadt.

Herbstrith, Waltraud 1998. *Never forget: Christian and Jewish Perspectives on Edith Stein; Carmelite Studies 7.* Washington, DC: ICS Publications.

Herbstrith, Waltraud 2006. *Edith Stein: ihr wahres Gesicht?, Forum Religionsphilosophie.* Berlin: Lit.

Hillesum, Etty & J. G. Gaarlandt 1996. *An Interrupted Life: the Diaries, 1941–1943; and Letters from Westerbork.* New York: Henry Holt.

Kempen, P. O. 1998. "Eyewitness in Westerbork." In *Never forget: Christian and Jewish Perspectives on Edith Stein,* W. Herbstrith (ed.), 272–6. Washington, DC: ICS Publications.

Koeppel, Josephine 1990. *Edith Stein: Philosopher and Mystic.* Collegeville, MN: Liturgical Press.

Lyne, Pat 2000. *Edith Stein Discovered: A Personal Portrait.* Leominster: Gracewing.

MacIntyre, Alasdair C. 2006. *Edith Stein: A Philosophical Prologue, 1913–1922.* Lanham, MD: Rowman & Littlefield.

Malham, Joseph M. 2002. *By Fire into Light: Four Catholic Martyrs of the Nazi Camps.* Leuven: Peeters.

Mosley, Joanne 2006. *Edith Stein: Modern Saint and Martyr.* Mahwah, NJ: HiddenSpring.

Müller, Andreas Uwe & Maria Amata Neyer 1998. *Edith Stein: das Leben einer ungewöhnlichen Frau: Biographie.* Zürich: Benziger.

Newman, John Henry, Edith Stein & Hanna Gerl-Falkovitz 2002. *Übersetzung von John Henry Newman, Briefe und Texte zur ersten Lebenshälfte (1801–1846).* Freiburg im Breisgau: Herder.

Newman, John Henry, Edith Stein & Hanna Gerl-Falkovitz 2004. *Übersetzung von John Henry Newman, Die Idee der Universität.* Freiburg im Breisgau: Herder.

Palmisano, Joseph Redfield, SJ, 2012. *Beyond the Walls: Abraham Joshua Heschel and Edith Stein on the Significance of Empathy for Jewish-Christian Dialogue.* Oxford: Oxford University Press.

Posselt, Teresia Renata de Spiritu Sancto & Edith Stein 1963. *Edith Stein: Schwester Teresia Benedicta a Cruce, Philosophin und Karmelitin; Ein Lebensbild, gewonnen aus Erinnerungen und Briefen durch Schwester Teresia Renata de Spiritu Sancto.* Freiburg im Breisgau: Herder.

Sawicki, Marianne 1997. *Body, Text, and Science: the Literacy of Investigative Practices and the Phenomenology of Edith Stein; Phenomenologica, vol. 144.* Dordrecht: Kluwer.

Sawicki, Marianne 2008. "Edith Stein Chronology of Writings," www.husserlpage.com/hus_r2st. html (accessed June 18, 2013).

Schandl, Felix M. & Waltraud Herbstrith 1990. *"Ich sah aus meinem Volk die Kirche wachsen!": jüdische Bezüge und Strukturen in Leben und Werk Edith Steins (1891–1942), Sinziger theologische Texte und Studien.* Sinzig: Sankt Meinrad Verlag für Theologie Christine Maria Esser.

Sullivan, John 2000. *Holiness Befits Your House: Canonization of Edith Stein: A Documentation.* Washington, DC: ICS Publications.

Sullivan, John & Philip Lamantia 1987. *Edith Stein Symposium: Teresian Culture.* Washington, DC: ICS Publications.

Teresia de Spiritu Sancto, Susanne M. Batzdorff, Josephine Koeppel & John Sullivan 2005. *Edith Stein: The Life of a Philosopher and Carmelite; Text, Commentary and Explanatory Notes.* Washington, DC: ICS Publications.

Volek, Peter 1998. *Erkenntnistheorie bei Edith Stein: metaphysische Grundlagen der Erkenntnis bei Edith Stein im Vergleich zu Husserl und Thomas von Aquin, Europäische Hochschulschriften.* Frankfurt: Peter Lang.

Westerhorstmann, Katharina 2004. *Selbstverwirklichung und Pro-Existenz: Frausein in Arbeit und Beruf bei Edith Stein.* Thesis (doctoral), Ferdinand Schöningh, Paderborn University, Paderborn.

Wimmer, Reiner 1990. *Vier jüdische Philosophinnen: Rosa Luxemburg, Simone Weil, Edith Stein, Hannah Arendt.* Tübingen: Attempto Verlag.

Film

Maran-Film 1996. *Edith Stein*. Birmingham, AL: ETWN Global Catholic Network.

Website

Edith Stein Foundation, www.theedithsteinfoundation.com.

JONAS PRIMARY SOURCES

Jonas, Regina. "Echo of the Holidays," type-written manuscript now in the archives of the Stiftung Neue Synagoge Berlin–Centrum Judaicum.

Jonas, Regina 1999. *Fräulein Rabbiner Jonas: kann die Frau das rabbinische Amt bekleiden?; Eine Streitschrift*, Elisa Klapheck (ed., intro.), Hermann Simon (foreword). Teetz: Hentrich & Hentrich.

Jonas, Regina 2004. "Halachic Treatise: Can Women Serve as Rabbis?" In Elisa Klapheck, *Fräulein Rabbiner Jonas: The Story of the First Woman Rabbi*, 100–192. San Francisco, CA: Jossey-Bass.

JONAS SECONDARY SOURCES

Brandt, Kim 2003. *Darf eine Frau Rabbinerin werden? Die Ordination im Judentum anhand der Geschichte der Rabbinerin Regina Jonas (Broschüre)*. Munich: Grin Verlag.

Centrum Judaicum Foundation 2000. "New Synagogue Berlin–Centrum Judaicum Foundation," http://mysql.snafu.de/cjudaicum/index.html (accessed September 23, 2008).

Dayan, Aryeh 2004. "A Forgotten Myth," *Haaretz*, May 25, www.haaretz.com/hasen/pages/ShArt.jhtml?itemNo=431619&contrassID=2&subContrassID=20&sbSubContrassID=0&listSrc=Y (accessed September 23, 2008).

haGalil 2008. "Regina Jonas: The First Woman Rabbi in the World," www.hagalil.com/deutschland/berlin/rabbiner/jonas.htm (accessed September 23, 2008).

Hermann, Karl. *Sammlung*. Terezin: Archiv Pamatnik.

Herweg, Rachel Monika 2008. "Regina Jonas," www.hagalil.com/buch/campus/jonas.htm (accessed September 23, 2008).

Katz, Lisa 2008. "Regina Jonas: The First Woman Ordained Rabbi," http://judaism.about.com/od/womenrabbis/a/reginajonas.htm (accessed September 23, 2008).

Klapheck, Elisa 2004. *Fräulein Rabbiner Jonas: The Story of the First Woman Rabbi*. San Francisco, CA: Jossey-Bass.

Nadell, Pamela Susan 1998. *Women Who Would be Rabbis: A History of Women's Ordination, 1889–1985*. Boston, MA: Beacon Press.

Sheridan, Sybil 1999. "History of Women in the Rabbinate: A Case of Communal Amnesia," www.bet-debora.de/jewish-women/history.htm (accessed September 23, 2008).

Sheridan, Sybil 1994. *Hear Our Voice: Women Rabbis Tell Their Stories*. London: SCM Press.

von Kellenbach, Katharina 1992. "Fräulein Rabbiner Regina Jonas: Eine religiöse Feministin vor ihrer Zeit." *Schlangenbrut* 38: 35–9.

von Kellenbach, Katharina 1993. "Die Majorität ist gegen Sie: Der Leidenweg der Regina Jonas, Rabbinerin in Nazi Deutschland." *Aufbau* 59(6): 4.

von Kellenbach, Katharina 1993. "Regina Jonas." In *Jüdische Frauen im 19. und 20. Jahrhundert: Lexikon zu Leben und Werk*, J. Dick, M. Sassenberg, Moses Mendelssohn & Salomon Ludwig (eds), 196–8. Reinbek bei Hamburg: Rowohlt.

von Kellenbach, Katharina 1994. "Fräulein Rabbiner Regina Jonas (1902–1945): Lehrerin, Seelsorgerin, Predigerin." In *Yearbook of the European Society of Women in Theological Research* 1994: 97–102.

von Kellenbach, Katharina 1994. "'God Does Not Oppress Any Human Being': The Life and Thought of Rabbi Regina Jonas." *Leo Baeck Institute: Yearbook* 39: 13–225.

von Kellenbach, Katharina 1999. "Reproduction and Resistance during the Holocaust." In *Woman and the Holocaust*, E. Fuchs (ed.), 19–32. Lanham, MD: University Press of America.

von Kellenbach, Katharina 2001. "Denial and Defiance in the Work of Rabbi Regina Jonas." In *In God's Name: Genocide and Religion in the Twentieth Century*, O. Bartov & P. Mack (eds), 243–58. New York: Berghahn Books.

von Kellenbach, Katharina 2008. "Rabbi Regina Jonas (1902–1944)," http://faculty.smcm.edu/kvonkellenbach/jonas.htm (accessed September 23, 2008).

Weiss, Iris 2008. "Regina Jonas: Zwischen Tradition und Aufbruch," www.hagalil.com/buch/campus/jonas-i.htm (accessed September 23, 2008).

GERMAN JEWISH HISTORY

American Jewish Committee 1935. *The Jews in Nazi Germany: A Handbook of Facts Regarding Their Present Situation*. New York: The American Jewish Committee.

Baader, Benjamin Maria 2006. *Gender, Judaism, and Bourgeois Culture in Germany, 1800–1870*. Bloomington, IN: Indiana University Press.

Banki, Judith Herschcopf & John Pawlikowski 2001. *Ethics in the Shadow of the Holocaust: Christian and Jewish Perspectives*. Franklin, WI: Sheed & Ward.

Bartov, Omer & Phyllis Mack 2001. *In God's Name: Genocide and Religion in the Twentieth Century*. New York: Berghahn Books.

Benz, Wolfgang, Arnold Paucker & Peter G. J. Pulzer 1998. *Jüdisches Leben in der Weimarer Republik [Jews in the Weimar Republic]*. Tübingen: Mohr Siebeck.

Bookbinder, Paul 1996. *Weimar Germany: the Republic of the Reasonable*. Manchester, UK: New York.

Bor, Josef 1963. *The Terezín Requiem*. New York: Knopf.

Bullock, Alan 1964. *Hitler: A Study in Tyranny*, rev. edn. New York: Harper & Row.

Craig, Gordon Alexander 1978. *Germany, 1866–1945*. Oxford History of Modern Europe. Oxford: Clarendon Press.

Dawidowicz, Lucy S. 1967. *The Golden Tradition; Jewish Life and Thought in Eastern Europe*. New York: Holt.

Dawidowicz, Lucy S. 1975. *The War Against the Jews, 1933–1945*. New York: Holt, Rinehart & Winston.

Eliach, Yaffa 1982. *Hasidic Tales of the Holocaust*. New York: Oxford University Press.

Elon, Amos 2002. *The Pity of It All: A Portrait of the German-Jewish Epoch, 1743–1933*. New York: Picador.

Ericksen, Robert P. & Susannah Heschel 1999. *Betrayal: German Churches and the Holocaust*. Minneapolis, MN: Fortress Press.

Fiorenza, Elisabeth Schüssler, David Tracy & Marcus Lefébure 1984. *The Holocaust as Interruption*. Edinburgh: T. & T. Clark.

Fischer, Klaus P. 1995. *Nazi Germany: A New History*. New York: Continuum.

Fischer, Klaus P. 1998. *The History of an Obsession: German Judeophobia and the Holocaust*. New York: Continuum.

Friedländer, Saul 1993. *Memory, History, and the Extermination of the Jews of Europe*. Bloomington, IN: Indiana University Press.

Friedländer, Saul 1997. *Nazi Germany and the Jews*. New York: HarperCollins.

Gay, Peter 1968. *Weimar Culture: The Outsider as Insider*. New York: Harper & Row.

Gay, Peter 1999. *My German Question: Growing Up in Nazi Berlin.* New Haven, CT: Yale University Press.

Gay, Ruth 1992. *The Jews of Germany: A Historical Portrait.* New Haven, CT: Yale University Press.

Gidal, Tim 1998. *Jews in Germany from Roman Times to the Weimar Republic.* Cologne: Könemann.

Gollwitzer, Helmut, Käthe Kuhn, Reinhold Schneider & Reinhold Niebuhr 1956. *Dying We Live: The Final Messages and Records of the Resistance.* New York: Pantheon.

Gutteridge, Richard 1976. *The German Evangelical Church and the Jews, 1879–1950.* New York: Barnes & Noble Books.

Heilbronner, Oded 1994. *Yehude 'Vaimar: 'Hevrah be-mashber ha-moderniyut, 1918–1933.* Jersualem: Hotsa'at sefarim al shem Y.L. Magnes-ha-Universitah ha-'Ivrit.

Herbstrith, Bernhard Maria 1984. *Daten zur Geschichte der Bundesrepublik Deutschland.* Düsseldorf: Econ Taschenbuch Verlag.

Heschel, Susannah 1995. *Transforming Jesus from Jew to Aryan: Protestant Theologians in Nazi Germany.* Tucson, AZ: University of Arizona.

Heschel, Susannah 1998. *Abraham Geiger and the Jewish Jesus.* Chicago, IL: University of Chicago Press.

Hilberg, Raul 1961. *The Destruction of the European Jews.* New York: Harper & Row.

Kaes, Anton, Martin Jay & Edward Dimendberg 1994. *The Weimar Republic Sourcebook.* Berkeley, CA: University of California Press.

Katz, Jacob 1986. *Jewish Emancipation and Self-emancipation.* Philadelphia, PA: Jewish Publication Society.

Kniesche, Thomas W. & Stephen Brockmann 1994. *Dancing on the Volcano: Essays on the Culture of the Weimar Republic.* Columbia, SC: Camden House.

Koltun-Fromm, Ken 2006. *Abraham Geiger's Liberal Judaism: Personal Meaning and Religious Authority.* Bloomington, IN: Indiana University Press.

Lederer, Zdenek 1953. *Ghetto Theresienstadt.* London: E. Goldston.

Lederer, Zdenek 1983. *Ghetto Theresienstadt,* 1st US edn. New York: Fertig.

Marrus, Michael Robert 1987. *The Holocaust in History.* Hanover, NH: University Press of New England.

Meyer, Beate & Hermann Simon 2000. *Juden in Berlin, 1938–1945: Begleitband zur gleichnamigen Ausstellung in der Stiftung "Neue Synagoge Berlin–Centrum Judaicum," Mai bis August 2000.* Berlin: Philo.

Morgan, Michael L. 2001. *A Holocaust Reader: Responses to the Nazi Extermination.* New York: Oxford University Press.

Myerson, Abraham & Isaac Goldberg 1933. *The German Jew, His Share in Modern Culture.* New York: Alfred A. Knopf.

Niewyk, Donald L. 1980. *The Jews in Weimar Germany.* Manchester: Manchester University Press.

Noakes, Jeremy & Geoffrey Pridham 1983. *Nazism, 1919–1945,* 4 vols. Exeter: University of Exeter.

Pierson, Ruth Louise 1970. "German Jewish Identity in the Weimar Republic." PhD dissertation, Yale University, New Haven, CT.

Polen, Nehemia 1994. *The Holy Fire: the Teachings of Rabbi Kalonymus Kalman Shapira, the Rebbe of the Warsaw Ghetto.* Northvale, NJ: J. Aronson.

Reinharz, Jehuda & Walter Schatzberg 1985. *The Jewish Response to German Culture: From the Enlightenment to the Second World War.* Hanover, NH: University Press of New England.

Rosenberg, Arthur 1965. *A History of the German Republic.* New York: Russell & Russell.

Showalter, Dennis E. 1982. *Little Man, What Now?: Der Stürmer in the Weimar Republic.* Hamden, CT: Archon Books.

Strauss, Herbert Arthur, Rainer Erb & Michael Schmidt 1987. *Antisemitismus und jüdische Geschichte: Studien zu Ehren von Herbert A. Strauss.* Berlin: Wissenschaftlicher Autorenverlag.

United States Holocaust Memorial Museum 2008. "Germany: Jewish Population in 1933," www.ushmm.org/wlc/article.php?lang=en&ModuleId=10005276 (accessed June 18, 2013).

GERMAN AND GERMAN JEWISH WOMEN'S HISTORY

Beyer, Karl 1933. *Die ebenbürtigkeit der Frau im national sozialistischen Deutschland: Ihre erzieherische Aufgabe.* Leipzig: Armanen-Verlag.
Bridenthal, Renate, Atina Grossmann & Marion A. Kaplan 1984. *When Biology Became Destiny: Women in Weimar and Nazi Germany.* New York: Monthly Review Press.
Cowle, Christine 1997. "Deviant Desire: Gender Politics and the Cultural Metamorphosis of George/Christine Jorgensen." *Australian Humanities Review* (August), www.australianhumanitiesreview.org/archive/Issue-August-1997/Crowle.html (accessed June 18, 2013).
Deutscher Lyceum-Club 1912. *Bahnbrechende frauen.* Berlin: Vita, Deutsches Verlagshaus.
Dick, Jutta, Marina Sassenberg, Moses Mendelssohn & Salomon Ludwig 1993. *Jüdische Frauen im 19. und 20. Jahrhundert: Lexikon zu Leben und Werk.* Reinbek bei Hamburg: Rowohlt.
Anon. 1994 "Enough is Enough! Against the Masculinization of Women." In *The Weimar Republic Sourcebook,* Anton Kaes, Martin Jay & Edward Dimendberg (eds), 659. Berkeley, CA: University of California Press.
Felstiner, Mary Lowenthal 1994. *To Paint Her Life: Charlotte Salomon in the Nazi Era.* New York: HarperCollins.
Fout, John C. 1984. *German Women in the Nineteenth Century: A Social History.* New York: Holmes & Meier.
Freidenreich, Harriet Pass 2002. *Female, Jewish, and Educated: The Lives of Central European University Women.* Bloomington, IN: Indiana University Press.
Fuchs, Esther 1999. *Women and the Holocaust: Narrative and Representation, Studies in the Shoah.* Lanham, MD: University Press of America.
Gerl-Falkovitz, Hanna-Barbara 1995. *Freundinnen: christliche Frauen aus zwei Jahrtausenden.* Munich: Wewel.
Glückel of Hameln 1932. *The Memoirs of Glückel of Hameln,* Marvin Lowenthal (ed.). New York: Harper & Brothers.
Gurewitsch, Brana 1998. *Mothers, Sisters, Resisters: Oral Histories of Women Who Survived the Holocaust, Judaic Studies Series.* Tuscaloosa, AZ: University of Alabama Press.
Herbermann, Nanda, Hester Baer & Elizabeth Roberts Baer 2000. *The Blessed Abyss: Inmate #6582 in Ravensbruck Concentration Camp for Women.* Detroit, MI: Wayne State University Press.
Koonz, Claudia 1987. *Mothers in the Fatherland: Women, the Family, and Nazi Politics.* New York: St Martin's Press.
Mayer, Gabriele 2003. *Post-Holocaust Religious Education for German Women.* Tübinger perspektiven zur pastoraltheologie und Religionspädagogik. Münster: Lit.
Ofer, Dalia & Lenore J. Weitzman 1998. *Women in the Holocaust.* New Haven, CT: Yale University Press.
Orfali, Stephanie 1987. *A Jewish Girl in the Weimar Republic.* Berkeley, CA: Ronin.
Paletschek, Sylvia & Bianka Pietrow-Ennker 2004. *Women's Emancipation Movements in the Nineteenth Century: A European Perspective.* Stanford, CA: Stanford University Press.
Petersen, Vibeke Rützou 2001. *Women and Modernity in Weimar Germany: Reality and Its Representation in Popular Fiction.* New York: Berghahn Books.
Pore, Renate 1981. *A Conflict of Interest: Women in German Social Democracy, 1919–1933, Contributions in Women's Studies.* Westport, CT: Greenwood Press.
Quack, Sibylle 1994. *Between Sorrow and Strength: Women Refugees of the Nazi Period.* Cambridge: Cambridge University Press.

Raphael, Melissa 2003. *The Female Face of God in Auschwitz: a Jewish Feminist Theology of the Holocaust*. London: Routledge.

Redlikh, Egon & Saul S. Friedman 1992. *The Terezin Diary of Gonda Redlich*. Lexington, KY: University Press of Kentucky.

Reicke, Ilse 1984. *Die grossen Frauen der Weimarer Republik: Erlebnisse im "Berliner Frühling."* Freiburg im Breisgau: Herder.

Saidel, Rochelle G. 2004. *The Jewish Women of Ravensbrück Concentration Camp*. Madison, WI: University of Wisconsin Press.

Stephenson, Jill 1975. *Women in Nazi Society*. New York: Barnes & Noble.

Stoltzfus, Nathan 1996. *Resistance of the Heart: Intermarriage and the Rosenstrasse Protest in Nazi Germany*. New York: W. W. Norton.

Usborne, Cornelie 1992. *The Politics of the Body in Weimar Germany: Women's Reproductive Rights and Duties*. Ann Arbor, MI: University of Michigan Press.

von Argyriadi, Amanda 2008. "Women of the Weimar Republic," http://mason.gmu.edu/~avonargy/typoassignment (accessed September 23, 2008).

QUEER THEORY, FEMINIST THEORY, ETHICS

Abelove, Henry, Michèle Aina Barale & David M. Halperin 1993. *The Lesbian and Gay Studies Reader*. New York: Routledge.

Ahmed, Sara 2006. *Queer Phenomenology: Orientations, Objects, Others*. Durham, NC: Duke University Press.

Aizley, Harlyn 2006. *Confessions of the Other Mother: Non-Biological Lesbian Moms Tell All*. Boston, MA: Beacon Press.

Alcoff, Linda 1997. "Cultural Feminism versus Post-Structuralism: The Identity Crisis in Feminist Theory." In *The Second Wave: A Reader in Feminist Theory*, L. J. Nicholson (eds), 330–55. New York: Routledge.

Alcoff, Linda 2006. *Visible Identities: Race, Gender, and the Self*. New York: Oxford University Press.

Anderson, Pamela Sue & Beverley Clack 2004. *Feminist Philosophy of Religion: Critical Readings*. London: Routledge.

Appiah, Anthony 2005. *The Ethics of Identity*. Princeton, NJ: Princeton University Press.

Battersby, Christine 1998. *The Phenomenal Woman: Feminist Metaphysics and the Patterns of Identity*. New York: Routledge.

Benhabib, Seyla & Drucilla Cornell (eds) 1987. *Feminism as Critique: On the Politics of Gender*. Minneapolis, MN: University of Minnesota Press.

Benhabib, Seyla, Judith Butler, Drucilla Cornell & Nancy Fraser 1995. *Feminist Contentions: A Philosophical Exchange, Thinking Gender*. New York: Routledge.

Boyarin, Daniel, Daniel Itzkovitz & Ann Pellegrini 2003. *Queer Theory and the Jewish Question*. New York: Columbia University Press.

Butler, Judith 1990. *Gender Trouble: Feminism and the Subversion of Identity*. New York: Routledge.

Cixous, Hélène & Catherine Clément 1986. *The Newly Born Woman*. Minneapolis, MN: University of Minnesota Press.

Cornell, Drucilla & Adam Thurschwell 1987. "Feminism, Negativity, Intersubjectivity." In *Feminism as Critique: on the Politics of Gender*, S. Benhabib & D. Cornell (eds), 143–62. Minneapolis, MN: University of Minnesota Press.

Davidman, Lynn & Shelly Tenenbaum 1994. *Feminist Perspectives on Jewish Studies*. New Haven, CT: Yale University Press.

de Beauvoir, Simone 1953. *The Second Sex*, H. M. Parshley (trans., ed.). London: Jonathan Cape.

Fanon, Frantz & Charles Lam Markmann 1968. *Black Skin, White Masks*. New York: Grove Press.

Foucault, Michel & Robert Hurley 1990. *The History of Sexuality: An Introduction*. New York: Vintage Books.

Frankenberry, Nancy. "Feminist Philosophy of Religion." *Stanford Encyclopedia of Philosophy*, Edward N. Zalta (ed.), http://plato.stanford.edu/entries/feminist-religion (accessed September 23, 2008).

Frazer, Elizabeth, Jennifer Hornsby & Sabina Lovibond 1992. *Ethics: a Feminist Reader*. Oxford: Blackwell.

Fuss, Diana 1989. *Essentially Speaking: Feminism, Nature and Difference*. New York: Routledge.

Garber, Marjorie B 1993. *Vested Interests: Cross Dressing and Cultural Anxiety*. New York: HarperPerennial.

Gilligan, Carol 1993. *In a Different Voice: Psychological Theory and Women's Development*. Cambridge, MA: Harvard University Press.

Gross, Rita M. 1996. *Feminism and Religion: An Introduction*. Boston, MA: Beacon Press.

Halperin, David M 1995. *Saint Foucault: Towards a Gay Hagiography*. New York: Oxford University Press.

Heilbrun, Carolyn G 1989. *Writing a Woman's Life*. New York: Ballantine Books.

Herminghouse, Patricia & Magda Mueller 2001. *German Feminist Writings*. New York: Continuum.

Heyes, Cressida 2007. "Identity Politics." *Stanford Encyclopedia of Philosophy*, Edward N. Zalta (ed.), http://plato.stanford.edu/entries/identity-politics (accessed June 6, 2007).

Hochschild, Arlie 1989. *The Second Shift*. New York: Viking.

Irigaray, Luce 1985. *This Sex Which Is Not One*. Ithaca, NY: Cornell University Press.

Irigaray, Luce 1985. *Speculum of the Other Woman*. Ithaca, NY: Cornell University Press.

Jaggar, Alison M 1983. *Feminist Politics and Human Nature, Philosophy and Society*. Totowa, NJ: Rowman & Allanheld.

Jagose, Annamarie 1996. "Queer Theory," *Australian Humanities Review* (December), www.australianhumanitiesreview.org/archive/Issue-Dec-1996/jagose.html (accessed September 23, 2008).

Jagose, Annamarie 1996. *Queer Theory: An Introduction*. New York: New York University Press.

Joy, Morny, Kathleen O'Grady & Judith L. Poxon 2002. *French Feminists on Religion: a Reader*. London: Routledge.

Le Dœuff, Michèle 1991. *Hipparchia's Choice: An Essay Concerning Women, Philosophy*. Oxford: Blackwell.

Le Fort, Gertrud 1962. *The Eternal Woman, The Woman in Time [and] Timeless Woman*. Milwaukee, WI: Bruce Pub. Co.

Lewis, Reina & Sara Mills 2003. *Feminist Postcolonial Theory: A Reader*. New York: Routledge.

Meyers, Diana 2008. "Feminist Perspectives on the Self." *Stanford Encyclopedia of Philosophy*, Edward N. Zalta (ed.), http://plato.stanford.edu/entries/feminism-self (accessed September 23, 2008).

Moessner, Jeanne Stevenson 1996. *Through the Eyes of Women: Insights for Pastoral Care*. Minneapolis, MN: Fortress Press.

Nicholson, Linda J. 1997. *The Second Wave: A Reader in Feminist Theory*. New York: Routledge.

Phelan, Shane 1994. *Getting Specific: Postmodern Lesbian Politics*. Minneapolis, MN: University of Minnesota Press.

Pickett, Brent 2006. "Homosexuality." *Stanford Encyclopedia of Philosophy*, Edward N. Zalta (ed.), http://plato.stanford.edu/archives/win2006/entries/homosexuality (accessed September 23, 2008).

Probyn, Elspeth 1996. *Outside Belongings*. New York: Routledge.

Rosario, Vernon A. 2002. *Homosexuality and Science: A Guide to the Debates, Controversies in Science*. Santa Barbara, CA: ABC-CLIO.

Sedgwick, Eve Kosofsky 1991. *Epistemology of the Closet*. London: Harvester Wheatsheaf.
Sölle, Dorothee 1993. *Celebrating Resistance: the Way of the Cross in Latin America*. London: Mowbray.
Sölle, Dorothee 1993. *Stations of the Cross: A Latin American Pilgrimage*. Minneapolis, MN: Fortress Press.
Sölle, Dorothee 2001. *The Silent Cry: Mysticism and Resistance*. Minneapolis, MN: Fortress Press.
Theory.org 2008. "Queer Theory," www.theory.org.uk/ctr-que1.htm (accessed September 23, 2008).
Trinh, T. Minh-Ha 1989. *Woman, Native, Other: Writing Postcoloniality and Feminism*. Bloomington, IN: Indiana University Press.
Weed, Elizabeth & Naomi Schor 1997. *Feminism Meets Queer Theory*. Bloomington, IN: Indiana University Press.
Welch, Sharon D 1985. *Communities of Resistance and Solidarity: A Feminist Theology of Liberation*. Maryknoll, NY: Orbis Books.
Wistrich, Robert S. 1999. *Demonizing the Other: Antisemitism, Racism, and Xenophobia, Studies in Antisemitism*. Amsterdam: Harwood Academic.

JEWISH FEMINIST WRITINGS

Adler, Rachel 1988. "The Virgin in the Brothel and the Other Anomalies of Character and Context in the Legend of Beruria." *Tikkun* (November/December): 28–32, 102–5.
Adler, Rachel 1998. *Engendering Judaism: An Inclusive Theology and Ethics*. Philadelphia, PA: Jewish Publication Society.
Beal, Timothy K. 1997. *The Book of Hiding: Gender, Ethnicity, Annihilation, and Esther*. London: Routledge.
Biale, David 1992. *Eros and the Jews: From Biblical Israel to Contemporary America*. New York: Basic Books.
Biale, David 1992. "Eros and Enlightenment." In *Eros and the Jews: From Biblical Israel to Contemporary America*, D. Biale (ed.), 149–75. New York: Basic Books.
Biale, Rachel 1984. *Women and Jewish Law: An Exploration of Women's Issues in Halakhic Sources*. New York: Schocken Books.
Greenberg, Blu 1998. *On Women and Judaism: A View from Tradition*. Philadelphia, PA: Jewish Publication Society of America.
Hauptman, Judith 1998. *Rereading the Rabbis: a Woman's Voice*. Boulder, CO: Westview Press.
Heschel, Susannah 1983. *On Being a Jewish Feminist: A Reader*. New York: Schocken Books.
Hyman, Paula 1995. *Gender and Assimilation in Modern Jewish History: the Roles and Representation of Women*. Seattle, WA: University of Washington Press.
Jastrow, Marcus & Henrietta Szold 2008. "Beruriah," www.jewishencyclopedia.com/view.jsp?artid=940&letter=B (accessed April 15, 2008).
Kaplan, Marion A. 1979. *The Jewish Feminist Movement in Germany: The Campaigns of the Jüdischer Frauenbund, 1904–1938*. Westport, CT: Greenwood Press.
Kaplan, Marion A. 1981. *Die jüdische Frauenbewegung in Deutschland: Organization und Ziele des Jüdischen Frauenbundes, 1904–1938*. Hamburg: Hans Christians.
Kaplan, Marion A. 1991. *The Making of the Jewish Middle Class: Women, Family, and Identity in Imperial Germany*. New York: Oxford University Press.
Kaplan, Marion A. 1996. *Between Dignity and Despair: Jewish Women in the Aftermath of November 1938*. New York: Leo Baeck Institute.
Kaplan, Marion A. 1997. *Jüdisches Bürgertum: Frau, Familie und Identität im Kaiserreich, Studien zur jüdischen Geschichte*. Hamburg: Dölling und Galitz.
Kaplan, Marion A. 1998. *Between Dignity and Despair: Jewish Life in Nazi Germany, Studies in Jewish History*. Oxford: Oxford University Press.

Kaplan, Marion A. 2001. *Der Mut zum Überleben: Jüdische Frauen und ihre Familien in Nazideutschland*. Berlin: Aufbau-Verlag.

Kaplan, Marion A. 2003. *Geschichte des jüdischen Alltags in Deutschland: vom 17. Jahrhundert bis 1945*. Munich: Beck.

Kaplan, Marion A. 2005. *Jewish Daily Life in Germany, 1618–1945*. New York: Oxford University Press.

Kaplan, Marion, Beate Meyer & Monika Richarz 2005. *Jüdische Welten: Juden in Deutschland vom 18. Jahrhundert bis in die Gegenwart*. Göttingen: Wallstein.

Katz, Lisa 2008. "What is the Eshet Chayil (A Woman of Valor) Hymn?" http://judaism.about.com/od/shabbatprayersblessings/f/eshetchayil.htm (accessed April 14, 2008).

Koltun, Elizabeth 1976. *The Jewish Woman: New Perspectives*. New York: Schocken Books.

Meyer, Alfred G 1985. *The Feminism and Socialism of Lily Braun*. Bloomington, IN: Indiana University Press.

Parush, Iris 2004. *Reading Jewish Women: Marginality and Modernization in Nineteenth-Century Eastern European Jewish Society, Brandeis Series on Jewish Women*. Waltham, MA: Brandeis University Press.

Peskowitz, Miriam & Laura Levitt 1997. *Judaism Since Gender*. New York: Routledge.

Plaskow, Judith 1991. *Standing Again at Sinai: Judaism From a Feminist Perspective*. San Francisco, CA: HarperSanFrancisco.

Polgar, Alfred 1994. "The Defenseless: A Conversation between Men (1928)." In *The Weimar Republic Sourcebook*, Anton Kaes, Martin Jay & Edward Dimendberg (eds), 204. Berkeley, CA: University of California Press.

Rudavsky, Tamar 1995. *Gender and Judaism: The Transformation of Tradition*. New York: New York University Press.

Ruether, Rosemary Radford 1993. *Sexism and God-Talk: Toward a Feminist Theology; With a New Introduction*, 10th anniversary edn. Boston, MA: Beacon Press.

Ruether, Rosemary Radford 1996. *Womanguides: Readings Toward a Feminist Theology*. Boston, MA: Beacon Press.

Umansky, Ellen M. & Dianne Ashton 1992. *Four Centuries of Jewish Women's Spirituality: a Sourcebook*. Boston, MA: Beacon Press.

Wallach-Faller, Marianne, Doris Brodbeck & Yvonne Domhardt 2000. *Die Frau im Tallit: Judentum feministisch gelesen*. Zürich: Chronos.

Wegner, Judith Romney 1988. *Chattel or Person? The Status of Women in the Mishnah*. New York: Oxford University Press.

Weissler, Chava 1998. *Voices of the Matriarchs: Listening to the Prayers of Early Modern Jewish Women*. Boston, MA: Beacon Press.

Wengeroff, Pauline 2010. *Memoirs of a Russian Grandmother*. Stanford, CA: Stanford University Press.

Wolfson, Elliot R. 1995. *Circle in the Square: Studies in the Use of Gender in Kabbalistic Symbolism*. Albany, NY: State University of New York Press.

PHILOSOPHICAL WRITINGS

Arendt, Hannah 1958. *The Human Condition*. Chicago, IL: University of Chicago Press.

Arendt, Hannah 1968. *Men in Dark Times*. New York: Harcourt.

Bhabha, Homi K. 1990. *Nation and Narration*. London: Routledge.

Bhabha, Homi K. 1994. *The Location of Culture*. London: Routledge.

Deal, William E. & Timothy K. Beal 2004. *Theory for Religious Studies*. New York: Routledge.

Leydet, Dominique 2006. "Citizenship." *Stanford Encyclopedia of Philosophy*, Edward N. Zalta (ed.), http://plato.stanford.edu/entries/citizenship (accessed September 23, 2008).

Sawicki, Marianne 2006. "Edmund Husserl (1859–1938)." *The Internet Encyclopedia of Philosophy*, www.iep.utm.edu/h/husserl.htm (accessed September 23, 2008).

Sellner, Timothy 2008. "Theodore Gottlieb von Hippel," www.pinn.net/~sunshine/whm2003/ hippel.html (accessed September 23, 2008).

Taylor, Charles 1989. *Sources of the Self: the Making of the Modern Identity.* Cambridge, MA: Harvard University Press.

Woodruff Smith, David 2008. "Phenomenology." *Stanford Encyclopedia of Philosophy*, Edward N. Zalta (ed.), http://plato.stanford.edu/entries/phenomenology (accessed September 23, 2008).

Zunz, Leopold 1845. *Zur geschichte und literatur.* Berlin: Veit.

OTHER

Arendt, Hannah 1978. *The Jew as Pariah: Jewish Identity and Politics in the Modern Age*, Ron H. Feldman (ed.). New York: Grove Press.

Armstrong, Karen, Feisal Abdul Rauf, Susannah Heschel & Jim Wallis 2005. *Fundamentalism & Violence.* Video recording, Episcopal Cathedral Teleconferencing Network. New York: Trinity Church.

Bell, Susan G. and Marilyn Yalom 1990. *Revealing Lives: Autobiography, Biography, and Gender.* Albany, NY: SUNY Press.

Bokenkotter, Thomas S. 1986. *Essential Catholicism.* Garden City, NY: Image Books.

Börsig-Hover, Lina, Hanna Gerl-Falkovitz & Winfrid Hover 1989. *Unterwegs zur Heimat: Martin Heidegger zum 100. Geburtstag.* Fridingen: Börsig-Verlag.

Brenner, Rachel Feldhay 1994. "Ethical Convergence in Religious Conversion." In *The Unnecessary Problem of Edith Stein*, H. J. Cargas (ed.), 77–100. Lanham, MD: University Press of America.

Cabezón, José Ignacio & Sheila Greeve Davaney 2004. *Identity and the Politics of Scholarship in the Study of Religion.* New York: Routledge.

Castiglioni, Niccolò & Edith Stein 1992. *Liedlein: Für Kinderchor und Instrumente.* Milan: Ricordi.

Ever, Isasc Hirsch & Judah Heschel Levenberg 1939. *Harov Y.H. Le'venberg: zayn lebn un 'kamf.* 'Kli'vland: Farlag "Ivri".

Foucault, Michel & Jeremy R. Carrette 1999. *Religion and Culture.* New York: Routledge.

Foucault, Michel & Robert Hurley 1990. *The History of Sexuality: An Introduction.* New York: Vintage Books.

Funkenstein, Amos 1993. *Perceptions of Jewish History.* Berkeley, CA: University of California Press.

HaHomash HaManukad Bereshit 1999. *HaHomash HaManukad Bereshit.* Jerusalem: Horev Publishing.

Hartman, Geoffrey H. & Sanford Budick 1986. *Midrash and Literature.* New Haven, CA: Yale University Press.

Herbstrith, Otto 1935. *Die Freizeichnungsklauseln bei Lieferungsverträgen.* Doctoral thesis, C. Pfeffer, Universität Heidelberg, Heidelberg.

Heschel, Abraham Joshua & Susannah Heschel 1996. *Moral Grandeur and Spiritual Audacity: Essays.* New York: Farrar, Straus & Giroux.

Heschel, Susannah, Michael Galchinsky & David Biale 1998. *Insider/Outsider: American Jews and Multiculturalism.* Berkeley, CA: University of California Press.

Idel, Moshe 1986. "Infinities of the Torah in Kabbalah." In *Midrash and Literature*, Geoffrey H. Hartman & Sanford Budick (eds), 141–56. New Haven, CT: Yale University Press.

Klutznick, Philip M. and Ethel and Menaham Mor 1992. *Jewish Assimilation, Acculturation, and Accommodation: Past Traditions, Current Issues, and Future Prospects.* Omaha, NE: University Press of America.

Koyré, Alexandre, Edith Stein, Hedwig Conrad-Martius & Hanna Gerl-Falkovitz 2005.

Übersetzung von Alexandre Koyré, Descartes und die Scholastik. Freiburg im Breisgau: Herder.

Kristeva, Julia 1982. *Powers of Horror: An Essay on Abjection*. New York: Columbia University Press.

Labanyi, Jo 2002. *Constructing Identity in Contemporary Spain: Theoretical Debates and Cultural Practice*. Oxford: Oxford University Press.

Le Dœuff, Michèle 1991. *Hipparchia's Choice: an Essay Concerning Women, Philosophy, etc.* Oxford: Blackwell.

Leo Baeck Institute 1958. *The Leo Baeck Memorial Lecture*. New York: Leo Baeck Institute.

Leo Baeck Institute 1994. *Yearbook XXXIX*. London: East and West Library.

Liedtke, Rainer & Stephan Wendehorst 1999. *The Emancipation of Catholics, Jews and Protestants: Minorities and the Nation State in Nineteenth-Century Europe*. Manchester: Manchester University Press.

Lustiger, Jean-Marie 1986. *Dare to Believe: Addresses, Sermons, Interviews, 1981–1984*. New York: Crossroads.

Lustiger, Jean-Marie, Jean Louis Missika & Dominique Wolton 1991. *Choosing God, Chosen by God: Conversations with Jean-Marie Lustiger*. San Francisco, CA: Ignatius Press.

Lyotard, Jean François 1984. *The Postmodern Condition: A Report on Knowledge*. Minneapolis, MN: University of Minnesota Press.

Maier, Hans, Theo Stammen, Heinrich Oberreuter, Paul Mikat & Hanna Gerl-Falkovitz 1996. *Politik, Bildung, Religion: Hans Maier zum 65. Geburtstag*. Paderborn: Schöningh.

Margolis, Max Leopold 1955. *The Holy Scriptures According to the Masoretic Text: A New Translation With the Aid of Previous Versions and With Constant Consultation of Jewish Authorities*. Philadelphia, PA: Jewish Publication Society of America.

Mendieta, Eduardo 2005. *The Frankfurt School on Religion: Key Writings by the Major Thinkers*. New York: Routledge.

New Jewish Agenda 1984. *The Shalom Seders: Three Haggadahs*. New York: Adama Books.

Pelaia, Ariela 2008. "What is Yizkor?," http://judaism.about.com/od/deathandmournin1/f/yizkor.htm (accessed May 6, 2008).

Plaut, W. Gunther 1981. *The Torah: A Modern Commentary*, Bernard Jacob Bamberger & William W. Hallo. New York: Union of American Hebrew Congregations.

Redmont, Jane 1992. *Generous Lives: American Catholic Women Today*. New York: W. Morrow and Co.

Redmont, Jane 1999. *When in Doubt, Sing: Prayer in Daily Life*. New York: HarperCollins.

Rosenzweig, Franz 1985. *The Star of Redemption*. Notre Dame, IN: Notre Dame Press.

Sachar, Howard Morley 1996. *A History of Israel: From the Rise of Zionism to Our Time*. New York: Alfred A. Knopf.

Scherman, Nosson, Hersh Goldwurm, Avie Gold & Meir Zlotowitz 2000. *The Chumash: The Torah, Haftaros and Five Megillos*. Brooklyn, NY: Mesorah Publications.

Scholem, Gershom 1961. *Major Trends in Jewish Mysticism*. New York: Schocken Books.

United States Conference of Catholic Bishops 1991. "New American Bible, Esther, Introduction," www.nccbuscc.org/nab/bible/esther/intro.htm (accessed April 30, 2008).

INDEX